Encounters and Dialogues with Martin Heidegger

1929–1976

HEINRICH WIEGAND PETZET

Encounters and Dialogues with Martin Heidegger

1929–1976

Translated by Parvis Emad and Kenneth Maly

With an Introduction by Parvis Emad

The University of Chicago Press

Chicago and London

Heinrich Wiegand Petzet, art historian and literary critic, is known to American readers through Rilke's *Letters on Cézanne*. Parvis Emad and Kenneth Maly are founding coeditors of the journal *Heidegger Studies*.

The University of Chicago Press, Chicago 60637
The University of Chicago Press, Ltd., London
© 1993 by The University of Chicago
All rights reserved. Published 1993
Printed in the United States of America
02 01 00 99 98 97 96 95 94 93   1 2 3 4 5 6
ISBN (cloth): 0-226-66441-4

Originally published by Societäts-Verlag as *Auf einen Stern zugehen: Begegnungen und Gespräche mit Martin Heidegger, 1929–1976,* © 1983 Frankfurter Societäts-Druckerei GmbH.

Library of Congress Cataloging-in-Publication Data

Petzet, Heinrich Wiegand, 1909–
    [Auf einen Stern zugehen.   English]
    Encounters and dialogues with Martin Heidegger, 1929–1976 / Heinrich Wiegand Petzet ; translated by Parvis Emad and Kenneth Maly; with an introduction by Parvis Emad.
        p.   cm.
    Translation of: Auf einen Stern zugehen.
    Includes bibliographical references and index.
    1. Heidegger, Martin, 1889–1976.   2. Philosophers—Germany—Biography.
I. Emad, Parvis.   II. Title.
B3279.H49P44613   1993
193—dc20
[B]   92-30966
                                                                                 CIP

To Arnold Stadler

For the wind that blows through Heidegger's thinking, like that which still sweeps toward us after thousands of years from the work of Plato, does not spring from the century he happens to live in. It comes from the primeval, and what it leaves behind is something completed, something which, like everything complete, falls back to the primeval.

Hannah Arendt

Offer testimony. I was there, although no one knew me.

Hugo von Hofmannsthal, *Der Turm,* act 5

Contents

Illustrations follow page 96

Translators' Note

The English translation of *Auf einen Stern zugehen: Begegnungen und Gespräche mit Martin Heidegger, 1929–1976* is based on a slightly revised text. Most of the revisions consist in the correction of dates or the deletion of certain words and passages (on the following pages of the German edition: 11, 16, 17, 34, 39, 45, 51, 52, 54, 86, 136, 137, 139, 156, 185, 191, 195, 196, 214, 238, 239, and 240, and in the Chronology).

The Biographical Notes and the numbered notes at the back of this edition were prepared by the translators.

This translation owes a great deal to the generous help it has received from Professor Stephen C. Doty. We thank him especially for his expert and resourceful assistance in the last stages of the work.

We thank James Ryan for carefully typing the first draft of the manuscript. And very special thanks go to Nancy Trotic for her exquisite work of copyediting. Last, we wish to thank Gertrude Emad for her invaluable assistance in preparing the index for this volume.

P. E. and K. M.

Introduction

Elements of an Intellectual Portrait in H. W. Petzet's Memoirs

Parvis Emad

The publication of *Encounters and Dialogues with Martin Heidegger, 1929–1976* makes accessible to the English-speaking public a work that sketches, in measured strokes, an intellectual portrait of one of the important philosophers of the twentieth century. Written by the art historian and literary critic Heinrich Wiegand Petzet, the book is based on Petzet's friendship with the philosopher, a friendship that grew out of a recognition of the significance of Heidegger's work and that lasted nearly half a century. Through its singular focus on Heidegger, the book opens an interesting vista into the intellectual history of the Germany of his time. It presents a panorama of people and events in which the philosopher appears as a man supremely dedicated to his work, entangled in the political realities of his day, and developing intricate personal relationships with many of his contemporaries, including Clara Rilke (the wife of the poet), Hertha Koenig (Rilke's personal friend), Jean Beaufret (the French philosopher), Ludwig von Ficker (the editor and literary critic), Erhart Kästner (the writer), Paul Celan (the poet), and Andrei Voznesensky (the Soviet poet). Although the book would be highly relevant for an intellectual biography of Heidegger—which has yet to be written—it is not itself a biography, even as it presents elements of an intellectual portrait of the philosopher. It depicts him in the decisive period of his inaugural lecture "What Is Metaphysics?" as rector of the University of Freiburg, and as the emeritus who continues to offer courses and seminars. The book also shows Heidegger engaged in conversations and dialogues that center on politics in the Third Reich and on many important intellectual figures—for example, Jean-Paul Sartre, Karl Jaspers, and Gottfried Benn. The intellectual portrait receives its finishing touches from some of Heidegger's most revealing letters and from assessments of him and his work by the literary historian Max Kommerell and by the writer Rudolf Krämer-Badoni.

I

Considering this book's genre, we find that it combines elements present in Johann Peter Eckermann's *Conversations with Goethe* and in Norman Malcolm's *Ludwig Wittgenstein: A Memoir*. Like Eckermann, Petzet records a series of dialogues; and like Malcolm, he recalls what transpired in the course of his long association with the philosopher. Dialogues with Heidegger are so important to this book that when in August 1986 I proposed to Petzet the present title for the English edition of his book, he unhesitatingly approved it, although it omits the main title of the original German.

Dialogues and conversations with Heidegger are among the first and strongest threads that are woven into the intellectual portrait of the philosopher. The dialogues happen unpredictably, do not follow a preconceived course—as is true for all genuine dialogues—and cover a wide range of topics. These topics include Heidegger's plans for some of his courses and seminars, his gradual disappointment with and distance from academic philosophy, his reaction to being a public figure and being recognized in public, his impressions of a Klee exhibition, his opinion of Karl Jaspers and Gottfried Benn, his political involvement during the Third Reich, the new Stuttgart edition of Hölderlin, and Sartre's visit to Freiburg.

Closely connected with the dialogues and conversations is a series of encounters between Heidegger and others, as well as his formal appearances before the Bavarian Academy of Fine Arts in Munich and elsewhere. The record of these encounters contributes significantly to a tighter weaving of the intellectual portrait of the philosopher. Some of these encounters are initiated by Heidegger (like the visit he pays to Clara Rilke), and some are instigated by others (like the visits of the Soviet poet Andrei Voznesensky and of a Buddhist monk). What distinguishes these encounters is the openness—a central theme of *Being and Time*—within which they occur. Unlike those who want to convert others to the "truth" which only they seem to possess, Heidegger always *lets* the other person *be* in his or her autonomy. He never expects the other person to correspond to a preconceived image. Petzet's long association with the philosopher allows him to capture effortlessly moments of this openness in Heidegger's encounters with other human beings. He thus concretely shows Heidegger's respect for human beings—a respect that comes from the recognition of an openness which is not created by us but is given to us. Heidegger never allows this openness to collapse, as it certainly would if he were to claim the other with little regard for his or her freedom to choose certain existential possibilities.

The scene of the encounter between Clara Rilke and the philosopher offers glimpses of this openness. Here Petzet writes at his best. A Rilke scholar himself, who years earlier had assisted Clara Rilke in editing her husband's *Letters on Cézanne,* Petzet tactfully arranges the visit. When we read the account of this encounter, we would do well to bear in mind Heidegger's essay on Rilke entitled "What Are Poets For?" (written in commemoration of the twentieth anniversary of the poet's death). Petzet describes the scene of the encounter in a way that allows the reader to participate in it and to listen in on the conversation that follows. Clara Rilke tells Heidegger that while in Paris she and her husband used to read Kierkegaard together; she mentions a poem of her husband's that belongs to that period and that she saw only a few days ago but can no longer find. When Heidegger accidentally finds the poem in one of the small volumes on the shelf, we witness one of the liveliest scenes in the entire book.

The encounters with Clara Rilke and with others are connected to threads in the intellectual portrait that point decisively to Heidegger's relation to painting. This is the domain in which the art historian Petzet is at home. What he remembers and records of Heidegger's relation to and views on modern art allows the portrait of the philosopher to appear in a way that mirrors the way color and light mold a painting. From "The Origin of the Work of Art," we know how significant van Gogh was for Heidegger's thinking about art. Petzet completes the web in the portrait of Heidegger and art when he highlights the philosopher's relationships to Paul Cézanne, Georges Braque, and Paul Klee. Since the appearance of Petzet's book in German, Heidegger's views of Cézanne have become more accessible through a number of studies devoted to that topic. It is fair to say that as van Gogh marks the beginning of Heidegger's way into art, Cézanne and Klee mark the last stage of the way. Petzet records Heidegger's plan for another philosophical essay on art which was to focus on Klee's paintings. (Heidegger also maintained a strong interest in the work of Picasso, but as a more distanced observer.)

Another strong thread in the intellectual portrait of Heidegger is provided by a number of letters that are reproduced in this book. Three of these are especially worthy of attention. The first two are letters that Heidegger wrote to Petzet; the third is from Max Kommerell to his wife, Erika Kommerell.

In one of the two letters addressed to Petzet, we find Heidegger's remarks on the present world-historical epoch in conjunction with Heinrich Vogeler's life, and in the other a *philosophical* response to Karl Löwith's indictment of Heidegger's involvement in the politics of national socialism.

The subject of the first letter is Petzet's book about the painter Heinrich Vogeler. Heidegger received a prepublication copy and an invitation to the celebration that preceded the book's appearance. He read the book quickly but thoroughly, and wrote a thought-provoking letter to Petzet. Heidegger refers to and comments on three intricately interrelated factors: Heinrich Vogeler the man, his works of art, and significant events in his life, such as his emigration to the Soviet Union. According to Heidegger, we may regard these factors as pertaining to the artist's biography, or we may treat them in the context of art history. We must not, however, mistake them for the painter's hidden destiny (*Geschick*). For, as Heidegger points out, that destiny "is not accessible to art history or biographical interest."

To what, then, is Vogeler's hidden destiny accessible? Heidegger's response would probably be: To a thinking that is fundamental-ontological and recognizes the historical character of being's unfolding, its handing over (*Geschichte des Seins*). Such a thinking is laid out in *Being and Time* and in *Beiträge zur Philosophie (Vom Ereignis)* (Contributions to Philosophy [On Appropriation]). Art history and biography, with no way of knowing how Heinrich Vogeler was claimed and appropriated by being, do not reach the domain in which his hidden destiny unfolds. That is why they can only talk about the man, his work, and certain events of his tragic life.

The second letter has to do with Karl Löwith, a former student of Heidegger's who, at the time the letter was written, was professor of philosophy at the University of Heidelberg. Petzet had brought to Heidegger's attention Löwith's derogatory remarks about Heidegger's involvement in Nazi politics. When read carefully, Heidegger's response to Petzet contains something very revealing.

Rather than directly taking issue with Löwith on the questions pertaining to national socialism, Heidegger makes a number of statements about his own philosophical concerns, thus intimating that Löwith must have known that Heidegger's thinking had left behind "the metaphysics of subjectivity." Moreover, he suggests that Löwith must have known that he had "communicated the notion of a turning (*Kehre*)" as early as his lecture "Vom Wesen der Wahrheit."

When we read this letter, two questions come to mind. Given the fact that "subjectivity" and "turning" directly point to the thinking of being, we wonder (1) what this thinking has to do with Löwith's remarks on Heidegger's involvement in national socialism and (2) whether Heidegger is not presuming too much about Löwith's understanding of his thought. For in this same letter Heidegger says that in 1929 Löwith characterized *Being and Time* as a "concealed theology," a characterization that shows his grave misunderstanding of this work. How can Heidegger then presume that Löwith must have known that in 1927 he "dealt with the question of being and not subjectivity for four hours every week"? How can he presume Löwith's access to and understanding of issues such as "subjectivity" and "turning" that directly point to the thinking of being, when in fact Löwith's relation to this thinking is based on a misunderstanding of it? To be sure, Löwith was a student of Heidegger's. But does this guarantee familiarity with the thinking of being and proper reflection on the question of being? Does not Heidegger himself, years before the letter was written, point out to Jean Beaufret that "for humans to be able to measure up (even to some small extent) to this reflection on this question, a silence for two or more decades may be necessary"?[1] Does not Heidegger know that Löwith, who considered *Being and Time* to be a "concealed theology," is not capable of such silence?

If we take these questions seriously, then we must read this letter for its suggestiveness rather than for what it presumes about Löwith. The letter suggests that if we wish to assess Heidegger's involvement in the politics of national socialism, we must take into account Heidegger's thinking of being as a thinking that has "left subjectivity behind and heeded the turning." Simply put, the involvement with national socialism is not an isolated incident that has nothing to do with Heidegger's thinking of being. On the contrary, it must be judged in accordance with intricate issues that pertain to this thinking.

I dwell on this letter because what it suggests seems to complete Petzet's presentations in chapters 2 and 4 of this book. As we shall see, the thread in the intellectual portrait of the philosopher that represents his interest in politics is a weak one unless his relation to the politics of his time is seen within the perspective of his thinking of being.

The third letter, written by Max Kommerell to his wife, captures aspects of Heidegger's work world that are important for his intellectual portrait. Kommerell vividly describes Heidegger at work in the hut at Todtnauberg, as well as its surroundings. Built in 1922, the hut was not simply a place for rest and recuperation but was the philosopher's actual workshop. Kommerell sees Heidegger in his workshop through the eyes of a novelist.

II

Petzet's intellectual portrait of the philosopher nears completion when he takes up Heidegger's interest in politics and his involvement in national socialism. This thread appears to be the most fragile in the portrait, the one that could snap under pressure. Petzet looks at Heidegger's assuming the rectorate of the University of Freiburg from a distance—he was not in Freiburg at the time—and touches upon Heidegger's rectoral address (*Rektoratsrede*) only as it was repeated at another university. He does not deal with the *philosophical core* and *intention* of the address.

Petzet's accounts of the period of Heidegger's rectorate (chapters 2 and 4) strike me as interesting but essentially incomplete. These chapters should be read against the background of "The Self-assertion of the German University," the address Heidegger delivered upon assuming the position of rector. It is not enough simply to narrate the details of Heidegger's interview with the newsmagazine *Der Spiegel* and to mention some of the facts that pertain to this period in Heidegger's life. Those details and facts must be considered in the light of the philosophical core of the rectoral address "The Self-assertion of the German University." As in Löwith's case, we must consider the historical documents and eyewitness accounts *together* with the address.

The philosophical core of the address is captured in these few words: *das Wesen der deutschen Universität*. It is difficult to find an appropriate English word for Heidegger's term *Wesen; Wesen* is not the German translation of the Latin *essentia* and cannot adequately be rendered by the English *essence*. Even if we used the word *essence*, in order to stress the component of being, we would still miss the proper sense of *Wesen*, for *Wesen* does not mean only being. Rather, it indicates a special way (which varies from case to case) for something to be—"to be" understood in the sense of enduring, whiling, abiding, issuing forth, and emerging. What exactly, then, is the *Wesen* of something—say, of the German university?

First, this *Wesen* is given in advance—it is not the contrivance of human endeavor. But it is not given in a solidified and fixed manner (as is, for example, an amount of money or the definition of a vehicle). The

Wesen of something is given in advance in the sense that thinking must *do* its share of opening it up and disclosing it.[2] When Heidegger talks about the *Wesen* of the German university, he means something about this university that is given in advance and that at the same time must be disclosed and opened up in and by thinking. To capture fully this sense of *Wesen* in English, we must look for a word or a combination of words that does not reflect the solidity and constancy implied by the word *essence* but that does indicate this need for opening up and disclosing.

Kenneth Maly has suggested the expression "root-unfolding" for capturing the ongoing movement of enduring, abiding, whiling, emerging, and lasting that distinguishes *Wesen*.[3] While the component "unfolding" indicates the openness to further development and evolving that is crucial to the occurrence called *Wesen*, and thus to the disclosing that is to be accomplished by thinking, the term "root" runs the risk of indicating the solidity and constancy of substance that is inimical to *Wesen*.[4] Nevertheless, the expression "root-unfolding," when heard in its full resonance, captures in English far better than the word *essence* the enduring and abiding character of being's unfolding that is given in advance to thinking.

Heidegger has this dimension of *Wesen* in mind when at the beginning of the rectoral address he says that "the self-assertion of the German university is the original shared will to its root-unfolding."[5] This characterization of the self-assertion of the German university brings to the fore its special way of being, its abiding and its root-unfolding, which is given in advance—given not completely and permanently, but such that it must be opened up and disclosed in thinking. This is a process that *needs* to be carried out—there is a *necessity* about it. Moreover, everyone is involved in this process, faculty and students alike. On this point Heidegger is quite specific; he speaks of the "shared will" that is directed or should be directed to the being of the German university. Finally, he indicates that this whole process is related to the origin (*Ursprung*) by stating that the self-assertion of the German university is original. And what is this origin? It is the beginning (*Anfang*) that the Greeks made in the West with "the breakthrough [*Aufbruch*] of Greek philosophy."[6] Thus Heidegger's rectoral address is built on the idea of an origin which was put forth by the beginning that the Greeks made. Heidegger suggests that the German university can assert itself only when faculty and students share the thinking and questioning that would open up and disclose the being of the

German university, its root-unfolding as given in advance in the origin that the Greeks brought forth.

Heidegger intimates that the beginning that the Greeks made in philosophy is not a beginning as historiography understands the term. For historiography, a beginning is the starting point that is left behind. By contrast, the nonhistoriographical beginning is not left behind. As Heidegger puts it, "The beginning still *is*. It does not lie *behind us,* as something that was long ago, but stands *before* us."[7] Seen in this manner, the beginning that the Greeks made is like a task: it forms and shapes the future. Heidegger stresses the impact of this beginning on the self-assertion of the German university when he says, "The beginning has penetrated our future. There it awaits us as a distant command bidding us to retrieve its greatness."[8]

Faculty and students together face the task of the German university's renewal, its self-assertion, by enacting a thinking that opens up the origin through questioning. This is a special way of questioning with which the readers of *Being and Time* are familiar—a questioning that involves the whole human being, that does not lead quickly to an answer: "Questioning is then no longer a preliminary step, to give way to the answer and thus to knowledge, but questioning becomes itself the highest form of knowing."[9] When faculty and students carry through this questioning and thinking, then an "original conception of science" will emerge. In the rectoral address, Heidegger does not have the time to indicate clearly that this "original conception of science" is original because it is not identical with the modern and humanistic ideals of science. Those ideals, according to Heidegger, have lost their binding power—as can be seen in the increasing departmentalization of sciences, which has resulted in the lack of unity and purpose in the university. An original conception of science, however, has such binding power as to "become the power that shapes the body of the German university. This implies a twofold task: both faculty as one body and students as another, each in its own way, must be *seized* and *remain* seized by the concept of science."[10]

On the part of the faculty the impact is unmistakable because the faculty unfolds its capacity for "a spiritual legislation" that shapes a human being into "the *one* spiritual world of the people."[11] Such a task requires that departmental barriers be torn down and that "professional training" be hindered from losing itself "in what is stale and counterfeit."[12] The task facing German students is far more demanding. Rather than being determined from the outside, students take over the task of determining their own being. They, too, enact the thinking that discloses and opens up the origin through questioning. The result is three bonds that bind students to the community of the German people—through a service (duty) that utilizes labor, a service that aims at defense (resistance), and a service through knowledge.

The establishment of these bonds and the exercise of services within each one of them require a special kind of leading and following. The relation between leading and following is a special one because it is not based on any form of total obedience. On the contrary, Heidegger perceives a kind of following from which blind obedience is banned: "All following, however, bears resistance within itself. This essential opposition of leading and following must not be obscured, let alone eliminated." [13] A following that harbors the seeds of resistance is nurtured by questioning and thinking. Obviously, such following has nothing in common with the blind execution of a command.

It has become clear that the self-assertion and spiritual renewal of the German university depends on an original conception of science, which can be attained by returning to the origin—the breakthrough of Greek philosophy. But what is it that would ensue from this original conception of science? The conception of science that dominates the German university and that Heidegger rejects presents science as "an accident we fall into or the settled comfort of a safe occupation, serving to further a mere progress of information." [14] By contrast, the new and original conception of science that Heidegger wants to achieve reflects one of the crucial concerns of his philosophy, namely, to bring about an altered relation to things. For science rooted in modernity, the relation to things is marked by calculation, manipulation, and domination; the new and original conception of science is the prerequisite for a relation with things that is not calculative, manipulative, and domineering. In the rectoral address Heidegger only hints at this altered relationship.

Let us gather together what we have said about the philosophical core of Heidegger's rectoral address: (1) Heidegger appeals to the faculty and students of the German university to join forces in a thoughtful way for the spiritual renewal of this institution; (2) the renewal is to take place by returning to and unfolding an origin, a beginning, whose appropriation is the prerequisite for an original conception of science heralding a new relation to things; (3) the return to that beginning presupposes a leading and following—a following that fosters resistance and is not based on blind obedience.

III

What about the intention of the rectoral address? We must deal with this question quite carefully, as it concerns a philosophical work. For this reason I propose to deal with it at three different but interrelated levels.

At the first and most basic level, the intention of the rectoral address is to communicate a philosophical message. The same intention is behind Heidegger's other speeches and lectures. At this level, then, the intention of the rectoral address is to enter the domain of philosophical discourse. By entering this domain, Heidegger's address tacitly makes the claim to *philosophical appropriation and interpretation.*

At a second, more specific level, the address presents a *philosophical program* for the renewal of the German university. To appreciate properly such a program, one must take seriously the situation of the German university at the time. At this level of a purely *philosophical diagnosis* the following questions are addressed: Did the German university incorporate the modern conception of science, with its calculative, manipulative, and domineering relation to things—a relation practiced through increased departmentalization and specialization of disciplines? Was the German university threatened by the imminent total control of the National Socialist regime?

The philosophical analysis of modernity in Heidegger's work since 1930 and the historical facts pertaining to the situation of the German university in the Third Reich make it necessary to answer both questions in the affirmative. After 1930 Heidegger's thinking increasingly takes cognizance of the historical character of being's unfolding. Accordingly, Heidegger sees modernity and its conception of science as representative of a will that wants to control and dominate everything through calculation and manipulation. In the arena of politics, the Ministries of Culture had tightened their grip on the German universities. The decision to appoint the rector and the deans rather than allow them to be elected by the faculty is one of several historical facts that led both to Heidegger's assumption of the rectorate and to his resignation from this office. (Among other historical facts pertaining to Heidegger's rectorate were the hanging of anti-Jewish posters in the buildings of the University of Freiburg and book burnings, which were some of the first political actions that Heidegger faced and prevented as rector.)[15]

At the third level at which we can pursue the intention of Heidegger's rectoral address, the speech presents an attempt at securing the support and cooperation of the National Socialists for its philosophical program.

This intention is corollary to the assumption that Heidegger in 1945 and in retrospect, puts in the form of a hypothetical question: "What would have happened and what would have been saved [*verhütet*], had around 1933, all capable forces aroused themselves and joined in secret in order to gradually purify and moderate the 'movement' that had come to power?" [16] The most important reason Heidegger sought this support, then, was purification and moderation of the National Socialist movement from within. More remote but nonetheless possible was the hope that such support would facilitate the spiritual renewal of the German university and thus counter the threat of total control by the Hitler regime.

What foremost distinguishes this attempt is a series of ambiguous terms designed to protect the philosophical message of the rectoral address. The first such word that stands out is *Kampf*, which in Nazi slogans means "struggle" or "battle." But Heidegger uses this word in the sense of "confrontation and contention," the sense that it has in Heraclitus's Fragment 53. [17] Thus *Kampf* has for Heidegger the intellectual sense of contention and not the physically violent meaning of battle and struggle. Another expression is *volklich-staatlich,* which Heidegger uses in connection with his crucial philosophical notion of *Dasein* (being here/ being there). [18] This expression combines the words *Volk* (people) and *Staat* (state). Heidegger understands these terms not racially as the Nazis did, but in Hölderlin's sense of *freien Gebrauch des Nationellen,* that is, a free use of the national element. [19] Specifically, Heidegger's understanding of *Volk* and *Staat* differs radically from the Nazis' understanding of these terms insofar as he considers the *Volk* an entity with an endowment (*das Mitgegebene*) and a task (*das Aufgegebene*). A *Volk* is endowed with certain gifts and faces certain tasks, tasks that it actualizes in accordance with its endowment. Depending on how a people's endowment molds a task, a state comes into being. Thus *volklich-staatliches Dasein* does not mean the racial and political existence of a people, as Heidegger's Nazi audience probably understood this expression. Rather, it means the way a people flourishes and thrives—according to its endowment and its task—and creates a state.

A third ambiguous term is *Dienst,* which means "service" but also implies "duty." As duty, *Dienst* need not be directed outward, as a service is. *Dienst* could just as well indicate a duty one has toward an inner task. Finally, there is the word *Wehr,* which usually means "defense" (as the Nazis always took it) but which Heidegger used "neither in a militaristic, nor in an aggressive sense, but as the action of resisting that comes through the need to resist [*Wehr der Notwehr*]."²⁰ This characterization of *Wehr der Notwehr* is important because *Notwehr* is defined (in the *Wahrig Deutsches Wörterbuch*) as *Abwehr eines rechtswidrigen Angriffs* (repulsion of an illegal attack), which obviously does not apply only to military situations.

But there was no guarantee that the Nazis would fall for the ambiguous language of the rectoral address. Soon they realized that what Heidegger had said was incompatible with Nazi ideology. By February 1934 they had ordered the text of the address banned.²¹

The attempt to secure the Nazis' support for the philosophical program of the rectoral address was doomed to fail because certain crucial elements of Nazi ideology were absent from this speech. No ambiguity of expression could hide the fact that the address did not have a single racial or anti-Semitic statement; in fact, it did not mention the issue of race at all. Moreover, there was no trace of the biologism of which racism is an offspring and which sustained nazism. The absence of racial and biological elements from the speech was not a strategic measure. In the Germany of the 1930s, it would have been absurd to be a racist and an anti-Semite and try to hide this from the Nazis.

The absence of the racial element was the logical outcome of Heidegger's sustained criticism of anthropologism and biologism in all their varied and sophisticated forms, as found in the philosophies of Nietzsche, Spengler, Ziegler, and Scheler. Long before he presented his rectoral address in 1933, Heidegger had laid out this criticism in his lecture courses (whose texts are now in print), rendering philosophically indefensible the anthropologistic, biologistic, and racist aspects of nazism.

Furthermore, the attempt to gain the support of the Nazis was in vain because there were more fundamental differences between what this speech said and what the Nazis were used to hearing. As their chief ideologist, Alfred Rosenberg (Commissioner for the Supervision of the Intellectual and Ideological Education of the Entire Nazi Party) repeatedly pointed out, nazism relied heavily on values and their lived-experience, notions that Rosenberg had taken from Max Scheler. But long before his rectoral address, Heidegger had criticized and rejected both the reliance on lived-experience and the assumption of values; the address never alludes to either. Heidegger's rejection of these notions becomes even more specific when, in a lecture course of the winter semester of 1934–35, he mentions Rosenberg by name, rejects his notion of a "race's soul" (*Rassenseele*), and adds, "This entire way of thinking, in any form, is deeply untrue and meaningless."²²

Finally, absent from the rectoral address are Hitler's name and the terms "Führer" and "national socialism." The rectoral address does not mention *anything* that would connect it to a totalitarian worldview. On the contrary, Heidegger introduces a daring notion of leading and following that is diametrically opposed to nazism. Heidegger talks about a leading and following in which resistance is present and which thrives on resistance. What could be more alien to nazism's demand for unconditional and total obedience?

The contrast between Nazi ideology and Heidegger's rectoral address is easier to grasp if we consider a passage from a speech Rosenberg gave on 22 February 1934. Unlike Heidegger's address, given a few months earlier, the speech is tainted with racism and is an adulation of Hitler:

> In the course of the development of the triumphant National Socialist movement, a deep mystery of blood became manifest which had seemingly died in the world war but was born again in this new movement. The thinking of all those who want to struggle for a new Germany and for a great future centers on this health-giving and newly born blood. This experience is accompanied by the appearance of a new science, by a new scientific discovery which we call *the science of race*. . . . Today, at the turn of a millennium, we declare that when Duke Widukind died in the eighth century, he triumphed in the person of Adolf Hitler.[23]

There was nothing in Heidegger's rectoral address, then, that made it palatable to the functionaries of the Nazi party. Nothing! The Nazis rejected it as "private National Socialism."[24] With the rectoral address there was an unfortunate collision between a totalitarian party that sought to consolidate its grip on everything (including universities) and a philosophical program. Heidegger and the Nazi party came together at the wrong time and in the wrong place.

Against my third-level analysis of the intention of the rectoral address, the objection may be raised that Heidegger was a member of the Nazi party; and although his speech did not represent the party's ideology, it was nevertheless written by a party member. But this objection overlooks three significant factors that differentiate Heidegger's membership in the Nazi party from a regular membership. Heidegger's membership was, as he put it himself, a *Formsache*, a pure formality, because it had no foundation in his philosophy and did not involve him in the activities of the party.[25]

The first of these factors was a simple one: Heidegger was *not* a member of the Nazi party *before* he became rector of the University of Freiburg. Existing documents indicate that he became a member of the party on 3 May 1933, one week *after* his official installation as rector.[26] This is important because his assumption of the rectorate, had he been a member of the party at the time, could be interpreted as an action that was brought about by the party's support. It was the outgoing rector, von Möllendorff, not the Nazi party, who proposed to Heidegger the assumption of the rectorate.[27] Moreover, had Heidegger already been a party member, his assumption of the rectorate would have been an occasion for him to implement the party's policies and to defend its ideology, which he did not do. His rectoral address is not a statement of the party's policy and does not articulate the party's ideology.

The second factor was an assumption on Heidegger's part that had lasting consequences for his own person and for his philosophy and that finally led to his critical reevaluation of and debate with the rectoral address. He assumed that with his membership in the party "a purification and clarification of the whole movement is possible."[28] This assumption is a significant indication that Heidegger's entanglement in the affairs of national socialism did not come about because of a mindless acceptance of its brand of nationalism and was not a case of transitory infatuation. By assuming that the party could be purified, moderated, and clarified, he approached the party and all its actions on the philosophical level. However we may look at the events in Germany in the 1930s, we cannot deny that "purification of the movement" by means of discursive/philosophical measures could claim a certain amount of plausibility. What if Heidegger's philosophical thinking could succeed in moderating and purifying the "nationalist movement"? As an outsider, Heidegger had no practical way to see whether such purification could be carried out.

The third factor was purely external but nevertheless weighed heavily on Heidegger. The minister of culture had demanded that all rectors, including Heidegger, become party members. Moreover, party functionaries had planned a book burning and the hanging of anti-Jewish posters on the premises of the university—events that Heidegger could not prevent as a nonmember (but that he did prevent after he joined the party). Furthermore, there was a deadline for becoming a member of the party, the so-called *Aufnahmesperrung,* after which no one could join the party.[29] It is obvious that if Heidegger wanted to implement his philosophical program by way of purifying and clarifying the party and thus prevent violent and aggressive actions such as book burnings, then he would have to join the party before the final and irrevocable deadline. He had little time for thinking through this situation. His assumption that it was feasible to influence the party by discursive/philosophical means gained the upper hand. When three party functionaries appeared at his office on 3 May 1933 and invited Heidegger to become a member, he accepted the invitation.[30] But he consented to membership only under the conditions that he would never be asked to participate in the party's meetings and that the party would not seek his advice in its affairs.[31] He acted as an academician whose concern was primarily with discursive/philosophical persuasion and who was intent on preserving the integrity of the university. It did not take him long to realize that persuasion by means of discourse was no longer possible. He recognized his error and after almost nine months resigned from the rectorate.

Heidegger's entry into and exit from the political scene of the University of Freiburg mark the beginning and the end of a brief involvement in politics by a philosopher who views the arena of political reality as one where philosophical thinking can make a difference. In this respect Heidegger is in the company of Plato and Marx. And Petzet reports Wolfgang Schadewaldt's sarcastic but quite appropriate question to Heidegger—"Back from Syracuse?" It was a succinct comment on Heidegger's rectorate by one of his respected colleagues.

Could one say that Heidegger shared Plato's hope as well as his disappointment? This hope meant that his whole entanglement in National Socialist affairs had, from the beginning, a discursive/philosophical orientation. He had to come to terms with this movement on purely philosophical grounds, which for him were provided only by the thinking of being. He had to depict the root-unfolding of what made something like Germany's national socialism possible. It is in his second major work, *Beiträge zur Philosophie (Vom Ereignis)* (Contributions to Philosophy [On Appropriation]), that he describes the phenomenon of nihilism, which makes something like national socialism possible. Published in 1989, this work was written between 1936 and 1938, years in which his philosophical rejection of nazism was a recurring theme in his lecture courses.

In a conversation with Heribert Heinrich on 14 October 1959, Heidegger addresses the problem of his involvement in national socialism. Heinrich summarizes some of Heidegger's remarks:

It was with the catastrophe of Stalingrad and the disasters of the air war that most Germans began to see through Adolf Hitler, that thief and criminal of the century. But when he [Heidegger] summons before his conscience his own responses, he realizes that he already recognized the total disaster in 1938 and revised his relationship to national socialism.[32]

In this conversation, Heidegger admits that not until 1938 did he recognize how Hitler betrayed the trust of the German people and destroyed German civilization and its national aspirations. The five years between 1933 and 1938 that Heidegger took to see the realities of national socialism are the years in which he was philosophically most productive. In this fact we may find a clue to what Heidegger calls retrospectively "a guilt incurred by a fundamental failure."[33] Perhaps this guilt provides a better understanding of the silence he maintained about his political entanglement.

IV

One of the recurring topics in chapters 2 and 4 of this book is Heidegger's persistent silence about his political involvement while he was rector. According to Petzet, Erhart Kästner was one of many friends and colleagues who kept urging Heidegger to take a public stance and refute the charges made against him. But Heidegger refused until he granted the interview to the newsmagazine *Der Spiegel* in 1966. Chapter 4 carefully and vividly describes the background issues that led to that interview and what transpired in it. Petzet does not discuss the philosophical substance of the interview simply because it is in print and accessible.

It seems to me that despite this interview, the question of Heidegger's silence needs to be addressed with care and assessed philosophically. We came upon this silence for the first time when we considered Heidegger's letter to Petzet about Löwith. We saw then that Heidegger's silence was masked by references to his philosophy. In order to look at the full range of his silence, I propose to begin with the following question: While he held the office of rector of the University of Freiburg, how did Heidegger himself react to his failed attempt to "purify the movement" from within? This question has a strong bearing on how we understand Heidegger's silence over the years, as well as his remark about "a guilt incurred by a fundamental failure."

From the beginning of his rectorate to the end of his life Heidegger never ceased to conceive his confrontation with the political as fundamentally *a philosophical and not a political* matter. This emerges clearly from an examination of the rectoral address and from a careful weighing of his various assertions during and after his rectorate. We find him making statements during his rectorate that on the one hand show a lack of confidence in its philosophical program and on the other hand a desire to strengthen that program. These statements indicate his own critical debate with the rectoral address.

While still rector of the University of Freiburg, he writes (on 30 August 1933) to his Jewish friend Elisabeth Blochmann that the new constitution of the university, which is being debated by the rectors and the deans, could be a "disastrous instrument." It is not difficult to imagine that participation in that debate led Heidegger to the pessimistic prognosis for the new constitution of the university and led him to draw a clear distinction in his own mind between the university-reform act that had the support of the Nazis and his own philosophical program for a spiritual renewal of the German university. In the letter he adds, "Everything depends on the education of the educators. As primary educators, these educators must first educate themselves so as to attain a secure form. Otherwise everything would stifle under increased organization." [34] This self-education of the educators is considerably closer to what is needed for the spiritual renewal of the German university than the new, Nazi-supported university-reform act. While the spiritual renewal of the German university calls for a return to the Greek beginning, the element of organization stressed in the university-reform act would stifle such a return. The letter to Blochmann articulates a significant difference between Heidegger's philosophical program for the German university and the Nazi reform of its constitution.

In a speech Heidegger gave three months after resigning from the rectorate, we note another significant point of contention, concerning the role of the state in the renewal of the German university. This speech, "On the German University," specifically addresses the role of the state with a precision and clarity that is absent from the rectoral address, which passes rather quickly over the role of the state by incorporating the state into the national existence of the people. Commenting on Wilhelm von Humboldt's design for founding the University of Berlin, Heidegger fully supports Humboldt's idea of the university but regrets that this idea could not be maintained and was later falsified under the already-existing power (*Vormacht*) of the modern conception of knowledge. It was this conception that hindered Humboldt's idea of the university from becoming a reality. In Heidegger's words, Humboldt put the main emphasis not on external organization but on calling upon the most qualified men, that is, creative thinkers and exemplary teachers. Wilhelm von Humboldt wrote at the time, "We need to call upon qualified men, and the rest will gradually follow." Thus the influence of the state was limited as far as possible, and the university obtained the freedom to teach and to learn. The philosophy faculty became the sustaining and determining center of the new university.[35]

What Heidegger says here about restricting the role of the state must be viewed as a significant addendum to his rectoral address.

By the fall of 1937, Heidegger, in a speech before the science and medical faculty of the University of Freiburg, goes so far as to clearly dissociate his own views on people as a national entity from the Nazi notion of people as a racial entity. His purpose in doing so is to reject the Nazi notion of a people-oriented (*völkisch*) science: "One day, perhaps, people will begin to realize what I demanded, wanted, and began with the rectoral address, [namely, something compared to which] the crude, absurd, and naive claim of a new, people-oriented science [*neue völkische Wissenschaft*] went completely awry."[36] This is not only an attack on the naiveté of the Nazis' conception of science, but also a critique of the notion of science presented in the rectoral address—a notion that is not adequately differentiated and analyzed in order to make it impregnable to Nazi misunderstanding. Apparently, Heidegger was dissatisfied with his own way of talking about the *Volk* (people) in the rectoral address. For had he expressed his views completely and thoroughly, his conception of an original science would have had enough persuasive force to unmask the Nazis' so-called *Völkerkunde* (science of people) and *Rassenkunde* (science of races) as pseudodisciplines that objectified humans according to race. In contrast to the rectoral address, in the 1937 speech Heidegger characterizes these Nazi-inspired pseudosciences as new forms of self-stupefaction. *LoL.*

By pulling together the series of direct and indirect criticisms to which Heidegger subjected the philosophical program of his rectoral address and by adding to these criticisms what he stated in the fall of 1937, we readily perceive the line of opposition that he took against Nazi ideology and the Nazi regime. Looking back at his failed rectorate, he said clearly what he planned to do next:

> Giving up and renouncing everything? No. Blindly affirming everything? No. Adjusting to everything? No. The only thing to

do is to build ahead [*vorausbauen*]. . . . [This means] to stay and try to exhaust the possibility of coming into contact with individuals [*Einzelne*]. To stay, but not in order to prepare the university—this is absurd now. Rather, to stay in order to preserve the tradition [*Überlieferung*]; in order to show exemplary figures, in order to occasionally implant a new claim in those essentially rare individuals [*Einzigen*]—somewhere, sometime, and for someone. This is neither a resignation nor a way out, but a necessity that originates from within the essentially philosophical task. . . . To bring on a knowledge but to do so only when the exigency of truth is experienced. And this requires above all knowing about the forgetting of being and the destruction of truth.[37]

This is clearly a new program that unmistakably replaces the program enunciated in the rectoral address. One element of this new program is building ahead in the sense of preserving the tradition, and the other is claiming rare individuals—all after the experience of the forgetting of being and the destruction of truth. It does not require a great deal of philosophical acumen to realize that this program is not a program of political action; it relies on a completely different kind of action, one that occurs at the level of thinking when thinking engages in disclosing and opening up what shows itself, emerges, and is manifest. Heidegger performed such an action in the rectoral address when he disclosed the Greek beginning as the origin to which the German university must return. The new program relies solely on the active character of thinking, which comes to the fore when thinking discloses such phenomena as preservation of tradition, claiming of individuals, forgetting of being, and destruction of truth.

That this new program was put into effect is shown by the now-available texts of Heidegger's lecture courses during his most productive period and especially by the text of his second major work, *Beiträge zur Philosophie*. When we study them, we find that the attempt to disclose and open up what shows itself is carried through with unprecedented care and clarity. One of the outcomes of this process is Heidegger's detection of the foundation of nazism in nihilism. A corollary to this detection is the continuing attack on and criticism of Nazi ideology in his lecture courses during the period in which he was writing *Beiträge zur Philosophie*. These attacks—as a result of which Heidegger and his family were in constant peril—were often directed at Alfred Rosenberg's explication and defense of nazism. Firsthand accounts of those like Siegrid Bröse,

Elisabeth Schmid, and Franz Büchner, who heard Heidegger's critique of nazism, testify to the passionate and courageous way in which he carried out this critique.[38]

When we take into account the realization of the new program, Heidegger's persistent silence appears in a new light. Heidegger remained silent about the political entanglement of his rectorate because he was fully aware that the final verdict on this entanglement would come not from persecutorial journalism but from his unpublished writings. The realization of the new program, which exposed the philosophical foundation of nazism, sustained his silence even while—as Petzet points out—allegations and untrue accusations increased. When, under mounting pressure, he finally agreed to the interview with *Der Spiegel,* it proved to be more a philosophical document than a carefully prepared defense that would satiate the journalistic curiosity. Heidegger's philosophical excursions in the course of the interview into the domain of technology and the will to power, his cryptic remarks on communism, national socialism, and democracy, and his very ambiguous statement that "only a god can save us" are philosophical issues that are deeply rooted in his philosophy and not at all accessible to the philosophically uneducated public for which *Der Spiegel* is a forum. This interview leaves the impression that Heidegger did not, after all, break his silence.

What motivated Heidegger's friends and colleagues to urge him to take a public stance? Presumably, it was the desire to see him vindicated and placed in a morally appropriate light. But what does "morally appropriate light" imply? It implies restricting the emergence and root-unfolding of action to the domain of morality. Is such restriction compatible with the kind of action for which Heidegger stands and in which he is engaged—the action in thinking for disclosing and opening up what shows itself and is manifest? However we may assess the period of Heidegger's rectorate, we cannot deny that the rectoral address documents a significant action in thinking that discloses and opens up the Greek origin and beginning. And such disclosure does not fall in the domain that restricts action only to moral action.

Heidegger is less concerned with morality, which relies heavily on arguments, than with the experience of guilt and shame. It seems to me that it is this experience, rather than the restrictive conception of action, that renders Heidegger's silence intelligible. The experience of guilt and shame is original and occurs at the pretheoretical level. Heidegger shows this to be the case—at least as far as guilt is concerned—in *Being and Time.* Rather than restricting the emergence and root-unfolding of action to the domain of morality, this experience provides an understanding of action that does not need moral argumentation and theoretical manipulations. There is a sense in which guilt points to situations and conditions into which we are "thrown" (*geworfen*) and with which we must come to terms. Heidegger has this sense of guilt in mind when, thinking back on the period of his rectorate and its political entanglement, he speaks of "a guilt incurred by a fundamental failure."

Heidegger was profoundly ashamed of having been associated with the Nazis. In two letters to Karl Jaspers, dated 7 March 1950 and 8 April 1950, Heidegger speaks of this shame. In the letter of April 8 he sums up what he has communicated to Jaspers: "What I report here can excuse nothing. Rather, it can explain how, when over the course of years what is virulently evil [*das Bösartige*] became manifest, my shame grew—the shame of directly or indirectly having been involved in it." [39]

If we assume that the philosophical background outlined here completes the accounts given in chapters 2 and 4, how does this outline affect the intellectual portrait of the philosopher that is woven in this book? The portrait reminds me of a notion in Heidegger's later thinking that he used in describing his friend Hans Jantzen, in the eulogy that he gave on the occasion of Jantzen's death. Heidegger characterized the departed friend as one who "was gifted with that rare way of existing (*eksistieren*) by which we mortals are capable of seeing through to what is most high and enduring (*das Hohe und Bleibende*). . . . I call this capability 'forthcoming holding-in-reserve' (*Zuvorkommen in der Zurückhaltung*)." [40]

The portrait that Petzet presents is striking because it shows the philosopher as a man who in coming forth—that is, in emerging—involuntarily kept something of his being in reserve. Are not the guilt and shame that we talked about already indicators of a deep-seated reserve that protected the philosopher from the persecutorial rage of the journalist and from the objectifying look of the biographer, a reserve that kept him sheltered in his work? Perhaps the reader should dwell on this question when carefully reading this book.

Encounters and Dialogues with Martin Heidegger

1929–1976

Martin Heidegger. Lithograph by Bernhard Heiliger.

Preface

It is still too early to write a biography of Martin Heidegger. His literary remains will not be available for a long time; his letters are dispersed and inaccessible; the complete edition of a largely still unpublished body of writing is only in its initial stage. Given such an inadequate foundation, a biography of Heidegger would have to be fragmentary. Then there is the issue of Heidegger's own aversion to putting his biography before his work. He repeatedly stressed that his life was entirely uninteresting and that only a study of his work was important. But regardless of our opinion on these issues, a critical debate concerning the person of Heidegger is hardly possible today without a further distortion of this controversial figure—as has already been made often enough by his opponents.

This book attempts something of a different kind. My aim is to outline especially the later years of the philosopher's life by drawing upon memories that often include seemingly unimportant personal details and events of marginal significance and that cover almost half a century. To do so, I shall make use of letters, sketches, and recorded conversations. I have proceeded from the assumption that at a time preoccupied with calculating and cataloguing, it would make sense to reflect on a life that was concerned exclusively with what is "necessary" without disregarding simple human affairs. This book has fulfilled its mission if it can serve to commemorate this man in such a manner.

Strictly speaking, a book such as this should narrate only what the author himself has experienced. Given the ways in which things are interconnected, however, I could not ignore the testimony of others. A historian obviously should place a decisive value on reliability. Thus the present work is based on my own notes taken over many years, on Heidegger's letters to me and to some of his friends, and on numerous other references from this circle. I must, however, point out that I did not intend to write a scholarly work, and for this reason I dispensed with a scholarly "apparatus." Those who miss footnotes and references in this book—the kind that accompany, for example, the edition of Thomas Mann's letters—should understand clearly that such an apparatus would have contradicted the whole character of this presentation. Wherever possible, I have included dates and bibliographic references in the text.

Heidegger's friendship and trust during a long and often-turbulent period were a great gift to me, even as they placed me under an obligation. To fulfill this obligation by publishing a book that lays the foundation for a future biography of Heidegger requires reckoning with some objections concerning the person as well as the issues. Yet the following presentation can be justified in good conscience. It is intended to be more than mere confession. However the future may judge Martin Heidegger, it is clear that, as one of the most significant figures of the twentieth century, he was subject to both approval and rejection. In this respect Heidegger could have summed up his life in Goethe's words: "How can I deny that I am disagreeable and odious to many people and that they will try to present me in their own way to the public? On the other hand, I know that I have never deliberately worked against those who bear me ill will, but have maintained uninterrupted activity and, although that activity was challenged, continued it to the end."

H. W. P.

On the Way with
Martin Heidegger

"It runs from the Hofgartentor to Ehnried. The old linden trees of the Schlossgarten preside over it from above the walls." [1] These are the opening lines, translated into many languages, of the short essay "Der Feldweg," which made Heidegger famous even beyond the international circle of his philosophical readers. That short piece of German prose, which carries something of the tranquillity and simplicity of Adalbert Stifter, is as much linked with Heidegger's name as is his famous work *Being and Time,* with which he stirred the thinking of an entire epoch.

"Der Feldweg," or country path, became a symbol for what distinguishes the philosopher Heidegger. For the *Weg,* or pathway, recurs as one of Heidegger's basic words. Even those taking only a cursory look into his writings frequently come upon the word *Weg* in various connections. For example, readers will find themselves from time to time on the "path" already traveled by an author. "An author who traverses the paths of thinking [*Denkwegen*] can only indicate the paths, without being oneself a sage, a *sophōs.*" Long is the most necessary *Weg* of our thinking—"and yet there are at first few signs to show the *Weg.*" But "questioning opens up a way." And, further on, "On the way to language." One must continue to ponder that "a way is always in danger of becoming a wrong way."

The opening stanza of *Aus der Erfahrung des Denkens* reads:

Go with and bear up under
Errancy and question
Along your one path. [2]

In his "attempts at thought," Heidegger is always concerned with the *Weg,* with the pathway, with being under way, without ever anticipating a destination. Whoever reads the present book and pursues its pathways should bear in mind the significance of *Weg,* which is anything but a preconceived system, because it is contrary to every fixed determination. But we are less concerned with *Denk-Wege*—pathways of thinking—than with a stretch of life, a pathway running parallel to pathways of thinking. We are dealing with outlines, contours, hints.

I would like to clarify my intention of pursuing in the following account something different from a mere biography by referring to an old Chinese legend. We are told of a famous old painter who, with his students, stands before a painting that he has just completed. Everyone praises the painting, the landscape with the trees and the mountaintops fading away in the distance. Some of the students ask the master to explain to them in detail this or that fine point. But then something strange happens. The painter steps onto the path that leads to the depths of the painting and, to everyone's astonishment, walks on until he vanishes at a turn in the pathway. Disconcerted, the students wait for a long time, far into the night. The painter, however, does not return. He is totally absorbed into his work.

This can only mean that the work is all that counts. It refers to the insignificance Heidegger attached to private events, saying that a preoccupation with such events would only divert attention from the one thing that is important. And yet, if this were wholly the case, would not something important still be left out of account—that pathway which leads the painter into and through his picture, a pathway that was and remains part of the whole? Would not a stretch of the way—which with its turnings, stops, and perils belongs to the completed work—be overlooked? If this pathway had taken a different direction, would not the whole of the work have turned out differently?

I am concerned here with looking at this pathway and its relation to the whole. At some junctures, as one looks ahead or looks back, something flares up that is more deeply related to the meaning of the way in its beginning, something that perhaps only later is disclosed. Thus it seemed to me not only meaningful but also necessary to record this stretch of Heidegger's pathway for posterity before my personal memories of it no longer exist. These memories and experiences are needed to establish a living connection with the letters and notes, which will later be condemned to a sterile existence in the archives. If these letters and notes occasionally touch something that is private, they are meant nevertheless to manifest connections that point beyond what is private.

Experiences and occurrences that would resonate as familiar to those who knew Heidegger may sound novel and even strange to the members of the younger generation. The following pages have been written for this younger generation, which is no longer familiar with the figure and the influence of the man who at the time of his death was called "the greatest thinker of the century" and who has often been misrepresented to that generation.

These pages contain nothing sensational. They hold perhaps a provocation and, it is to be hoped, an inducement. The intellectual landscape into which they lead spans half a century—and what a century! But to be on the way in such a landscape means that one must pause here and there, to look around and reflect. Sometimes obstacles blocked the way, and the one who came after barely saw the one who was there before. That the one who came after always managed to find the way again and to advance a bit further into what until then was pathless—to that this book would gratefully like to give testimony. In his book *Wege und Begegnungen*, Hofmannsthal wrote that one cannot conceive anything more strange and mysterious than the seemingly arbitrary contours of a human life. Do these contours outline a senseless going, roaming, and seeking? "Sometimes they leave behind a trace that glows for a long time . . . that radiates such that it does not vanish."

What Martin Heidegger knew at the end of his long way (did he know it about himself?) he captured in a short poem entitled "Cézanne":

Kaum noch bemerkliches Zeichen des Pfads
der in das Selbe verweist
das Dichten und Denken.
das nachdenksam Gelassene,
das inständig Stille
der Gestalt des alten Gärtners Vallier
der Unscheinbares pflegte
am chemin des Lauves.

(Hardly noticeable anymore, the sign of the pathway
which alludes to the same:
poetic saying and thinking.
thoughtfully left as is,
the urgent stillness
of the figure of the old gardener Vallier
who tends what is nonappearing
on the chemin des Lauves.)

1

The First Encounter

The Metaphysics Lecture of 1929

"By nature, my friend, there is something of the philosopher hidden in the man!" I read this statement from Plato's dialogue *Phaedrus* in my Greek classes at the old Bremen gymnasium and heard it again in the course of my preliminary studies in philosophy (designed to give the graduates of the year 1928 a foretaste of university studies), and it has stuck in my mind. For I took the great philosopher's statement as a consolation in the face of the confusing and wide-ranging field of philosophical knowledge, scattered as it is among many disciplines. The statement first of all referred the inquirer back to himself or herself and to his or her own ability to inquire—an ability that need not be subordinated to somebody else's opinion, no matter how authoritative.

It was, of course, never my intention to study philosophy or to become a professional philosopher. To turn a phrase of Nietzsche's around, abstract thinking meant for me more a pain than a feast. The closer I got to the end of my studies in the gymnasium, the stronger grew my desire to devote myself to history—although I was not able to see the goals clearly. Later, when I considered a profession in my native Hanseatic city of Bremen, I had to respect my father's wish that I first complete a study of jurisprudence. Because it had prominent professors in several disciplines, the University of Freiburg (where more than half of my Bremen classmates went to study) offered me the possibility of enjoying along with jurisprudence, other sciences that enticed me more.

At that time Gerhard Ritter attracted a large number of students to his history courses, and the lecture hall where the famous phenomenologist Edmund Husserl held his lectures was no less crowded. My attempt to follow Husserl's presentations failed, however; his efforts seemed like a play of glass beads. During the first vacation of the semester, I somewhat disappointedly talked to my old German teacher, who had taught the preliminary course in philosophy. He said that recently a new star had risen in the heavens of philosophy in Freiburg—namely, Martin Heidegger, who had come from Marburg—and that I should attend one of his lectures.

This was the time in which, as Hannah Arendt later wrote, Heidegger's name traveled across Germany like the rumor of a secret king. Long before being called to succeed his teacher Husserl, Heidegger, who was not yet forty years old, attracted students from all over the world, gathering large audiences in front of his lectern. They came from all walks of life in a world uprooted by the great war and from places far beyond Germany and Europe—even from the Far East. That rumor hinted at the rigor of thinking linked with the new and unfamiliar name of Heidegger, as well as at an unprecedented liberation from what education traditionally offered. Martin Heidegger attracted the youth of this period like a magnet.

My first encounter with him in the lecture hall remains unforgettable. In the summer semester of 1929, Heidegger gave a lecture course as an introduction to academic studies, in the course of which he explicated Plato's simile of the cave. Every corner of the lecture hall—it was Room V, where we struggled each morning with the Civil Law—was filled when Heidegger entered in his quick gait. Many people, like Bollnow, Biemel, and von Weizsäcker, have described their impressions of his entrances. They all say that even in outward appearance Heidegger was quite different from what people imagined him to be. He had nothing about him of the scholar, but rather gave the impression of a peasant or a woodsman. But as soon as one noticed his eyes, one was spellbound by his gaze and knew: That could only be Heidegger. As Gadamer put it, Heidegger was "one who sees, a thinker who sees." When he turned to his lecture notes, he did not actually read from the text; in his speaking, he created anew what he presented—sometimes deviating from his notes, sometimes adding to them. For those who listened carefully, even the most difficult train of thought became simple and intelligible. His high tone of voice, warmed with a powerful Alemannic timbre, almost without modulation and yet not monotonous, demanding one's last ounce of concentration; his obviously intense devotion to the matter of thinking, which was enacted anew in every lecture session—all this contributed to the unusual fascination with this man and his lectures. As Bollnow observed, "Perhaps Fichte impressed his audience in the same way. The comparison with Luther also suggests itself. Here in the lecture hall, philosophy took place (*er-eignete sich*) in the emphatic sense that Heidegger has given to this word."

The lecture course made us restless and disturbed the neatly organized academic program. What we had learned in the humanistic gymnasium, especially the glimpse we had had of the Greek world, suddenly took on new and different colorings and altered dimensions. Yet what this "introduction" dealt with did not lie somewhere far away in the past, in a worn-out culture, but was actually close at hand insofar as we involved ourselves in it. The "Introduction to Academic Studies" was definitely different from what this novice had imagined it would be. Nevertheless, these weekly afternoon sessions, couched in the darkness of the allegory of the cave, remained an unshakable constant in the midst of the multifaceted thirst for knowledge that marked the beginning of my academic studies, extending from physiology to the modern German novel. And yet, how very different was this poetic allegory of Plato's, and how much more it spoke to us than did the well-prepared lectures of Jonas Cohn on the system of ethics, which was supported by more or less traditional platitudes.

Heidegger did not give answers to the many questions put to philosophy—or, at most, he responded in such a way that a new question emerged immediately behind his response. He questioned inexorably and piercingly. And the students, who might resist at first, were either finally swept along by this questioning, forced to jump into uncertainty—or found themselves trapped in an aporia. The students who entrusted themselves to the direction taken by the relentlessly questioning Heidegger were by no means given a handle with which to deal with the sciences, which were still unfamiliar to them. Instead, this "introduction" led in an increasingly alarming manner beyond the closed circle of the sciences. But led to where? In retrospect, it seems to me as if the allegory of the cave had been placed like a weighty riddle over the auditorium, where the audience sat and listened breathlessly, a riddle for which there was no final solution—as though we were not yet standing in the full light but were still under a covered sky. Only the small, dark man who commanded all attention, there at the lectern, seemed to have the light and the key in his hands.

The memories of that semester in Freiburg are all too vague. Too many paths opened up for me then, none apparently the right one. In spite of all my preparation for philosophy, I did not feel up to Heidegger. The abundance of other claims on my time made evasion quite easy. The months were bright, made more pleasant by wine; and they brought so much contact with important figures of the period (notably in the circle of friends at the academic literary society to which Ernst Zinn introduced me) that my studies often suffered a little. How many different worlds!

There were the psychologist Ludwig Klages, the philosopher Nikolai Berdyayev, the Jewish religious scholar Martin Buber, the Catholic theologian Erich Przywara, the architect and city planner Ernst May, the writer Alfred Neumann, and the architect Moholy-Nagy. But I did not forget Heidegger. Occasionally, a pang of conscience told me that I had missed something significant, for my fellow students reported to me on what was going on in that large lecture course. I attended it once, but I no longer found any connection. Otherwise, it seemed as if Heidegger dominated the intellectual scene of the university even where he was not actively involved—finding opposition as well as agreement. While some were enthusiastic about him, others resisted and mocked him. The enormous neologisms in his language were facetiously twisted or maliciously distorted. Or one made fun of his clothes, which did not seem to be appropriate for a respected full professor. He appeared in breeches and a short jacket, whose raised collar was reminiscent of the costumes of Hessian peasants. (Stefan George also dressed like that.)

However, the mockeries soon ceased. The time came when I, like so many others who followed him without being professional philosophers, had to see the true significance of the man, the master who determined my whole life, far beyond any academic discipline.

It was 24 July 1929. In a festive setting with golden scepters and silken gowns (which in the old university gave these occasions color and dignity), Heidegger gave his inaugural lecture, "What Is Metaphysics?" The lecture had an unexpected and amazing effect on me. It was as if a tremendous streak of lightning split apart the dark sky that had hung over the allegory of the cave. The things of the world lay open and manifest in an almost aching brilliance. The way that was offered was not well trodden and not without danger; it was neither well marked nor certain of its goal. Rather, it was a path full of dangers all the way to its last consequence, a path that was inconvenient and that contradicted everything familiar. We were dealing not with an object of scholarly research, but with something thought, and there was no getting away from its demands. We were dealing not with a "system," but with *existence*!" [1] Blinders fell away from my eyes; what had been offered by education and easily believed now disappeared. And now Kant's fourth question emerged as even more troubling: "What is it to be a human being?"

When I left the auditorium, I was speechless. For a brief moment I felt as if I had had a glimpse into the ground and foundation of the world.

In my inner being something was touched that had been asleep for a long time. Heidegger awakened it with his question, "Why are there beings instead of nothing?"[2]

My last semester in Freiburg was entirely dominated by the lecture course "Basic Questions of Metaphysics (World, Finitude, and Individuation)."[3] I cannot forget the place and the time: four times a week between five and six o'clock in the afternoon in the largest auditorium of the university. At that time, however, I did not have a personal relationship with Heidegger. And I did not try to have one. I was much too shy in the presence of this man and the fire that burned in him. (I was reminded immediately of my encounter with Heidegger when, in the fifties, the director of a Basel museum, Georg Schmidt, talked to me about his visit with Picasso. He mentioned the difficulties he had had while speaking with the painter, out of fear that one single trivial remark of his might prevent an inspired stroke of the brush of this man, who was so full of passion for his work.) Even the customary, brief presentation of the student registration booklet almost required courage, because Heidegger used to examine closely everyone who approached his lectern, saying barely a word. There was in the auditorium an intellectual tension that can hardly be imagined today.

Conversations during that winter were fed by reports brought back by participants in the "Davoser Hochschulkurse," in which Heidegger debated Ernst Cassirer.[4] These reports reminded us of the period of the important *disputationes* during the Middle Ages, when the best minds of the time struggled with one another. It seemed that a rich tradition, which protected goods declared holy, was again under attack. One specific statement by Heidegger excited those whose minds had become sleepy on their convenient paths of thinking. Heidegger had said that the task of philosophy is "somehow to jolt human beings out of their laziness and in a certain sense back into the rigor of their destiny, using only the works of the mind." Who could not have paid attention to this? It was no wonder that this statement, which fifty years earlier could have come from Sils Maria,[5] was ardently discussed in the lecture halls of the University of Freiburg and even became a topic for evening discussions in ski huts. This venture into a meditation on thinking was not about theoretical points of view, but rather about the very roots of one's own being. The first session of the lecture course in that semester had begun with a statement from Novalis: "Philosophy is actually homesickness—it is a desire to be at home everywhere." It was difficult for me to leave Freiburg. I have always felt homesick for the place where the event of thinking became visible to me for the first time.

The Visit to Bremen

I visited my old German teacher Jordan again during the Easter vacation of 1930, in order to tell him about Heidegger. We soon agreed to try to get the author of *Being and Time* to give a lecture in Bremen. Rumor had it that Heidegger was inaccessible for such an event and, at best, would only speak in a university town. Would he be more inclined to accept an invitation brought to him in person? At any rate, I volunteered to bring him an invitation myself. I must admit that the prospect of exchanging unfamiliar Bonn for a few days in my beloved Freiburg contributed considerably to my vigorous support for this proposal. In June we succeeded. Once again I sat in the old auditorium. At the end of a lecture session, and with some palpitation, I asked Heidegger whether he would be willing to give a lecture in Bremen the following autumn. After briefly considering the proposal, he said, "Why not? After all, Knittermeyer is the director of the Philosophical Society in Bremen. I know him. They should just write to me."

I happily reported my success to the people in Bremen, and the matter took its course. Jordan was pleased to have such a jewel for the beginning of his winter program. And my mother was pleased to put the house at the disposal of the guest. (She always did this for important events, such as the annual Göttingen University Weeks, when we had to house a speaker.) Our guest book, with its heavy leather cover in the Jugendstil,[6] recorded the names of these speakers. Among them were the archaeologist Theodor Wiegand, the historian Karl Brandi, the astronomer Hans Kienle, literary critics such as Fritz Kern and Fritz Strich, and the constitutional- and international-law experts Erich Kaufmann and Carl Schmitt. To these was added, from the sixth to the ninth of October 1930, the name of Martin Heidegger.

From the correspondence that preceded his arrival, it was clear that Heidegger wished his host to keep everything as simple as possible. He also wrote that he would not be accompanied by his wife, since she would be needed at home with the children. As the time of the visit drew nearer, I managed to suppress the happiness of anticipation and warned my parents that it would not be easy to show the philosopher—who lived in an atmosphere totally different from that of most of Bremen—things that he would find really interesting. No significant intellectual figures had left their trace in our city; and Heidegger could not be expected to be impressed by ships, shipyards, and commerce. This sounded slightly disturbing to my father, who was a director at Lloyd's. Somewhat puzzled, he asked, "What am I supposed to do with him?" He could not entertain Heidegger, he said, with reminiscences of his own "philosophicum" at the University of Munich. I suggested that he show Heidegger our old cathedral, the city hall with its golden chamber, and the art galleries, especially Worpswede.

When, on the afternoon of 6 October, I was sent to the train station to meet our guest, I missed him. (This happened again some twenty years later, and it gave Heidegger the chance to make an amusing remark about "the Bremen tradition.") Annoyed, I returned home and learned that Heidegger had arrived some time earlier; I was to present myself to him immediately. As I stood before him in our guest room, with its wide view into the autumnal garden, Heidegger looked me straight in the eye and said, "It *was* you, then! Last winter semester you always sat in the corner, near the aisle, in the third row on the left." He had recognized me on the spot, even though it was said that he did not notice anyone in the auditorium.

As so often happened at the round table beside the fireplace in the large living room of our beautiful house (which had been decorated by the Jugendstil architects Bruno Paul and Richard Riemerschmid), the tea hour turned into a small feast. With her reserved and delicate grace, my mother reigned as hostess. Initial bashfulness quickly disappeared. Conversation centered on the Black Forest, which my parents liked very much. Heidegger spoke with pleasure about how he had "caroused around in powder snow" one day last winter near his ski hut. How irrelevant my anxiety-filled preparations had been became evident when my father asked Heidegger what he would like to see the following day, adding, "My son wanted to suggest . . ." Heidegger interrupted my father and said, "Herr Petzet, what I would really like is to see the port and the ships and to experience something of the life of the city and its connections overseas." Later, my father reproached me in strong terms: "Ignorant young man! What nonsense you were talking! One can discuss everything important with that man."

My diary has the following entry for the same evening: "Went to the performance of the Philharmonic Orchestra. Old Pembaur played Chopin's Piano Concerto in B Minor. Then Bruckner: much too long." But our guest—who was stared at because, even on such an occasion, he was wearing the garb mentioned above—appeared to be pleased with the virtuosity of the performance, which I had thought could hardly have touched him. Many years later he was delighted with a concert held at Helmken's house in Bremen; the church organist, Hans Heintze, played Johann Sebastian Bach's "The Musical Offering" in Heidegger's honor. Music had a place near Heidegger's heart, something not everyone knew. For example, C. F. von Weizsäcker remarked that music is hardly ever mentioned in Heidegger's lectures on art. It would be wrong to conclude, however, that he was therefore out of the reach of music; on the contrary. He loved Mozart above all else. On the two hundredth anniversary of Mozart's birth, at the beginning of a lecture session, he offered a beautiful testimony by citing a verse of Angelus Silesius:

> A heart as deeply quiet as God wants it to be will be pleased to be touched by God.
> Such a heart is God's string music.

And Heidegger added: "Mozart is God's string music."

The following afternoon, after sightseeing in the city and at the port, we went on an excursion to Worpswede. At that time, Worpswede had not yet been so alienated by tourism. It still mostly preserved its old, rustic character and recalled the founders of its painters' colony. Philine Vogeler, sister-in-law of the painter Heinrich Vogeler (who had emigrated to Russia), welcomed us in her beautiful gallery, which had been constructed by Bernhard Hoetger. She showed us paintings from Paula Becker-Modersohn's Worpswede period as well as some of Becker-Modersohn's very last paintings from Paris, by which the artist had achieved her European fame. Heidegger had never seen an original painting by Becker-Modersohn and was deeply impressed. He took a reproduction of *Elsbeth* (with the bluebell) as a gift for his wife, who had early memories of Worpswede. Afterward, we visited the painter's grave in a cemetery high on the hillside. We remained there for a long time. Nineteen years later, when Heidegger and I were standing on the same spot, enveloped in a light snowfall, he said to me, "Petzet, you have no idea how often, in my thoughts, I stand at this grave." The destiny and art of this painter were quite dear to him.

Before returning to the city, we once again walked over to the hilltop of the Weyerberg with its view of the distant valley, dim in the evening light, on whose horizon the towers of Bremen rose—a powerful impression of a German lowland scene. But we could not stay too long. The sun was setting, and guests were already waiting at home. During Heidegger's stay in our house, my parents invited some of their friends for lunch and dinner. Their manner and conversation gave Heidegger some idea of that special Bremen spirit which, after the legendary days of the Goldene Wolke,[7] was still to be found in many houses of this Hanseatic city. Bremen's love of art, at a time when an extremely materialistic attitude prevailed, created an atmosphere that was contrary to the drive for pure profit and in which deep thoughts and important works of art could emerge and have an effect. There were people who preserved some of this atmosphere beyond the world war. They included the maritime senator Hermann Apelt, who from his youth onward had the aura of Weimar about him; his wife Julie, who participated in everything in a spirit of excitement; the sovereign Meta Sattler, the much-traveled translator of Italian literature, who had once been friends in Florence with the essayist Karl Hillebrand and the sculptor Adolf von Hildebrand; and, finally, Mayor Theodor Spitta, a statesman educated entirely in the spirit of German classicism, who with dignity embodied its freedom. Spitta not only created the 1919 constitution of Bremen, but later was also one of the founding fathers of the Federal Republic of Germany.

Heidegger had lively conversations with all these people, conversations that never lacked interest and that he had not expected to find in Bremen, the city of business. That Bremen became known as "the only big city that fascinated Heidegger" is ultimately due to these encounters, among which the relationship with Spitta lasted for many decades.

The gathering on the evening of 7 October, when we returned from Worpswede, was different from that at midday. Besides Doctors Knittermeyer and Jordan, representing the Philosophical Society, there were some young people who came to chat around the fire. Among them were those young women students from Bremen who were proud to have learned from Heidegger not only the beginning of philosophizing, but also how to ski. Since his Marburg days, when Heidegger took some young theologians from Bultmann's circle to his hut during Christmas holidays, it was considered a special honor to be invited to Todtnauberg for winter sports. That evening Bultmann's circle was represented by Mayor Spitta's son, who was already acting as pastor. On the theme of the evening, my diary laconically remarks, "Insight into the theologian's confusion." The writer of this diary apparently did not understand much of the discussion, which, as he remembered, was for the most part a passionate one. It was getting late, and the old Westminster clock struck twelve as the guests left.

On the next day, Heidegger withdrew to the library, as was his custom, for concentration and preparation. He emerged only for one hour at lunch. In the evening, he gave his lecture. The great hall of the *Real-gymnasium*,[8] one of the largest lecture halls in Bremen, was filled to over-flowing. The morning edition of *Bremer Nachrichten* published one of the extremely rare photos of the philosopher, which I had obtained from Freiburg and supplied to the newspaper. Thus I had the pleasure of both savoring the lecture and reporting on it. This was my first journalistic effort—a little bold and arrogant, but halfway successful; and I did not have to be ashamed of it.

The title of the lecture was "Vom Wesen der Wahrheit." [9] At the time, few were aware that this lecture—presented in other cities and later pub-lished (in 1943), often being reworked and expanded—represented a de-cisive step beyond *Being and Time.* However, every attentive member of the audience would have noticed that this lecture accomplished some-thing of the highest order in thinking. However much may not have been comprehended in this discussion (which transformed the question of how truth unfolds or *is,* into the question concerning the truth of this very unfolding, its being—thus leading the discussion back to the question of being), what became fixed in one's mind was the Greek idea of truth as un-concealment, *a-letheia:* "stealing (*Raub*) from what is hidden." The last sentence of the lecture—which is not in the later published ver-sions—points out, "It is not a question of bending, but of breaking."

After the lecture, a large number of guests gathered around Heideg-ger at the home of the wholesale merchant Kellner. Heidegger realized that he was received quite differently here than in the academic circles more familiar to him. After initial shy attempts, the conversation got bogged down in the question of whether one human being can change places with another, and the danger emerged of senseless, psychologizing talk. Heidegger suddenly turned to his host and said, "Herr Kellner, would you please bring me the *Parables of Chuang-tzu?* I would like to read some passages from it." The silence that followed must have made clear to Heidegger that he had made something of a faux pas here in Bremen, namely, embarrassing the host by requesting a completely un-known book. Nevertheless, Kellner did not hesitate for a moment, simply excusing himself so that he might go to the library upstairs. In a few min-utes he returned with Buber's new edition of the *Parables.* There was much astonishment and relief all around, and Heidegger began to recite the legend of the joy of the fishes and the joy felt by the one who stands on the bridge above the brook and watches the play of the minnows in the water. The deep meaning of the legend cast a spell on all who were present. With the interpretation he offered of that legend, Heidegger unexpectedly drew closer to them than he had with his difficult lecture, which remained inaccessible to most of them.

This gathering again lasted well beyond midnight, because an increasing number of people found the courage to put questions to the man who appeared more open and human than they had previously assumed. And they received patient responses, as it was always Heidegger's custom to give in such situations. When we finally returned home, my parents asked him not to leave the next morning as planned, but to stay one day longer. This Heidegger did happily. Thus there came about a postlude.

Hilde Roselius, the daughter of the coffee merchant and founder of the Böttcherstrasse in Bremen, invited us to breakfast (after we had visited Paula Becker-Modersohn's house and the picture gallery). While serving Weserlach and Chablis, she asked Heidegger what he especially liked about Bremen (for everyone sensed that he liked being in this city). Smiling in a sly manner, he passed the question on to the other person at the table: "Well, Petzet, as a Bremenian, you can best respond to this question." Somewhat embarrassed, I said that perhaps the reason was that there was no university here. Heidegger laughed and said that there was some truth in this, adding, "My dear Fräulein Roselius, in Bremen professional philosophers do not ask me stupid questions that do not lead anywhere. Reticent and untouched by philosophy as you are, you Bremenians are concerned only with essential matters, even if these are the simplest things. And this is what gives me a good feeling." Our hostess replied that this honored the people of Bremen. Two decades later Heidegger was sorry not to meet this intelligent woman again, who was so open to life.

"Who Is This Heidegger, Anyway?"

As a token of his gratitude for the friendly days spent in Bremen, days not disturbed by any discord, Heidegger sent a copy of *Being and Time* to my parents with a dedication that included their son: "To the Petzet family in memory of the October days in Bremen. From 6 to 9 October 1930." For her part, Elsa Petzet gave Heidegger as a memento one of the beautiful books from the Bremenian Press of her brother, Willy Wiegand, entitled *Der Deutsche in der Landschaft* (The German in the Country), prepared by Rudolf Borchardt. I saw the dedication that she had written in this book—from a work of Goethe's—when Frau Heidegger returned the volume to me, as a remembrance, after her husband's death. Between my mother and the philosopher there quickly developed, without words, a deep confidence. Indeed, he sensed the inner solitude of this woman, who even then suspected her serious illness. Later, Heidegger often remembered her. In a letter with New Year's greetings in January 1931, he wrote that the days he had spent in Bremen had made that year a memorable one. It certainly says a great deal that Heidegger, who did not use clichés, chose to use the word "memorable." Many years later, whenever I visited him in the house at Rötebuck and we drank toasts with wine served in glasses from Bremen (a birthday present), Heidegger never failed to remember my parents.

That New Year's letter is remarkable for a different reason. In Berlin, where I had been studying law since the winter semester of 1930, there was often talk of Heidegger among my fellow students, especially after he refused a call to the University of Berlin. Max Dessoir's question made the rounds: "Who is this Heidegger, anyway, who makes the world so restless?" In the capital of the Reich—a city that considered itself the center of the world not only in art and related matters, but also in everything intellectual—Heidegger was resented for rejecting the call. The circles in this city that were devoted to art and that tried hard to attract every new celebrity could not understand such a refusal. It was assumed that everyone should try to move up from the belittled "provinces"—a prejudice that often led to misunderstanding. The allegation of provincialism, which was assumed to be behind Heidegger's refusal, was brought against him later in a more serious and general way. It appeared strange and suspicious to some people that because of his own person, his teaching, and his work, Heidegger succeeded, around 1930, not only in gathering more and more young people around him every year, but also in attracting countless students to Freiburg, instead of Berlin. The question "Who is this Heidegger, anyway?" was not raised accidentally.

There were lively discussions of this question in the highly intellectual circle of professors and lecturers to which I was introduced by Erich Kaufmann, an expert in constitutional and international law (and whose lectures I had already heard in Bonn). This circle—which met regularly in an old, fashionable house in Blumeshof in Berlin for lectures and discussions and which included the theologian Erich Seeberg and the historian Gerhard Maszur—was not unaware of the fact that I had a personal relationship with Heidegger. So the request was made that the young student (twenty-two years old at the time) present a paper on Heidegger. Resistance was of no avail, and Kaufmann wrested a yes from me.

When I became ill during the Christmas vacation, I looked for a way out of the commitment I had made. But in this regard I did not know my mother well enough. She had studied *Being and Time* intensively and had also read the new Kant book. She played on my pride and wrote to Heidegger asking whether I might discuss my concerns about this paper with him. Heidegger's reply was that I could come with all my questions but should not make it too heavy a task; that is, the simpler these questions were, the easier it would be to respond to them, to the extent that he could respond at all.

Encouraged by this, I went to Freiburg at the beginning of the second half of the semester. I had never before been in the philosopher's house in Rötebuck. I stopped before the steps that led to the entrance in order to read an inscription above the door, which I had certainly not expected: "Shelter your heart with all vigilance; for from it flow the springs of life" (Proverbs 4:23). Heidegger received the newcomer in his study, which I entered then for the first time. He asked me to sit in the heavy leather chair near the writing desk (where I sat many times later, like so many other visitors). I was briefly cross-examined about the circle in Berlin to which I was to present my paper, and then Heidegger discretely brought the conversation around to the problems that troubled me. The entire huge ballast of preliminary and secondary questions that I had loaded upon myself collapsed like so many insignificant accessories. From out of the simple pathway of thought that he traveled with me, there emerged something like a guiding thread on which I would be able to rely. Some glimpses into his world, which now for the first time I could follow, seemed to take my breath away. But I had to stay strictly on the subject at hand. Although I can no longer say what in particular we were dealing with, I know that at the end of this hour and a half I felt refreshed and immersed in a rigor and clarity that had demanded a great deal of energy to keep up with. It was the lengthiest philosophical discussion that I had had with Heidegger. I was getting dizzy.

The next morning, before returning to Berlin, I was allowed to participate in the main seminar as a silent guest—the only time that this was granted to me, a nonphilosopher. Heidegger's wish was that I write my paper with the totally fresh impression I had gained from the work with him. Although I did not succeed at all in following the discussions (which for more than two months had centered on a certain thought), I was unusually touched by these two hours of seminar. In the end, it was only a pedagogical device that I kept remembering—especially since, in my own period of doctoral work and in working with other academic teachers, I had nowhere come across this trick. After the protocol of the previous session was read, Heidegger did not immediately ask another participant to do the protocol for this session. He moved on to deal with the text under discussion until, after more than an hour, he casually said, "Today Fräulein Schmidt will take over the protocol." Thus he managed to get all participants (there were perhaps thirty or more) to follow the questions, counterquestions, and objections with such undivided attention that every one of them would be in a position to do the protocol for that session.

Back in Berlin, I immediately began to work on my paper. Nothing remains of the mountain of sheets filled with closely written notes, the outcome of many days and nights of work. Today, it seems to have been a task like that of Sisyphus. Nevertheless, considering my own struggle and attempt at clarity, it was not entirely without meaning. In any case, this paper about Heidegger—whose final title I can no longer recall— was, thanks to the "instructions" I had received in Freiburg, appropriate in many respects for effectively confronting some of the grave misunderstandings about the "nihilist of the Black Forest." I presented the paper on a March evening to a board of "seven wise men," who listened with benevolence. But the energy and conviction which I had for the subject matter did not achieve much. In the end, I had a close brush with defeat. For in circles like that, which operated with presuppositions totally different from those of Heidegger's thinking, Heidegger came, so to speak, under the guillotine. What I tried to present had, of course, nothing to do with humanistic ideals and traditional religious values. For the question of being (and the shock that comes from this question) was inaccessible to this circle. "Being" was hastily identified with "God," and with that identification the access to Heidegger was closed. That evening I believed that I had lost a battle. Of what value were all those friendly expressions at the end, which implied assurance that they already knew everything there was to know about the philosopher?

Only one of the participants caught up with me in the dark, snow-covered streets and held a long and intelligent conversation with me. He encouraged me by citing a verse of George. His name was Walter Elze, the young professor of history (called to succeed Delbrück) who was to become my mentor a couple of years later. I never forgot him as the one who gave me this emotional lift.

The report back to Freiburg—which I felt committed to make—must have been a little severe. The response, which came back soon, was significant. Heidegger wrote that, above all, I should not let myself be intimidated by the heavy-handed behavior of the grand gentlemen from Berlin. More importantly, I should not lose courage. What was important for me now was to work very calmly and to grow deeply with things: "It is quite essential that you preserve and practice respect for things, so as to be immune from the danger of merely talking about them. I have never entertained the idea that I will have an effect. That is the fate of philosophy." If the gentlemen of the Berlin circle were now satisfied that they had "finished him up" and so could move on to the next fashionable thing of the day, then this was quite all right. "We, the others, should take no notice of that."

Is this a haughty and arrogant statement? It may seem so. But this would be a misunderstanding, one for which the writer of the statement would be not entirely without fault. For one tends to interpret as arrogant someone who wrote so many statements that were not understood. (His inability to repeat clichés!) If that statement, however, is read in the context of the entire letter, then one sees what it really means. It shows neither despisal nor disdain of the other "colleagues" (although the "grand" gentlemen from Berlin were not to his taste); much less does it show any refusal to understand their views. Rather, Heidegger wanted to make clear to the young beginner that he should not be misled by an authority that presumes to have monopolized the truth or believes it has the better arguments. He should not allow the path of inquiry (*Weg*) to be distorted by great proclamations that carry hidden within them, from the very beginning, a refusal to understand. This is basically a refusal to be prepared to want to listen—and thus to be able to listen. Heidegger, who truly knew how to listen, must have learned where one would be led if listening were replaced by "mere talking." He knew exactly why he quoted with delight Goethe's word to the magician of the north: "Hamann, listen!"

If a statement such as that reflected upon here is taken superficially, it might appear to testify to an excessive self-conceit. But Heidegger's statement is free from any such attitude. Heidegger must have known *who* he was—but precisely because of this he was not spared deep suspicions and severe attacks. No one knows what he had to come to terms with in his own solitude. This mirrors what happened to Nietzsche, behind whose seemingly arrogant statements, such as "Why I am a Destiny," were hidden the most difficult of conflicts, an enormous struggle and suffering. Heidegger could become ironic, but any form of cynicism was alien to him.

It will become apparent in the course of Heidegger's way that hidden behind all this was the thinker's extreme vulnerability, which often had to seek protection in the shadow of silence. He did not have a thick skin, and wounds inflicted on him healed only with difficulty. For this reason, he did not like to defend himself publicly. The public did not understand this, and enemies intentionally took advantage of it. When in 1931 he wrote about the gathering of professors in Berlin, saying that not for one moment was he under any illusion about the "effect" he had on people, his statement should have confirmed the destiny of philosophy: Thinking demands its victims.

2

In the Third Reich

Chancellor of the University of Freiburg, 1933*

"Aber—Herr Heidegger!" [1] With this phrase—which is the title of a pamphlet directed against Heidegger—Samuel Beckett responded to a question of mine during a conversation in Bern in the early fifties. I had been trying to highlight the intellectual ties that could perhaps be shown between the poet's plays and Heidegger's philosophy; and in the end I had asked him what and how much he knew of the philosopher's work. The irritating and astonishing phrase "Aber—Herr Heidegger!" is as characteristic as it is suggestive. For wherever Heidegger's name is mentioned—with or without approval—this "aber," whether stated explicitly or simply thought, is always used to express reproach or regret. The phrase refers to the 1933 episode of Heidegger's chancellorship of the University of Freiburg. Depending on one's position, this episode at the very least appears to be a historical blemish with which even those who recognize Heidegger's significance can come to terms only with difficulty, or it indicates a serious degradation of his actions at that time and a rejection of his philosophy in general.

If, in the following, I look at these interconnected issues and take up a topic that has already been discussed—one would have to say excessively—in the past decades, then I must proceed with great caution, as I myself did not live in Freiburg in 1933. I would like to report here (as well as in this entire book) only what I heard from Heidegger himself and what I have critically thought through, or what I have seen in my own

---

*This account of Heidegger's chancellorship was written in 1981–82—before the new publication of his *Rektoratsrede* and thus with no knowledge of *Tatsachen und Gedanken* (hereafter *T&G*), written in 1945 but added to the text of the speech and published for the first time in the early part of 1983. Heidegger had discussed with me most of the facts contained in this addendum—facts and intentions mostly unknown, to the extent that they were not mentioned later in the *Der Spiegel* interview—so that after his death I could include them in the manuscript of this book. After the appearance of *T&G,* I had to correct only a few gaps and lapses of memory. My initial writing of the text corresponded closely with Heidegger's remarks. For the sake of clarity, I refer at certain points in this book to Heidegger's later published apology by indicating the pages of *T&G.* HWP

experience. In this regard one must take to heart the words of Julien
Green (referring to the mistake of many older writers): "When they recall
who they once were, they attribute to that distant young man an experience he completely lacked at that time." Nevertheless, it is possible (and,
indeed, has been confirmed for me in the course of my life) that as a
twenty-five-year-old, and despite being emotional, I did have some insights. Precisely because the present generation has difficulty placing itself
in the situation of those who lived around 1933 and precisely because
this generation believes it must reproach and reject those who were responsible for those times, it should expect a person from those times to
say and to write—to the best of his knowledge and in good conscience—
what happened then. Years of intimate friendship and confidential relationship, through good days and bad, does not automatically mean there
will be a twisting and glossing over—which would only succeed in dis-
torting the picture of Martin Heidegger. Besides, there are not many left
who experienced those times by participating in them.

"He who thinks greatly must err greatly." These words from *Aus der
Erfahrung des Denkens* (Out of the Experience of Thinking) do not sig-
nify a quick and handy justification, as has been occasionally suggested,
and much less do they give a superficial psychological explanation. These
words state a truth. Beginning with Plato, who became involved with the
tyrant of Sicily because he believed he could set up his ideal state there,
up to Hamsun, who embraced Hitler's cause of faith in the Germanic race
and was bitterly disappointed by him, one could mention a host of names
of those who held high intellectual rank but who nevertheless fell victim
to the temptation of power. To turn to the time in question here, not
everyone had the strength of character and the unbending steadiness of a
Ricarda Huch. But almost all those (like Gottfried Benn, Ernst Jünger, or
even Gerhart Hauptmann) who let themselves be swept away by the great
waves of those days and somehow succumbed to the national frenzy were
excused their "faux pas," even if reluctantly and admonishingly, by the
consciousness of a later time. Somehow that "faux pas" was canceled out
by their work and intellectual significance. Whether a Hamsun was really
close to national socialism and believed in it is unimportant today in the
face of his literary (and human) greatness. Why is it different for Heidegger? Why does his case still evoke that "aber"? It is not taken into account that Heidegger, like those mentioned above, clearly distanced himself from national socialism—in fact, much earlier than everybody else.
What is at work here? Is the reluctance to acknowledge this distancing
due to a resistance not so much to his obvious and acknowledged per-

sonal mistakes, but to a thinking that he set in motion and that cannot be annihilated?

After initially reaching a large number of people with the precise formulations of the metaphysics lecture of 1929 (in the long-standing, traditional setting of the German university), this thinking was later noticed by a much larger circle of people (again in the academic setting in Freiburg) after the much-maligned, little-read, and even less understood *Rektoratsrede* (rectoral address) of 1933. This speech was attacked because it radically challenged ideas that were cherished far too much but basically emptied of meaning long ago. For in this speech Heidegger decisively bade farewell to the humanistic concept of the university, which grew out of the upper-middle-class ideas of the nineteenth century. He led "science" back to its original ground, Greek philosophy, and thus back to a rigor of questioning that had nothing to do either with a fragmented erudition or with the kingdom of self-satisfied specialists that the university—long cut off from people, preparing the young for "distinguished" professions—was increasingly becoming. What came out of the philosopher's mouth in Freiburg sounded different: "Science means a persevering (*standhalten*) questioning in the midst of things in totality—a totality that always hides itself. The enactment of this perseverance is aware of its weakness in the face of destiny." For two and a half millennia, the progress of human action, both in theology and in technology, has strayed from the original unfolding of science as known to the Greeks. Nevertheless, that beginning still continues. It is important to regain the greatness of that beginning so that once again science might become "an inner necessity of Dasein"[2] and cease to be a harmless occupation promoting a mere progress in knowledge. The philosopher spoke of the abandonment of contemporary humanity in the midst of beings—an abandonment in which the perseverance in being exposed to what is concealed and uncertain becomes transformed. Here questioning itself becomes the highest form of knowing. (Twenty years later, in Munich, Heidegger came up with another formulation: "Questioning is the strength of thinking.")

The opposition that gathered toward the thinking of the philosopher was unable—or did not want—to take seriously these allusions to the Greeks and to the conception of the university that derived from them. Heidegger was blamed for wanting to dismantle what were basically old and fossilized institutions, and he was ridiculed for the "self-decapitation of the German university."[3] But quite different voices were also heard. For example, Werner Jäger, who had succeeded Wilamowitz in Berlin and who left Germany soon thereafter because his wife was Jewish, wanted to publish Heidegger's speech in the journal *Die Antike*. He saw in this speech—which was modeled, in terms of form as well as diction, on the example of the classics—an excellent testimony to the continued effectiveness of the ancient heritage. For the speech contains hardly anything that could be interpreted as a "concession" to the political power of the time, although the spirit of that time undoubtedly blows through it. I do not know what obstacles kept it from publication. I also do not recall whether I asked Jäger about this when, in the autumn of 1938, I visited him one evening in Chicago—after nearly five years had passed, during which time things had changed considerably and become more acute. I probably heard about this intention to publish the speech only much later.

Nor do I recall when I first heard about Heidegger's acceptance of the chancellorship and his speech. At that time, the summer semester of 1933, I was studying at the University of Kiel. I had little time to be concerned with events in another university, since I had to strive to keep my head above water and maintain a relatively acceptable course in the midst of the "purges" that were being stringently carried out at the University of Kiel. (This university had been considered a model of modern jurisprudence, but it was now swamped with national socialism, both in staff and in organization.) Thus it was with a great deal of anticipation that we students awaited a lecture by the chancellor of the University of Freiburg, which was to be given in July 1933. Because the various archives of the University of Kiel were later destroyed in air raids, no published version of this lecture exists. However, if we compare some handwritten notes with the text of a lecture delivered on 30 June of the same year at the University of Heidelberg, we can assume that we are talking about one and the same lecture, with hardly any changes. Some prominent sentences that we remembered corroborated this.

The lecture was entitled "The University in the New Reich." Anyone familiar with the *Rektoratsrede* would have had to notice that something like a continuation of that speech was being presented here; the lecture at times presupposed what was said in that address. At any rate, this speech turned out quite differently than party members and political functionaries in Kiel had expected. It was widely believed in lecture halls and laboratories that the revolution had been victorious. But Heidegger emphatically denied that. He started with the notion that the university was possibly condemned to death and that the very last vestige of education's power was being forfeited, even if "self-administration" was left to the

universities. Nevertheless, it was important that the university again become a force that educates out of knowledge for the sake of knowledge.
He reproached teaching that had no goal and research that lacked direction. But, he said, it is not enough to account for what is new by putting
a little political color over everything. As he had done already in Freiburg,
Heidegger warned against the so-called "new concept of science," which
was just the same as the old one except that its foundation was a bit more
anthropological. "All this talk of the political is a disturbing nuisance,
because this talk will not end the old routine."

This sounded harsher than the statements reported from Freiburg.
How would things turn out? Then Heidegger demanded the courage to
decide on the basic questions of science. For this secular decision would
determine whether the Germans wanted to remain a people committed to
knowledge in the highest sense. University teachers should not simply
impart knowledge. Rather, they should be concerned with letting students learn and with bringing students to learning. And this requires that
one allow oneself to be pressured by what is unfamiliar, in order to master the unfamiliar by knowing and comprehending it; one must be uner-
ring as one looks for what is essential. The student must be forced out
into the insecurity of everything, from which there emerges the necessity
of involvement: "Academic pursuit must become once again a venture."

The members of the audience stared at one another. Did they correctly understand that academic studies should not support cowards—
those who would not have the courage to experience and to bear up
under the abysses of Dasein? This seemed to have gone way over the
heads of the academic audience. Could all this be compatible with the
day-to-day affairs of the university? Moreover, the speaker seemed to seriously offend the Christian Albrecht University of Kiel, where one was
particularly proud to have weeded out all Jewish persons and things—
including works in the library manifesting the Jewish spirit. And yet, not
once did this speech mention the issue of race.

This is an important point, because it brings up a decisive fact. Heidegger never advocated the official "theory of race" and never took it up
in his thinking. He was not a "racist." This means that the central element
of national socialism was absent—and not only from his statements as
chancellor. This is illustrated by a minor incident. Heidegger told me
about it while we were discussing the *Rektoratsrede*, which brought him
so much insult. During the dinner that followed the celebration of Heidegger's assumption of the chancellorship, the minister of culture, who
sat next to him, remarked, "But, Your Excellency, you did not say any-

thing about the issue of race." Heidegger responded caustically, "You noticed that?" After that, the dinner proceeded in a rather cool atmosphere. For Heidegger did not approve of the national-socialistic theory of race, much less its application.

This is an occasion to rethink some of the basic principles involved in Heidegger's attitude toward national socialism. We know how it came about that in April 1933 Heidegger accepted the office of chancellor of the university, after its Senate unanimously elected him. Professor of Anatomy von Möllendorff was first elected chancellor but, because of his political attitude, was thought to be unsuitable for this office. He turned to his politically blameless neighbor Heidegger as the most famous member of the university, and, given the delicate situation of the university (which was threatened with interference by a party functionary), asked him to take up the office of chancellor. In spite of Heidegger's initial reluctance (half a year earlier he had written to my father that he would like to avoid all administrative responsibilities in order to devote his life entirely to his work), the persistent urging of von Möllendorff and other colleagues led him to accept the offer.

There was more to this decision than just the wish to prevent the university from being delivered into the hands of a mere functionary of the party. Something that had occupied Heidegger in the preceding years of his teaching in Marburg and Freiburg became clear. At the beginning of his inaugural speech ("What Is Metaphysics?") we read, "Today only the technical organization of universities and faculties holds together the disintegrating multiplicity of disciplines (of the sciences). . . . The rootedness of the sciences in their essential ground has withered away." Heidegger strove to reopen access to this essential ground. Through every stiff and solidified organizational "setting of aims," he wanted to open the way to an alert readiness that only the youth know.

For Heidegger, the university—and the Albert Ludwig University of Freiburg stood for all German universities—embodied hope in the youth. This is perhaps more difficult to understand now than it was then, since today German universities have been reduced to merely vocational and professional schools that mold public opinion. But it is only this hope—which was connected with the high intellectual demands he made both on himself and on the youth—that makes understandable Heidegger's decision to commit himself so completely to the university in the spring and summer of 1933, setting aside for a while his own tasks of thinking. He committed himself to the university because he firmly believed that it could give rise to an internal as well as external regeneration of the Germans. In view of the course that history subsequently took, it sounds almost paradoxical to believe that national socialism should have been put at the service of the university as Fichte conceived it—and not the other way around. What a utopia!

Fichte is mentioned here for a reason. For what was obviously present in Heidegger's mind was intimately related to his sense of nationality—a notion and a spiritual reality that was exaggerated beyond measure, too much talked about, and finally destroyed by the ideology of national socialism and by every process that was influenced by it. Is there today still a genuine sense of nationality, of national values and national concern? To the younger and youngest generations, such a sense appears irredeemably exhausted and old-fashioned, if not worse. But for a man like Heidegger, and for many young men who returned from the First World War and found themselves belonging to a nation that was viewed with suspicion everywhere in the Western world, these questions had a profound meaning.

Not that Heidegger would have believed that he was cheated by the "ideals" of youth. His national German sense did not have any "Prussian" character. If Heidegger, who was not political to begin with, entertained hope for the Germans, then it was more like the hope of a Stefan George, a hope rooted in Hölderlin's vision that all would find themselves in the "highest feast." Thoughts and questions such as "Where is your Delos and your Olympia?" were not foreign to German youth at the time. These thoughts and questions excited and fulfilled the intellectual world of the young generation's fraternities. (Today it seems almost inconceivable that a great Jewish author like Rosenstock-Huessy expressed the idea that Hitler would fulfill Hölderlin's dream.)

Through Heidegger's national sense flowed much of the rigor that made the soldierly thought of Ernst Jünger so unusually attractive to German youth. I still remember quite well how alluring Jünger's works *Der Arbeiter* (The Worker) and *In Stahlgewittern* (The Storm of Steel) were for many of my fellow students in the university and how Jünger was revered as a kind of national figure. With its global vision and description of a new reality, *Der Arbeiter*—and what this book brought into question—became significant for Heidegger in many ways. As recently as 1980 Jünger mentioned, in a conversation in Paris, that Heidegger once gave a seminar on this book. We should note, however, that it was not a seminar but an elucidating discussion about this book—which at that time had already existed for a decade and was not understood in its "clairvoyant" manner—that Heidegger held in 1939–40 before a small group of university professors. (It is also worth noting that this discussion was watched by the police and finally terminated.) How important *Der Arbeiter* (as well as Jünger's work *Die Totale Mobilmachung*—"Total Mobilization") was for Heidegger can be seen in the fact that, in his public statements in 1933, the philosopher referred several times to *Der Arbeiter*. Heidegger said that the human being as worker is involved in coming to grips (*Auseinandersetzung*) with beings in totality and that humanity fulfills itself through work. The sense that Heidegger gave to the notion of work, however, had nothing to do with principles of Marxism or national socialism. As different as the philosopher and the writer were in their points of departure and their results (Jünger never left behind the realm of metaphysical thinking), they shared much common ground—and the fact that Jünger attended Heidegger's funeral has a peculiar symbolic power.

As occasional references in conversation led me to believe, the as-yet-unpublished correspondence between Karl Jaspers and Heidegger may give us more information on both the idea and possible realization of a deep spiritual and human rejuvenation through the younger generation in German universities.[4] Heidegger maintained a connection with Jaspers—his "philosophical neighbor" in Heidelberg—through correspondence and visits, until the spring of 1933. That this connection was never completely severed, in spite of what later separated the two men, was confirmed by a moving letter Jaspers wrote on the occasion of Heidegger's seventieth birthday. Heidegger, touched and pensive at the time, let me read it in strict confidentiality. The closeness of the two men over many years has a special significance for Jaspers's famous little volume *Die geistige Situation der Zeit* ("The Spiritual Crisis of Our Time"), published as no. 1000 Göschen's series of small volumes.[5] This closeness obviously extended to the proximity of the *Rektoratsrede*, where Heidegger concludes by quoting Plato: "All greatness stands in storm"—a statement that was too hurriedly connected to the National Socialist movement. That Heidegger's expectations from the "rebellion" of the younger generation were misunderstood—as happens frequently in the history of philosophy—was noticed by Viktor von Weizsäcker and by many other observers in those days. It may be a moot question whether Heidegger saw a deeper process, "about which others had no idea," at work behind the theories and facades of the day-to-day politics, as von Weizsäcker suggested. Rightly understood, however, a much-quoted statement from a lecture course of 1935—a statement about "the global movement," which was later construed as the continued glorification of national socialism—supports von Weizsäcker's conjecture that Heidegger saw such a deeper process.

Another characteristic of Heidegger's was his love for his homeland—which, like his national feeling, has been misconstrued as being related to national socialism. Later I shall talk about how deep this love went, what nourished it, and how it sustained the entire life of the philosopher. In his own way, Heidegger was in some respects a man with peasantlike qualities—which, of course, does not mean that he behaved in the manner that the city dweller somewhat derogatorily characterizes as "peasantlike" (*bäurisch*). Nevertheless, Heidegger was slightly suspicious of everything that had to do with the city and never quite felt comfortable in it, except in the only city that received his undivided sympathy. In simply getting close to a big city—with its proliferating dump sites, factories, and desolate housing developments, with the whole ugly atmosphere of formless and rampant growth that surrounds even old and beautiful cities—Heidegger, an extremely sensitive man, would be affected with almost physical abhorrence. Anyone who ever traveled with him across the country and remembers the arrival in a big city (like Zurich) knows how strong this feeling was. A big city embodied for Heidegger the basic feature of the epoch—namely, homelessness. After a visit to a new construction in Stuttgart, he commented, "Two farmsteads separated by a two-hour walk may be more like neighbors to each other than two apartments in a high rise."

He felt completely free within nature, most of all in his familiar Black Forest homeland. Heidegger *lived* with words—his style of speaking was never "sophisticated" while always very precise—and the language of his homeland was his most beloved medium. For Heidegger the homeland also included certain human beings—such as the old peasant woman who lived in the farmstead in the Rütte, where Heidegger wrote *Being and Time* and heard many a word that reached back into another layer of time to which the younger generation no longer has access. Albert Leo Schlageter was a special case among those who signified "homeland" for Heidegger. By curious accident, the men of the Third Reich who searched for "holy figures" with which to decorate their new pantheon also came upon those who actually had nothing to do with them. Schlageter was one of these. He had been shot by court order in 1923 because of sabotage during the French occupation of the Ruhr. This descendent of a line of farmers, who was a few years older than Heidegger, also studied at the gymnasium in Konstanz. Both were favorite students of the clergyman Sebastian Hahn, who came from Rast, near Messkirch, and who taught

Greek at that gymnasium. This may explain why, on 26 May 1933, Heidegger took part in the state-ordered celebration of the anniversary of Schlageter's execution. Heidegger honored this otherwise very problematic Schlageter merely because of these connections with his homeland—and his words of praise were at the same time addressed to the forests and mountains of this homeland.

If Heidegger lacked a certain "urbanity" and was estranged from everything pertaining to city life, this was particularly so in the case of the urbane spirit of the Jewish circles in the large cities of the West. But this attitude should not be misconstrued as anti-Semitism, although Heidegger's attitude has often been interpreted in that way.

I have already said that any form of racist fanaticism was alien to Heidegger. Nevertheless, because he used the word *völkisch* several times in public statements, people have tended to attribute that attitude to him.[6] Who took the time to notice that for Heidegger this word still carried the general sense it had for Fichte, a sense that differed from the tenor of the word in *Völkische Beobachter?*[7]

We should bear in mind that before 1933 the lists of participants in Heidegger's seminars contained many Jewish names, some of which became very important later on (for example, Herbert Marcuse). A large number of Heidegger's students were of Jewish descent, and with some of them—notably Hannah Arendt and Helene Weiss—he maintained sincere friendships for decades after the twelve dark years of Nazi rule. Many times he stepped forward to protect the Jewish students, and he assisted some of them in going abroad. But even Heidegger—who for a short time seemed to have a "position of power"—needed courage to go to Berlin to see the minister of culture, Rust, in order to intervene in matters that pertained to a Jewish student of his whom he regarded highly and who had lost her position (the attempt was of no avail, as one can imagine).[8]

When the University of Freiburg organized a celebration of the centennial of Husserl's birth, Heidegger asked me to take part in it, because he felt that it was not possible for him to do so after all the reproaches and accusations in matters concerning his former teacher. Soon thereafter I gave him an account of that dignified celebration, and he told me, not without emotion, that Husserl's daughter had visited him and reassured him that all rancor had now been put aside. Later, on a rainy evening in the hut, when we were not enticed by the usual walk, I took advantage of the occasion to ask him about his relations with Husserl and the rumors that had circulated in public. My friend Nagel, who was present, later recalled, "At the beginning it was not very easy for Heidegger to talk about this topic, and sometimes his responses came at first with great reluctance. But you did not let up drilling him; and in the end Heidegger seemed pleased to have finally discussed this difficult topic." We discussed everything—the fruitful yet stressful relationship between teacher and student; the whole string of petty allegations with their untruths, half-truths, and distortions; and finally Husserl's death and his funeral, which Heidegger did not attend. Heidegger never refused the old emeritus entry to the university or access to the library (similar insinuations were also untrue). That he did not participate in Husserl's funeral—which no one prevented him from attending—was a human failure that Heidegger clearly found unpleasant, and even painful. At that time, in 1938, Heidegger himself was one of those who were looked at with suspicion by the National Socialists.

We have already anticipated a great deal with these remarks. To return to the events of the summer of 1933, I had the opportunity to greet Heidegger briefly in Kiel, much to his pleasure. In response to a bouquet of flowers that I had sent for his wife, Heidegger, before departing Kiel, sent me a postcard in which he once again expressed his regret that our meeting had been too brief. He added heartfelt greetings to my parents and to Bremen. When I look at this official postcard today—"Chancellor of the University of Freiburg/Prof. Dr. Martin Heidegger"—what strikes me is the absence of any emblem. For the swastika was not there—the swastika which at that time was to be seen everywhere.

The winter of 1933 was difficult and bleak. For months I lay in the hospital of the University of Kiel; in January 1934 my mother died in Munich. Before the end of the year, Heidegger had written her a long and encouraging letter. In it he referred to his own situation with a single, distinctive statement: "I regret that I could speak only very briefly with your son last summer in Kiel; it troubles me at present that the business of my office and its various responsibilities do not leave me the time and energy anymore to devote myself to young people, as I want to." He added that one appointment was always followed by another. One senses in such words that the hope of bringing about a "breakthrough" in the university by means of the youth had proved to be unfounded. At any rate, the breakthrough that *Heidegger* wanted to make, under a banner that was basically not his own, had already failed. Did he overestimate his own power as well as that of the young people with whom he thought himself allied?

In those autumn months, events took place whose meaning I consciously understood only much later. Heidegger received "calls" (each connected to a "special political assignment") from the Universities of Berlin and Munich, and he refused both of them.[9] Such a refusal actually bordered on disobedience—the more so because the state obviously believed it could burden the professor (who at that time was still being wooed by the party) with a political task, one that would have dragged him deep into the activities of the party. How much he was already involved and how little he could pursue his original intentions are things that he must have noticed at the latest during that "Demonstration of German Science" held on 11 November 1933 in Leipzig—of which there exists a photograph showing Heidegger with Pinder and Sauerbruch. This affair, which was organized on the occasion of the election of the Reichstag, made it completely clear to him what he had sensed for a long time already—that he ran the risk of becoming a political puppet who was to be exploited because of the fame attached to his name, especially abroad. In November 1933, this development reached its climax. It was followed shortly by catharsis.

Heidegger later told me that he withdrew to the hut in December, earlier than was his custom, alone, in order to think clearly about himself and the future. The bitter outcome was the realization that he must give up the chancellorship, because things could not go on like that. He wanted to give up everything connected with this position, in order to devote himself solely to academic teaching and to his own work.

One has to be clear about the significance and consequences of this decision. Giving up the chancellorship long before the end of his tenure could have been interpreted as an insult that might cost him not only this office but also his chair. But he could not find any other solution. Heidegger did not obey the ministerial orders to dismiss Dean Möllendorff (from the medical faculty) and Dean Erik Wolf (from the law faculty). They were not National Socialists but, rather, scholars who were well known through their work and who could increase the prestige of the university. In Karlsruhe, however, they thought differently. Supported behind the scenes by dissatisfied circles within the university, who did not feel particularly comfortable with the "show-boy" Heidegger, Karlsruhe wanted to alter decisively the look of the University of Freiburg, which up until then was not at all adequately "colored" in terms of party and politics. When in February 1934 the Ministry of Culture in Karlsruhe categorically ordered Heidegger to dismiss both deans, he refused to carry out the order and submitted his resignation. With this step, the decision Heidegger had already made became a reality. The decision became known only when the newspapers reported the appointment of a new chancellor, who was glorified as the "first National Socialist chancellor of the university." No one referred to Heidegger any longer, and he did not participate in the transference of the chancellorship. That he returned the gold chain of the chancellor's office by mail is a story that was made up and disseminated with the intention to hurt him. To announce publicly the news of Heidegger's resignation was obviously not desirable; the resignation would have made much noise abroad and been exploited against the state—especially after the setback the state had just suffered from Stefan George's departure from Germany and his death soon thereafter in Switzerland.

In 1933 Benedetto Croce said to Karl Vossler, "I don't believe that Heidegger can do much in politics—our dictators don't give a hoot about theories." Heidegger did not feel like joking when Schadewaldt greeted him after his resignation by saying, "Herr Heidegger, are you now back from Syracuse?" To express himself publicly would have been suicidal for Heidegger. But even later he avoided openly addressing this issue for fear of unleashing new turmoil. He paid dearly for his faux pas. His own thinking on this matter during the early months of the spring of 1934 is reflected by what he said to a student with whom he had become close friends. Soon after Heidegger's resignation, this student let him know that she could not comprehend his entire activity as chancellor and the related political engagement. To this Heidegger responded, literally, that it was the greatest stupidity of his life.

Contact Renewed

After January 1934, my connections with Heidegger in Zähringen[10] were broken. His touching letter of condolence on the death of my mother got lost in the war. I did not know what was going on in Freiburg and heard of Heidegger's resignation only much later. My illness had interrupted my studies for more than a year, after which I had to get settled in Berlin under drastically changed circumstances. I had had to give up the study of law, a subject I did not particularly like, to return to history, which I had studied earlier. In order to shorten as much as possible the lengthy period of study, I concentrated on my dissertation (under Walter Elze's direction) and devoted myself to working with those historians who, after the forced resignation of Hermann Oncken, did not kowtow to national socialism.

Erich Kaufmann, who as a Jew had to give up his teaching positions both in Bonn and in Berlin, continued his seminar privately in Nikolassee until 1938. He met in his house with a large number of younger law students, among whom were a few that later became known in connection with the events of 20 July.[11] Guests from other faculties also participated in these evening lectures and discussions. It was here, in the winter of 1935, that I made the acquaintance of a young and elegant foreigner—the second attaché to the Peruvian embassy, Alberto Wagner de Reyna. It was apparent that his major function at the embassy was a social one. There were undoubtedly more-serious intentions hidden behind this activity, however. After I had met him frequently in the lecture halls and had become friends with him, he mentioned that his father, who was still living in Lima, came from Freiburg im Breisgau and that he (Alberto) would like to go to Freiburg—not just because of his many relatives, but also because of Heidegger, with whom he wanted to study. He had been interested in philosophy for a long time, but he did not know how to make contact with Heidegger. I made up my mind immediately to try to establish a connection between Heidegger and my friend, since we understood each other well on the subject of the philosopher. I also hoped that perhaps this would allow me to renew my contact with Heidegger.

I was very pleased when soon thereafter a long letter arrived in response, in Heidegger's unmistakable handwriting. Heidegger wrote that my friend Wagner could certainly participate in his lectures and could study with him, and he enclosed for my friend's perusal the titles of the lecture courses and seminars for the next semester. The letter concluded with a sentence that turned it into a very personal joy for me and showed that our relationship was intact. The sentence read, "Incidentally, I would be pleased if you would write in detail about what you are now doing and looking forward to, as well as what you find questionable and difficult." Whenever I took the road to Rötebuck 47[12] or the forest path to the hut in Todtnauberg in the following years, these last words accompanied and encouraged me.

Alberto Wagner studied for several semesters in Freiburg and had close contact with Heidegger, with whom he had long philosophical discussions. When they were able to reestablish their correspondence after the war, in 1946, Heidegger wrote to Wagner—who was now a diplomat and had been transferred to Bern—that he remembered their discussions with fondness. Then he wrote, "In the meantime, I have made a little progress in interpreting Greek philosophy and will be pleased to tell you about it." The closed borders at that time did not, however, allow personal contact to be reestablished. As secretary of the Peruvian embassy Wagner deserves credit for having helped Heidegger's family by sending packages of food (one of Heidegger's sons returned half-starved from the Russian POW camps in 1947, the other in 1949) until the situation returned somewhat to normal in the Federal Republic.

In the course of time, profession and life-style distanced the young diplomat from his years of study in Freiburg; but a bond remained intact. He always regretted not having completed his studies by earning a Ph.D. degree under Heidegger. While Wagner was still studying with Heidegger, the question of finishing these studies had been discussed. Heidegger proposed "The Problem of Substance in Descartes and Leibniz" as a topic for a doctoral dissertation. Having made this proposal, he waved it aside in the same breath: "Yes, since you are a foreigner and a diplomat, this arrangement can perhaps work out. But if you were German I would have to advise against it." For Herr Krieck of the Ministry of Culture in Karlsruhe, who evaluated university candidates and was highly regarded by prominent Nazis, always caused a great deal of difficulty for people who came from Heidegger to register for the comprehensive examination. And Heidegger had added, "No German student of philosophy works with me any longer on a doctoral degree. You do not want to have unpleasant experiences with Krieck and his department."

Alberto Wagner understood this hint and, with a heavy heart, abandoned the project of earning a Ph.D. degree at Freiburg. Later, he received the doctoral degree in his native Lima, with a dissertation titled "The Fundamental Ontology of Heidegger." This whole incident, together with its background, deserves to be mentioned here in detail because it clearly shows how Heidegger's position in the university during those years was suspect to the National Socialists and constantly threatened.

Wagner supported Heidegger not only with material assistance, but also by translating into Spanish, ten years later, various works of his teacher (for example, "Die Zeit des Weltbildes" / "La Imagen del Mundo") and by decisively speaking out against malicious allegations that Heidegger had been an "outright Nazi." Thus he contributed considerably to the dissemination of Heidegger's thought in the Latin American world.

A rather pleasant event from 1970 should conclude this look at what is indeed a lesser-known relationship of Heidegger's. Wagner, who was at that time the Peruvian ambassador to Bonn, came to Freiburg on a diplomatic mission and surprised me one evening in my apartment—not knowing that Heidegger was my guest. There was a happy and moving reunion between the former student and his aging professor, already eighty years old. There was much happiness and surprise, and red wine contributed to the good mood. It got very late. Before the arrival of the taxi we had called, I asked my guests to sign the old guest book, with its many inscriptions. After their cheerful departure, I looked at the guest book and found this entry: "Nothing comes to mind. Alberto." And beneath it: "Nor to mine. Heidegger." Truly worthy of reflection! In delightful moods, like the one of that evening, Heidegger used to say that he could do one thing particularly well—think nothing (*nichts denken*). Here again, unexpectedly, he came upon the "nothing"—a genuine Heideggerian ambiguity that often made me chuckle about the double meaning of this inscription.

Shortly after my Ph.D. comprehensive examinations in Berlin in May 1938, my father drove with me to Freiburg to visit Heidegger. This became a little "trip into the baroque," in which I, as the travel guide, could have earned Pinder's vote as "egregie." Coming from Weingarten, we roamed the area that lies between Pfullendorf and Überlingen, Heiligenberg and Haldenhof—an area that later on, in all its seasonal moods, became and has remained my favorite German landscape. We arrived in Freiburg on a warm May evening. In the Zähringer Hof hotel, which still existed at that time, we found Heidegger's card addressed to "Herr Doktor," inviting us to come to his house in Zähringen the next day for lunch and to spend the afternoon. It was a great pleasure to enter the familiar house again, with its view—which was then still open toward the east—extending over stretches of meadow and up to the ruins of the castle peeking out of the forest. My father was deeply impressed by the stillness of Heidegger's study with its dark bookshelves, in which he discovered the volume that my deceased mother had given to Heidegger as a remembrance.

After lunch we sat out on the terrace until evening. We talked about Bremen and the changes that had occurred there. Heidegger regretted very much Mayor Spitta's forced resignation from public life. He was also quite forthcoming with remarks that displayed his serious concern over the course of events in Germany. On a long trip to South America two years earlier on the *Cap Arcona*, my father had had long conversations with Hans Grimm, and he quoted some statements that showed the writer's equally grave concern over the development of German affairs. Grimm, through a friend in Cambridge, had provided me with an English book that was absolutely necessary for my dissertation but that I could not find in any German library. This was a chance for me to speak about my dissertation, which dealt with a historical theme from Cromwell's time—a rather transparent evasive maneuver. But Heidegger soon dropped the British issue (he was not interested in it) and came back to France.

Conversation turned to the necessary and possible agreement with our neighbor to the west; and in the course of the conversation we spoke about poets, like Ernst Stadler and René Schickele. Heidegger read to us a few paragraphs from his text *Wege zur Aussprache,* which he had published a few years earlier but which had gone unnoticed; he considered this text quite important. The essay was published in the same year that German philosophers had been invited to a congress in Paris to commemorate the three hundredth anniversary of the publication of Descartes's *Discours de la méthode.* But Heidegger was initially not included on the list that the Germans had prepared. When Heidegger later received the call from Berlin to travel to Paris—a call made in response to the French amazement that he had been omitted—he refused to go (not least because of the scandalous way the whole thing had been handled) and thus avoided any possible demonstration. Heidegger's response was *Wege zur Aussprache*—an essay that is today still quite worth reading and reflecting on. In his letter to Heidegger on Heidegger's eightieth birthday, in 1969, Jean Beaufret indicated that that exchange of views had less to do with the peculiarities of the two neighboring nations than with their common origin that is concealed within their neighborliness: "What in Europe still remains concealed: a question mark." That afternoon our reflective conversation was concerned with that very question. As we left in the evening, Heidegger offered my father an offprint of *Wege zur Aussprache.*

The next day I was again in Zähringen because Heidegger wished to talk to me about my future. During a long walk, I reported that I would be given an assistant professorship in Professor Elze's Department of History in late autumn, and that I could not yet foresee whether this would lead later to the *Habilitation.*[13] Heidegger understood such doubts and again warned against Krieck. After that he spoke about his current participation in the new edition of Nietzsche's works, of the research on Nietzsche's posthumous writings, and of the vehement debates going on over Alfred Bäumler's role in the "preparation" of *The Will to Power.* There was much bitterness in Heidegger's words—not least because of the falsifications that Nietzsche's sister Elisabeth Förster (who had recently died) had introduced into Nietzsche's letters.

In later years Heidegger would often remind me of this short visit to Freiburg, which had taken place entirely within the old atmosphere of cordial confidentiality. He often recalled "that afternoon in the house in Zähringen, the lively travelogues and thoughts and judgments of international significance for which the philosopher so much appreciated my father.

During the War

Soon after the outbreak of the war in September 1939, an intensive correspondence developed between the Heidegger and Petzet families. I had suggested to my father that, in case of an evacuation of Freiburg, Heidegger and his wife should move to our country residence in Bavaria. My father accepted the suggestion without delay. After Heidegger gratefully accepted the proposal, my father ordered that several rooms be arranged for the eventual refugees—who might possibly arrive soon—in the house in Icking, where he had lived in retirement since his departure from Bremen. Heidegger had indicated that it would in any case be dangerous in his native Messkirch—where he would go if necessary—because of its nearness to the military training ground in Heuberg.

The total uncertainty of those days was reflected in the letters that went back and forth. Rumors proliferated. Would the French cross the Rhine? Heidegger favored a wait-and-see attitude. Since the expected evacuation of Freiburg did not happen, examinations and awarding of Ph.D. degrees continued at the university. Heidegger indicated that one obviously must limit oneself during difficult times, but that he and his wife were used to simple living because of their dwelling in the hut. If it should really come to fleeing Freiburg, then he would be forced to teach either in the schools or at the University of Munich, which was not yet closed. He added, "To be sure, no airplanes can be built with philosophy; and the teaching of philosophy, seen from the outside, may appear to be a quite untimely activity."

As early as the beginning of September, Heidegger wrote that, besides the immediate members of his family, he was most concerned about his manuscripts, which contained a decade's worth of work. His brother in Messkirch kept the most important of these, but there were many others that needed a secure place. And so it was that finally, in place of the Heideggers, several large packages of manuscripts packed in clothes hampers (along with some additional household goods) took possession of the sanctuary that had been offered to the family. These hampers contained copies of the texts of lecture courses and unpublished larger treatises, to which handwritten notes had occasionally been added. (I remember this well because Heidegger later gave me permission to read the manuscripts.) For years they remained under my protection, even after the house in Icking was sold, until they were needed for the *Gesamtausgabe*.[14] Some blue folders also contained numerous poems, including "Der Tod" (Death) and "Die Fluh" (Rocky Cliff), which Heidegger later gave me as a gift.

On 26 September 1939, Heidegger turned fifty. My father had sent Heidegger his best wishes; in his response from Todtnauberg, Heidegger said, "We are still waiting in complete uncertainty." He added that he had spent his birthday, appropriately, arranging and packing manuscripts. He also wrote, "In these days, when we correspond with each other, I often think of the beautiful days that I spent at your house in Bremen and remember the mother of the house, who has returned home." But the thoughts of the author of these letters, as well as the thoughts of those who received them, were concerned mostly with the bleakness of the future, which could not be lightened by state-ordered pseudo-optimism. Heidegger wrote, "In any case, we must now detach ourselves in our inner life from everything that constituted our immediate surroundings and homeland. For beyond the possible war we must endure other tests, from which we can hardly protect ourselves." At that time I understood these words most precisely.

When my father died two years later, in the late summer of 1941, I received in Icking a moving letter of condolence from Heidegger. In thinking about the death of Arnold Petzet, he said, he did not have to look for consolation at all, since he knew that it was the completion of a life that "included a great deal of enterprise and real life as well as much suffering and deprivation, and thus this life was a genuinely human one." When held before the mind's eye, this life appeared in its fullness and exemplariness, and this was a good way to remember him. To the exhortation to preserve the legacy of my parents, Heidegger added his gratitude for this dear man's extremely magnanimous friendliness toward Heidegger and his wife two years earlier. For Heidegger, so much lay in the name of this place, Icking, that the memory of it stayed alive of its own accord and was connected to what now had to be endured: "If Germans ever experience quiet days again and if they poetize and unfold their own being and their innermost destiny, then one day you will come again to the beloved Black Forest and will find with us a warm welcome and a spirit of shared remembrance."

Four years later the nightmare of the Third Reich was destroyed in blood and tears. In spite of all the hope for the future that had been rekindled, misery, mourning, and uncertainty dominated Germany, and no one was spared difficulties and disappointments. While the world slowly began to breathe again after the destruction and devastation, people and things that had given help and strength in the bleak years of the war were not to be forgotten. In October 1946, Heidegger wrote to Alberto Wagner, "Strenuous intellectual concentration is an exertion that can be maintained in the long run only with much effort. But without it, nothing enduring comes about. Everything must now be sacrificed to recovering an intellectual world."

Since Christmas of 1941, when Heidegger had sent me a small, privately published offprint, I had not heard from him. I wondered how he was doing. I tried everything to establish contact with Zähringen, in order to visit Heidegger as soon as possible. Contact through the mail was difficult at that time, and it was not easy to cross the borders of the various occupation zones. After our correspondence was resumed in December of 1946, I thought I would surely be able to notify Heidegger of my visit in the spring. But it was much easier to get to our old Bremen home than to travel to Freiburg. I was working part-time for the American Art Collecting Point in Munich (taking care of libraries and of artworks stored in warehouses), and I finally succeeded, through the mediation of this agency, in securing a passport for the French occupation zone, where Freiburg was. I had to wait until November 1947 to travel, however. The official and approved purpose of the trip was to write a report for the newspaper on a first exhibition of modern French art—including Picasso, Braque, Gris, Léger, and Chagall—in Freiburg. But the real reason for the trip was to visit Heidegger.

Now it was in *his* house that he offered me accommodation. I had brought Frau Heidegger some food and coupons. During the day I was in the heavily destroyed city, at the exhibition—which made a stronger impression because it was set up in the makeshift rooms of a former *Konzertcafe*. But I had to be back at Rötebuck 47 before the beginning of curfew. After his time for work, to which Heidegger always held stringently, he devoted himself entirely to his guest. During that November in 1947, in the company of Martin and Elfride Heidegger, I got to know what it means to "find a warm welcome and a spirit of shared remembrance." He immediately felt that I was not happy with the attempts I was making in my new occupation; he knew how to rearrange the confusing threads of life and to give them a new meaning—to gain energy even from renunciation.

On the first afternoon, the two of us sat alone upstairs in Heidegger's study,with its view out toward the graying dusk that slowly slid into evening and night. It was a long, nearly endless conversation. First I had to give an account of my experience in Berlin, in closest proximity to the highest command of the armed forces, and of my work in the army's division of war history (work that had to do with Greece, of all things, which appeared to me to be an insult). Then I had to tell of the increasing pressure that I was under because of my becoming familiar with circumstances and events whose true and cruel nature had been concealed from the public. That evening I could express myself for the first time about something that burdened my conscience the most: the experience of that autumn evening in Moabit, where I unsuspectingly became witness to the transportation of hundreds of Jews—women, children, and elderly men—who, singing, were pressed into trucks and driven to their death. It was then that I suddenly saw and only half understood, with horror, what was unimaginable, what had been whispered about here and there. I could not say anything about this to anyone. My existence in Berlin was finally nothing but agony. And yet, to say that my later transfer to the eastern front meant a relief would have been a lie.

When I told Heidegger how an incautious remark of mine in Augsburg shortly before the end of the war had nearly cost me my life, he took this as an occasion to talk about the unfair things that had happened to him in those years and how he had been endangered. In the meantime, the desk lamp that had somewhat scantily illuminated the room had gone out, because the electricity was generally turned off, leaving the whole city in darkness. For two hours or more we sat in total darkness and only heard each other's voices. Perhaps it was exactly this situation, removed from everything irrelevant, that made our conversation more open and more intimate. Heidegger listened like a father, sometimes putting in a word of consolation. Then he began to reveal a great deal about himself of which I had not the slightest idea. I can only hint at a few things; and we never returned to this topic later. Heidegger spoke of the way he had been gradually and invisibly encircled, while he continued with his professional duties seemingly unchallenged. He spoke of how permission for publishing his new writings was denied and of how those approved were kept from appearing; of how they were collecting "evidence" against him and of how he was constantly spied upon after the numerous explicit statements he had made in his lectures became known to the police. He spoke of how an older participant in his seminar had come to him one day and confessed to being a Gestapo agent, charged with spying on him; but, in view of the work that Heidegger had accomplished in the seminar, the agent could no longer bring himself to perform his treacherous duty. On the other hand, he could not simply remain silent. That was why he wanted to alert Heidegger, before a possible order for something far worse deprived Heidegger of all freedom. Heidegger recalled that he had "a long conversation with the Gestapo agent, who was an excellent human being." He added, "I never saw him again; he was sent to the front and got killed" (cf. *T&G*, p. 41ff.).

More shocking than the intrigues and incredible schemes against the philosopher who had become an embarrassment was what he related about the period at the end of the war. Deemed "superfluous" [15] in his teaching profession, Heidegger was one of the first to be put on the list of those who were called to the *Volkssturm* [16]—surely in the hope of getting rid of him. This was an insidious plot that did not work. Leaving the bombed-out Freiburg, which was threatened by the Allies' entry, he finally made his way to his native Messkirch on a bicycle. But worse things awaited him upon his return to Freiburg: "When in December 1945 I was brought totally unprepared before the "settlement committee" and was confronted with the twenty-three questions of the inquisitorial hearing, and when I subsequently collapsed, the dean of the medical school, Beringer (who saw through the whole farce and the intentions of the accusers), came to me and simply drove me away to Gebsattel in Badenweiler. And what did he do? He just started walking randomly with me through the snow-covered winter forest. He did not do anything else. But as a human being he helped me, so that three weeks later I was again healthy and returned home."

How deeply wounded he was by the behavior of the university (which abandoned him) and the behavior of his colleagues, Heidegger did not have to say. For years, one could notice it whenever the conversation turned to these things. It had to do with his honor. This wound never entirely healed.

When the lamp on the writing desk lit up again, we were transported from the darkness of the discussions of the gloomy days of the past and back into the November evening in Freiburg. The mutual intimacy of those hours together became the foundation of our friendship, which nothing could ever destroy. Heidegger brought the conversation to an end in his inimitable way; he reached for a printed sheet and read to me his own translation of the great chorus song from Sophocles' *Antigone*. This is the song that deals with humanity and its destiny and concludes with the following verses:

Going out and everywhere under way,
inexperienced, with no way out,
he comes to the nothing.
Through no manner of flight
is he able to resist
the one way out, death—
even if he has managed to escape
every inevitable infirmity
with his cunning.

Though shrewd in mastering,
beyond every expectation,
the place of his power,
yet all at once he slips
fully into malice;
and then again he turns out
valiant and well.

He wanders through and between
the fixed rule of the earth
and the anchored sphere of the gods.
Rising high above his abode,
he is deprived of that abode,
he for whom what is goes on not being,
on behalf of courageous venturing.

But it was not Sophocles who brought to an end this evening in Zähringen. At a much later hour, when I was already in bed, there was once
again a knock on the door. Heidegger stood there in his pajamas, holding
a candle. He wanted to give me something else, a work on German literature that he said I absolutely must read. It was a treatise on the last
poems of Stefan George, poems such as *Wenn an der kimm mit sachtem
fall* and *du schlank und rein wie eine flamme,* and especially those like
wunder von ferne oder traum—a poem that had become Heidegger's constant companion "on the way to language." That night he also gave me
those poems, which at that time had not yet become my innermost possession. When I departed two days later, Heidegger offered me the chorus
song from *Antigone,* as a generous gift.

3
Heidegger's Work and Its Impact after 1945

In the Public Eye?

As late as the final trimester in the winter of 1944, before Freiburg was destroyed by bombing, Heidegger began a lecture course at the university entitled "Poetizing and Thinking"; but he did not complete it. Because the university and the occupation forces did not permit him to teach, he was barred from his professorial chair, and no one knew whether he would ever return to it. Thus Heidegger was deprived of his natural element, and his voice was silenced. He was also not allowed to publish. His situation was similar to that of the sick lion in La Fontaine's fable: the jealousy, ill will, lack of understanding, and malevolence were meant to inflict pain and harm on the former celebrity in every way, from petty annoyances all the way to slander. At that time there were very few who openly and unwaveringly supported him.

What Heidegger actually thought at the time of his persecution and exclusion from public life, and how he was able to look beyond his own scandalous treatment, can be seen from what he wrote to me in October 1948. About six months earlier I had been invited to Switzerland by Alberto Wagner de Reyna, who worked in the Peruvian embassy in Bern, in order to get away from the postwar situation. Having gratefully accepted my friend's invitation, I was able only with difficulty to get over the contrast between Germany's destruction and Switzerland's safety. After returning from the "ecstasy" of the days spent in Switzerland, I had serious doubts whether, after what Germany had experienced and suffered, there was any hope of something similar for this country, something like a *restitutio ad integrum*.[1] Sending along greetings and best wishes from his former student, I wrote Heidegger in detail about my stay in Bern; and I did not hide my reservations.

He responded in great detail on 26 October, taking my letter as an inducement to express himself on the current situation of the world. He was of the opinion that in Switzerland, and in similar circumstances elsewhere, people overlook "what really is." However terrible what befell the Germans may be, there are nevertheless hints everywhere that—perhaps

48

only after a few decades—the modern world of technological humanity will come to its end, its culmination. (That he was mistaken, at least with respect to the short term, he openly admitted later, in a speech in Messkirch.) He expressed the view that psychology—which had long ago turned into psychoanalysis—is taken in Switzerland and elsewhere as a substitute for philosophy (if not for religion) and that this psychology also falls under technology. Responding to my question more specifically, Heidegger wrote, "Nothing will be gained from renovation of the old, as long as we do not go through the fundamental experiences of Nietzsche and Rilke and as long as we do not take their views of the contemporary world-epoch seriously." But this does not mean that he wanted to turn thinking and poetizing into creeds or to pretend to be a kind of savior. It only means "that we keep hearing the distress that contemporary humanity suffers and keep hearing the cry of distress that this humanity itself cannot understand, in order to go on thinking ourselves, again and again." Beside the mania of "wanting to know and recognize the latest happenings, only to forget them on the evening of the same day," the great and simple words stand apart, as if they did not exist.

He added that these views have nothing to do with criticizing our time—which is the easiest thing to do. Rather, they are concerned with encountering "the simple claims of being." Finding this way may be wearisome, and it may appear paltry in comparison with everyday exertion. "Nevertheless, we must find our way back to the poverty of essential relations. One would think that the external situation would assist this from all sides."

At that time Heidegger was not the only one to think along these lines. Was not Rilke, during the German collapse in November 1918, already expressing similar views and hopes? We must doubt, however, whether the way back to "the poverty of essential relations" was ever seriously attempted. Was not the road sign already pointing in an entirely different direction, and thus the insight into a decisive separation of the ways unable to take root? There came the days of "great efforts to make things harmless"—about which Christoph Meckel wrote, "We were looking for new straw for the old nest." But Heidegger did what he could by calling us to mindfulness. Although he was officially forbidden access to the public, there were a few courageous people who did not heed the slanders and who wanted to hear the thinker himself speaking. A group of young people from Bremen paved the way, in the late autumn of 1949. A few months later they were followed by a great physician, Gerhard Stroomann from Bühlerhöhe, and soon thereafter by the newly founded

Bavarian Academy of the Fine Arts in Munich, in the person of Count Clemens von Podewils. Thus, unexpectedly, a threefold forum opened up for Heidegger, which he used to express himself. It was not until the winter semester of 1951 that he was allowed to return to the University of Freiburg.

When I look back on my experience of all these various places where Heidegger made an impact—in whose coming to pass I played a role—I see a clear difference from earlier situations. To put it simply, it was a totally different public and a different kind of publicity that confronted the philosopher, accustomed as he was to his old lecture hall at the University of Freiburg. Certainly there were young people, numerous students in overfilled lecture halls. But this was no longer the homogeneous element of a youth which, with its questions and philosophical and ideological doubts, was heading toward a new shore, needing a trustworthy and reliable boatman capable of deviating from the old course. Now his audience consisted of scholars of all kinds, artists of every orientation, men well recognized (or at least successful) in their professions, and women of high society who tried to follow the philosophical prodigy. And there were also more than a few curious people who were drawn to a name that was surrounded with so much suspicion. They gathered in the elegant rooms at Bühlerhöhe or in the lecture halls of the Academy in the capital city of Bavaria (which on the occasion of such meetings never forgot to brag about its legitimate Catholic element). But the small circle that gathered around the thinker in the Hanseatic city must not be included in these characterizations. That was the reason that Heidegger, in the 1950s, frequently and happily went to Bremen. Preparing for a lecture there, he once said, "I like the clean air in Bremen—and that is what counts."

Sometimes it was almost moving to see with what patience and courtesy he tried to become familiar with these totally different atmospheres, claims, and expectations—even when the whole thing threw him off and presumably hindered him from attaining all that he wanted. One small example may make this clear. The day after a lecture in Stuttgart, he and I went for a walk in the Schlosspark von Hohenheim, and we spoke about the issue of "creative personality" and the traditional concepts of personality. At this point Heidegger suddenly stopped and said that all this talk about personality really collapses completely ("that is done and over with once and for all"). However, people do not see this, and here, as elsewhere, they stick to the old ideas instead of "setting themselves free." As we continued with our walk, he said that for me, as a historian, there are significant insights here concerning what is history. Breaking off, he asked me not to raise these questions at all in the discussion scheduled for that afternoon in the house of a Stuttgart notable. To my astonished counterquestion, he responded that some would obviously have questions in mind aiming at "the practical" in the sense of "What should we do?" — as was recently the case in Bremen. But in an inquiry like the one we were pursuing, only two or three could participate, while most people would be unable to follow. I had the following entry in my notes regarding that discussion: "With angel-like patience and forbearance, Heidegger carefully and critically evaluates all theological and theoretical historical matters that are brought forward, such as Spengler and Toynbee, without frightening the participants. Therefore, they notice neither that 'being = God' is a fundamentally erroneous premise, nor that they actually are speaking about history and not about *Geschichte.*" [2] Nevertheless, in the end there was a fruitful dialogue about "thinking," because here in the heart of Swabia the reference to the line by the Swabian poet Mörike, "Denk es, O Seele!" received a thoughtful response.

What bothered Heidegger in this atmosphere, and what he had hardly experienced before, because he had dealt with generations of students, was "the public." All his life Heidegger distrusted the public, because the public is not a real vis-à-vis and in truth does not have a face at all. "What I am trying to do during these months, even toward the public, remains ambiguous and an inevitable tribute to *Ge-stell.*" [3] Thus it was a tribute to the technology that dominates the whole being of modern humanity. And Heidegger did not willingly carry out this tribute. Early on there were indications that he would have gladly withdrawn from the business of the public. Before a conference in Munich in May 1950, he said, "I dread the whole thing." A little later, he came to realize that "there is no point in what I am doing in Bühlerhöhe with Stroomann." That nowadays every oral or written expression necessarily gets entangled in ambiguity was a theme that was manifest in all his efforts. "Communication no longer succeeds, or does not yet succeed. There are indeed reasons that go way back in the past as to why people like us flee the university. It is becoming more and more urgent to pay heed to the necessary consequences. An appropriate and mature occasion for a thoughtful communication is not yet to be found."

Communication with whom and to whom? Heidegger meant, above all, those whom for decades he had seen before him in the lecture halls and seminars and with whom he was constantly associated—the youth. For a thinking such as his, which would change the world, sought and found its fallow ground above all in the youth. Thus it was typical of him that, when he quarreled for a while with the Academy in Munich because of an unfortunate misunderstanding, he regretted the consequence that young people would be deprived of opportunities that could serve them as occasions of illumination. And when he overcame his resentment, because of the matter at stake, and forced himself to accept the invitation to the Academy, he said that he had done so because he wished to be available to the youth. When it was arranged that the talk given in Munich, entitled "The Thing," would be given a second time at my house in Icking, he decided that only younger people should be invited to that meeting. He stood by this decision with such consistency that he did not even invite to the meeting in Icking his old friend Professor Manfred Schröter, the Schelling scholar, who because of other commitments had not been able to attend the lecture at the Academy in Munich. Heidegger wanted the young people to feel relaxed and not to be disturbed by the presence of an older and prominent gentleman.

No one ever thanked him for such considerateness. He soon noticed that young people, whom he wanted more than anybody else to address, did not receive their due in the large public lectures and that in most cases they were simply left out because of "urgent" social considerations. Most of the time there were not enough admission tickets for the students who were crowding in front of the doors. This also happened on the occasion of Heidegger's talk on Hölderlin, when a theater had to be rented as a lecture hall because the chancellor of the university of Munich, a religious zealot, would not allow Heidegger the use of the university's great hall.

Things like this increasingly spoiled for him the great lectures for which he was everywhere in demand and which he was, often enough, talked into giving. Even the high participation of students in his university lectures, which since 1951 he had been allowed to hold again in Freiburg, could not deceive him into overlooking the fact that something had changed drastically. So it happened that Heidegger, who was strengthened by the progress of his work, became urgently concerned with dialogue, thus shifting away from the customary form of modern publicity into the realm of dialogue. He was of the opinion that one could not trust "this society," where from the beginning one is already the loser, being forced to move in *its* arena: "The only possibility is to stay away. But where? I ask myself this question every day. Perhaps in a gathering of *your* generation, which can be a gathering rather than an organization and is not susceptible to the public."

The Club of Bremen

At a time when Heidegger was banned from the university by the occupation authorities, it had to cause a sensation that in 1949 he held a lecture in Bremen, in response to the invitation of an association of prominent representatives of business and the Hanseatic upper middle class, the Club of Bremen. In the next decade this lecture was followed by many others, always in the same context. However much circumstances had changed, Heidegger's name did not disappear from public awareness. This is reflected in, among other things, many Gottfried Benn's letters written before 1950 to his Bremenian friend, the businessman F. W. Oelze. The latter, who had close connections with Egon Vietta (the writer who popularized Heideggerian issues), obviously heard early on about the plans to explode the unworthy "ghetto" around the philosopher and communicated this to Benn. In the postwar period Benn considered Heidegger one of the three or four people who had something to say, and he kept to this opinion, even though his judgments vacillated greatly. In October 1949, Benn suggested that Heidegger was now overdoing it; "Now he travels around. This is not nice." Four years later, when Heidegger traveled to Bremen once more—even though he was allowed to hold lectures in Freiburg again—the poet asked Oelze with astonishment, "What is it that connects him with Bremen?"

Oelze, who had heard Heidegger's talk "Who Is Nietzsche's Zarathustra?" in May 1953, responded to Benn that "Heidegger's attachment to Bremen is because of a social stratum that he meets here and perhaps only here—a stratum that in such a compact majority does not exist in university towns and towns occupied by civil servants, not even in Bühlerhöhe; it is made up of big businessmen, specialists in overseas commerce, and directors of shipping lines and dockyards, for whom a famous thinker is a fabulous creature or a demigod." Oelze understood this only partially; since he was not close to the narrow circle of Heidegger's audience in Bremen, he was unable to draw the appropriate conclusion from his sociological statements. For he did not know, and indeed could not know, two things. The first was that the philosopher's appearance in Bremen, in a seemingly alien atmosphere, had nothing to do with his personal ambition. It was because of the initiative of a few men and women who were committed, over and above their professions, to self-examination and who wanted to revive a nonmaterialistic time. For this reason they were interested in allowing that thinker to speak publicly who, in spite of all hostilities, claimed his rank and brought to their city the fruitful uneasiness of questioning. The desire to work against the injustice done to Heidegger also played a strong role. For in the circle of this association, whose members represented the active public of a free city, Heidegger was not forbidden to speak.

The second factor was that Heidegger considered it in many ways a helpful and invigorating experience to confront what Oelze called "a compact majority"—one whose thinking was generally not deformed by academic opinions, but at most was molded by the old humanistic education and, in addition, was distinguished by a very free attitude. Here, perhaps, their contact with the world beyond Germany played a role. This was an audience that was certainly not philosophically trained; but, by the same token, it was less prejudiced and more willing to hear new ideas, and it was totally immune from admiring the philosopher as a "fabulous creature" or even as a "demigod." It was this that constituted what Heidegger frequently cited as the "clean air" that was very important to him. Such an atmosphere made him gladly return to Bremen (where he was spared the pain of being stared at)—not to "show off," as Benn completely unjustly said, but to own up freely to his thinking and to find himself received freely and with goodwill. A clear testimony to this was his dialogue with Hilde Roselius.

Heidegger carefully prepared his first public speech after many years of imposed silence. When the president of the Club of Bremen approached him in the late summer of 1949, Heidegger's first publication after the war (*Holzwege*) was being printed in Germany. It would have been feasible for Heidegger to select for his talk in Bremen one of the themes that he dealt with in this work (in the essays about Hegel, Nietzsche, and Rilke, in "The Origin of the Work of Art," or in "The Age of the Worldpicture"). In mid-October he wrote to me, "I am now inclined to present 'The Age of the Worldpicture' on one day in the first week of December. [The text of his speech differed from the printed text; *Holzwege* was not available in bookstores until mid-November.] On the next day, then, I would like to discuss what appears to me to be significant beyond 'Worldpicture.' I have a second plan in the background: to read something from a dialogue about 'The Thing' which leads us to the same realm of questioning." Clearly, he did not wish to present to the audience in Bremen what was already in print. He wanted to address this audience straightforwardly and with freshness. During the walks we took together on the heights above Todtnauberg, we reminisced about Heidegger's visit to Bremen in 1930; and this reminiscing became livelier as representatives of the Club of Bremen arrived, wanting to establish personal contact with Heidegger and to have a preliminary discussion of his speech before he withdrew to Messkirch for final work on the lecture. He looked forward to this trip that would take him out of an artificial isolation: "Perhaps we can stretch my stay in Bremen so that, despite shorter days, we can see something of the countryside and people"—a wish that was fulfilled by a trip to Worpswede.

Neither the president of the association nor its members, many of whom still remembered the speech of 1930, had any idea what would finally come out of Heidegger's secluding himself in Messkirch for work, or that the professor from Freiburg would have anything to say to them that in the changed historical circumstances would be more exciting than the insights he had presented earlier into "the root-unfolding of truth." It was surprising even to those who were close to him that in the end Heidegger did not take up any of those topics that had been considered for Bremen. The announcement for 2 December stated that he would talk about "Einblick in das, was ist" in the *Kaminsaal* of the new city hall. What he presented in Bremen for the first time were those statements about the metaphysics of technology that became famous and formed the foundation of his entire philosophical work for the last three decades of his life. They constituted a group of four speeches (the third of which was not given): "Das Ding" (The Thing), "Das Ge-stell" (Enframing), "Die Gefahr" (The Danger), and "Die Kehre" (The Turning). What he presented put unusual strain on his audience, who—to their credit, it must be said—held their own under the intellectual demands and listened to Heidegger attentively.

When Heidegger entered the auditorium of the city hall, one of the few large buildings not destroyed in the war-ravaged Hanseatic city, there was a great tension. Everyone felt that an unusual intellectual event was about to take place. Nonetheless, there was none of that snobbish curiosity that was to fill the lecture hall in Munich the next year. The audience that gathered in Bremen was made up not only of Club members, but also of many others who had traveled from afar. As on the first occasion, Mayor Spitta and Senator Apelt, representing their old official positions, took their seats in front of the lectern, which Heidegger approached with visible emotion. He began by thanking the old city that had invited him, and then said, "Nineteen years ago I gave a talk here and said things that only now are slowly beginning to be understood and have an effect. I ventured something then, and I would like to venture something again now."

Egon Vietta published a report several days later, which said the following: Heidegger deliberately chose the same Hanseatic city "in order to venture the boldest statement of his thinking," which attempts to lift, almost like a huge excavator, the scaffolding of our civilization from its dangerous self-confidence by elucidating the unfolding of the being of technology. The readily adoptable and misconstruable characterization of the root-unfolding of technology as *Ge-stell* was quickly repeated by every mouth without a proper grasp of the actual character of this abstract designation. Nonetheless, many other things from the far-reaching train of thought of the "Einblick" immediately stuck in one's mind, especially the "jug" that Heidegger, with poetic power, evoked as an instance of a thing and consequently as an instance of the "fourfold" (*Geviert*) of the earthly, heavenly, divine, and mortal. And here Heidegger spoke of the "mirror-play" (*Spiegelspiel*) of the four, in which each is mirrored in the other (the word "mirror-play" had once been used by Rilke, in 1924, in a dedication to Max Picard.)

In the 1950s, Heidegger came to Bremen eight times to speak. Between the "Einblick" series of lectures and the "Bild und Wort" (Image and Word) seminars, there were talks entitled "Logos—das Leitwort Heraklits" (Logos—The Guiding Word of Heraclitus), "Wer ist Nietzsches Zarathustra?" (Who Is Nietzsche's Zarathustra?), "Der Satz vom Grund" (The Principle of Ground), "Wissenschaft und Besinnung" (Science and Reflection), "Die Sprache" (Language), and "Kants These vom Sein" (Kant's Thesis on Being), which was presented privately. Each of these events was organized by the Club of Bremen. It planned to make available to the public the lecture "Einblick in das, was ist" as a publication of the Club. This was an idea that unfortunately could not be realized because of Heidegger's other publishing commitments. Nevertheless, when the lecture was published, it was remembered as being intimately connected with Bremen. Many notes and copies of this talk were circulating everywhere. Following the lectures, some of which were held in the city hall and some in the large Schütting auditorium, evenings of discussion took place. These were held in the city's Senate house (where Heidegger gladly stayed as a guest) or in private homes, where the best manner of Bremenian hospitality reigned. The residence of Senator Helmken in Oberneuland was frequently the site for meetings of a large circle. Often there were many guests from outside Bremen, the so-called Friends of Bremen, who were asked to join the smaller group of approximately a dozen participants. But Heidegger opted for a rigorous selection of these guests. Some people with whom he maintained a relationship might not receive an invitation (without ever knowing this) because Heidegger was of the opinion that that person did not fit well in the circle—whose homogeneity meant much to him. The core of this group was formed by some students currently enrolled in Marburg and Freiburg. From the broader "milieu" (as Benn called it) came a number of Bremenians with whom Heidegger had developed friendly relationships since his visit to Bremen in December 1949.

An epigram by Hermann Apelt from 1911 reads, "Denn Bremer Art ward nur einmal erfunden" (For Bremen style was invented only once). Heidegger appreciated and even loved this style—which was formed by the city's spirit and its free attitude toward the world—as much as the Bremenians who came into contact with Heidegger appreciated and loved him in turn, without everyone's necessarily having complete access to his thinking. It was his humanness that captivated people, a humanness without disguise that affected everyone, because he conducted himself quite freely in the atmosphere of Bremen. Neither academic considerations nor an excess of social conventions provoked his mistrust here, whereas pride of nobility or arrogance of money would have closed him off. Just as he was pleased with the city, with the activities of its people, and with their open gaze into the world beyond the seas, so Heidegger's friends in Bremen responded to his gratification by actively taking up his thinking and by noticeably trying to follow paths of thought that were little known to them. His attachment to this circle of friends from a younger generation so pleased Heidegger that he always found a way to stay several days longer just to do justice to everyone. Matter-of-factness, willingness, and distance from a ready-made conceptuality—these were the elements that made up the atmosphere there in Bremen, an atmosphere made more lively by the decidedly friendly attitude of that circle. In this city he was surrounded not by functionaries, but by human beings of independent thought and action.

The rigor that determined discussion and dialogue with Heidegger about essential issues of thinking relaxed into a trusting friendliness. It even progressed into a cheerful mood as soon as "life's niceties" were given their due—such as when the city hall's waiters, wearing red tuxedos, would place the carafe of wine on the table at the guesthouse in the Parkallee. In a way that is difficult to describe, Heidegger had liked this city ever since he had been in Bremen for the first time in my parents' house. Perhaps he somewhat overestimated the people of this city with regard to what he wanted to build with some of them in the early 1950s and what he apparently had in mind for putting into motion, in a humane way, against the pressure of the technological economy that was emerging throughout the world. This would have demanded that the philosopher stay much longer in Bremen and would have inevitably led to a kind of "organization," which he strongly rejected. It is certain that he did not intend to assume once more the unfortunate role of a "Plato in Syracuse," a role that had already been disastrous for him once.

The effectiveness of the semipublic forum that the initiative in Bremen offered Heidegger in the winter of 1949 would intensify ten years later in Heidegger's own realm—Socratic dialogue. Some of Heidegger's letters (from which I shall quote in the following) show clearly how carefully he prepared for the discussion that was to occur in the seminar he gave in Bremen, "Bild und Wort" (Image and Word). These letters also offer a glimpse into Heidegger's way of working. They show that as soon as the seminar (hoped for and asked for by friends for many years) began to take shape, Heidegger insisted that even the slightest semblance of a discussion without rigor was to be avoided.

I have already indicated that it was not possible for me to participate in the celebration of the philosopher's seventieth birthday. In February of 1959 Heidegger wrote, "In order not to jeopardize what is so essential to the discussions in Bremen, I consider it best to postpone them until the spring of 1960. Too much is happening in the fall of this year. By then I hope to be able to present something more on 'language'." Besides the honorary citizenship of his native city that was to be conferred on him, Heidegger at that time would need to deal with some personal matters in Freiburg and Messkirch that could not be ignored. However, the realization of the idea that had already been formed was only postponed. We agreed on the early summer of 1960 and chose as the site of the conference the house on the Lindenweg in Oberneuland that Helmken put at our disposal. The theme for this meeting was "Bild und Wort." Participants were to prepare by reading several texts, among them the essay by Wilhelm von Humboldt "On the Diversity of Human Language Structure and Its Influence on the Intellectual Development of the Human Species" (1836), as well as the address that Paul Klee gave in Jena on modern art.

On 1 May Heidegger wrote to tell me that he had reconsidered what the participants must read prior to the seminar: "Most of them are not going to be able to do that. Humboldt's essay alone is a tough nut. It is more advisable to read once again my works (*Vorträge und Aufsätze, Holzwege, Satz vom Grund,* and *Unterwegs zur Sprache*), which are somewhat familiar but not yet really known, and from there informally approach the topic 'Wort und Bild.' For ultimately we will discuss my thinking, and I myself would like to remain free vis-à-vis this thinking, to learn a few things from the dialogues. In an introductory lecture I shall outline this theme and thus the main thrust for the course of the discussion. The question remains whether I myself should direct everything as fits the style of an informal seminar or whether Helmken, for example, should lead the discussion. Both have their advantages and disadvantages. If we take the first approach, there would indeed be a greater and a more designed completeness. But this runs the risk of one-sidedness. Perhaps you can discuss this matter with Helmken, because how we proceed determines the way my initial 'lecture' will be laid out."

In the end the first approach was chosen. The participants prepared for the seminar by concentrating on five texts: a quotation from Augustine's *Confessions* (10.7–8), Heraclitus's Fragment 112, Chuang-tzu's simile of the carillon stand, the text of Paul Klee's lecture in Jena ("On Modern Art"), and Heidegger's couplet "Nur Gebild wahrt Gesicht / Doch Gesicht ruht im Gedicht" (Only image preserves the face / But the face rests in the poem). Thus we had the prerequisite foundation for the seminar discussion. It lasted two days and one evening and was held partly in the Bremen *Kunsthalle* (art gallery)—in front of a painting by Rembrandt and an abstraction by Manessier)—but for the most part in Oberneuland. These meetings basically showed that hardly anyone was really equal to Heidegger's method of inquiry, especially when preparation could not be as thorough as with students at a university.

At the end of the discussions that lasted several hours on both days—discussions that Heidegger always knew how to guide when they tended to become too loose—the dialogue focused on the question "What is a metaphor?" One example considered was fast-moving clouds/sailors of the air (*Eilende Wolken/Segler der Lüfte*). What seemed to be firmly worked out with this example soon began to waver. And the rounds of discussion that took place in the garden were gripped by that uprootedness (*Bodenlosigkeit*) that often set in with Heidegger's questioning, after one believed oneself to be completely sure of one's point.

Short notes I took that afternoon show only patches of thought. What is the relation between language and metaphor? Does the image have priority over the word? Is "image" more comprehensive than "language"? What does "image" mean in general? What does "word" mean in general? Language never images adequately. The theory of language as "sign" on the basis of correspondence (*Verabredung*) gets exposed, and the relation between representation and memory investigated. To what extent does word belong to image? Image-character of language? "As long as there is metaphor, there is metaphysics. . . ."

Some verses were compared, such as Homer's original Calypso scene from the *Odyssey* in translations by Voss and Rudolf Alexander Schröder with the prose translation by Schadewaldt—which Heidegger seemed to prefer considerably. Toward evening Heidegger concluded the conference with Eichendorff's stanza about the song (*Lied*) that slumbers in all things.

These scanty remarks may show that, as Heidegger later said, this venture of a seminar in Bremen fell noticeably short of expectations. He wrote the host, saying, "I knew that the discussion would become difficult. But it eventually got going and provoked many questions. In such cases there is nothing more to achieve." All of us, both those from Bremen and the guests from outside (among whom were Jean Beaufret from Paris, the clergyman Paul Hassler from Basel, Dr. Martin Nagel, and Heidegger's old friend Dr. Ingeborg Schroth), experienced something of what Georg Picht wrote about such seminar sessions—that Heidegger took them with a solemn seriousness and in a style that today one would reproach as "authoritarian." In this style there was nothing of what is nowadays called, rather thoughtlessly, a "discussion," since Heidegger considered something like that to be chatter: "One learned immeasurably much." In those days in Bremen, during which Heidegger treated us gently, we nonetheless noticed that "he lived in a landscape of thunder and lightning." The seminar sessions in Bremen had little to do with what he later achieved in the seminars at Le Thor in 1966 and 1973.

Heidegger was seriously interested in plans, discussed vaguely at first, for founding the University of Bremen anew and forming it independently of existing conceptions. He seemed to believe that here was promise for a beginning that would not be burdened by the past. He was greatly disappointed by what developed soon after the collapse of the first organizing committee and by the shift into a political program. What he ultimately thought about this development (not only with respect to Bremen but also in general) is documented in a letter he wrote in the year of student unrest to one of the members of the Bremen group. Having stated that the university will inevitably become a professional school, he continued, "That must be taken seriously. The political scientists will take over the task of the intellectual orientation of the students, and the task of rescuing the 'spiritual' tradition will be pushed aside. It is useless to fight the ravings of the technological world. All this must be seen without resignation, which is often not easy to do but is more productive than hopelessly trying to rescue what existed before. Behind the technological world there is a mystery. This world is not just a creation of human beings. No one knows whether and when humans will ever experience this emptiness as the 'sacred empty.' It suffices that this relation remains open" (Letter to Ingeborg Böttger, 25 February 1968). This statement touched again, briefly, upon the speech "Einblick in das, was ist."

There was another side to Heidegger's visits to Bremen, however. In 1930 he had shown a lively interest in various aspects of life in the Hanseatic city, to which he gained access from my parents' house and through my father's position as president of the Norddeutsche Lloyd. This interest continued later. Whereas in 1930 we could not show him any of the big American ships, now he wanted—not least because shipping technology had greatly changed since 1930—to be instructed about the rebuilding of the German merchant fleet, which was then beginning. In the mid-fifties—it must have been 1953—we were able to visit and inspect a large new vessel (belonging to the ARGO steamship line) in the free port of Bremen with the help of Karstedt, who was a Lloyd's director. He had followed Heidegger's lectures with enthusiasm and had even prepared a version of "Wissenschaft und Besinnung" that was supplemented with very reflective marginal notes. Heidegger was very pleased to visit the *Arion* and surprised the captain with all kinds of technical questions. Finally, he asked to see not only the bridge, deck, and loading spaces, but also the engine room. There he received detailed explanations about everything and had long conversations with the engineers and sailors. When he finally emerged from the depths of the ship, he turned to me—I had stayed behind with some reservations—and said with a broad and happy smile, "What do you think Jörg would say?" He was thinking of his oldest son, an engineer, before whom he now hoped to be able to hold his own.

Several years later, a trip to Bremerhaven was a disappointment for him. While he admired the sluiceways, the dockyards, and the huge Columbus-Kaje (Columbus Wharf), the real reason for the trip—an inspection of the reconstructed ship *Bremen*—proved to be a terrible failure. Heidegger showed no mercy for this colossal vessel. He found it a degradation of what a ship is supposed to be when he saw the *Bremen* equipped as a "floating hotel" (as the expression goes, which in this case was precise) with a colorfully trimmed collection of bars, boutiques, movie theaters, and all kinds of fancy shops that traveling Americans liked. He left with outright displeasure and remained taciturn until we returned to Bremen, angrily intimating that equipping a ship with such follies of fashion would certainly not have met with my father's approval.

Nevertheless, he continued to be very fond of shipping, shipowners, and businessmen. This is one of the reasons that in 1962 he was invited to the famous *Schaffermahlzeit* (Feast of the Captains), the oldest fraternity banquet in the world.[4] After I succeeded in allaying Heidegger's doubts, Dr. Eddo Blaum, who presided as First Captain of this group of friends, finally received Heidegger's enthusiastic acceptance of the invitation. The only thing that Heidegger categorically rejected was wearing the required tuxedo. This was accepted, since by that time a dark suit had managed to break through the social barrier of tradition. According to the rules, this feast, which businessmen shared with their captains, was to take place on the "second Friday in February, before the breakup of the winter ice and the annual beginning of merchant shipping." So on this day in 1962 Heidegger was again in Bremen. The "forerunner of existentialism"—as he was called in a newspaper's listing of the guests—sat at the diagonal table with the large Neptunian trident, which is set up in the great medieval hall of the city of Bremen each year for the celebration of the Feast of the Captains and decorated with flowers and silverware—a table that brought together members of the Haus Seefahrt (House of Seafaring), the captains, businessmen, their guests from all over Germany, honorary guests, and the mayor, who acted as host.

For fear that Heidegger might feel like a complete stranger in such an atmosphere, he was prudently seated opposite Henry Lamotte, one of the most likable, sociable, and witty men of big business in Bremen. This name deserves to be remembered, because Lamotte knew not only how to introduce Heidegger to all the customs and manners of drinking throughout the banquet, but also how to put him in good spirits by telling occasional stories, both serious and enjoyable, and simple anecdotes about Bremen—so that the older gentleman splendidly survived the prescribed four and a quarter hours of sitting at the table with all the speeches and songs. Around nine o'clock in the evening—the banquet began at three in the afternoon—Heidegger joined the company downstairs in the *Ratskeller*. His eyes betrayed how pleased he was with the whole thing.

I would like to conclude this glimpse into Heidegger's long-standing relation with Bremen with two of his own statements that show how intimately he felt connected to this city. When he was allowed to return to the University of Freiburg in the winter semester of 1951–52 and could hold lectures again, he received a package of wine from Bremen as a gift for this occasion. Since Goethe's time, this had been a custom for celebrating special occasions. In a letter of 21 November expressing his gratitude, Heidegger said, "The wine from Bremen, an excellent libation, arrived here at noon before the lecture—an appropriate time. Thanks for this present and for the thoughtfulness behind it. On this day *I remembered particularly the friends from Bremen,* who can lay claim to being the *first* to have risked letting me speak in public, some years ago. Once again it becomes clear to me how essential the spoken word is, even if this word is received by only a few people—and indeed unknown people—from among the many."

Another present from the friends in Bremen, one that I shall talk about later, was given to Heidegger in Freiburg on the evening before his seventieth birthday. It was the forty-volume edition of Goethe's works (his *Ausgabe letzter Hand*),[5] purchased in a secondhand bookstore in Bremen. In presenting this gift to Heidegger, each representative of the friends from Bremen used a quotation from Goethe to fit the occasion and, so to speak, to embellish the edition. In his thank-you speech to the guests invited that evening, Heidegger, noticeably moved, said that his friends now knew what is typically Bremenian, because they had just experienced it. He added that he accepted this gift of an *Ausgabe letzter Hand* as a quiet reminder that he should have his own work edited and published in the same way. To Senator Helmken, who initiated and organized this gift, Heidegger wrote, "I cannot properly and sufficiently thank you, even if I recall what I attempted to offer to the friends from Bremen in the past years . . . and what I perhaps still can offer them. The nature and the intention of this gift reflect the grandeur of the Bremen spirit."

Never before was Gottfried Benn's question as to what connected Heidegger to Bremen given a more fitting response.

Bühlerhöhe

On the last evening of his visit to Bremen in December 1949, before bidding farewell, Heidegger gave me a copy of his *Holzwege*, which had just appeared. At my request, he wrote in it Lessing's metaphor of the windmill: "I am truly a mill and not a giant. Here I stand, in place . . . alone. From the whole wide atmosphere I do not demand anything but that it use my sails for its own circulation. Only this circulation should be left to them." It was a good and invigorating experience for Heidegger to have

Bremen open up this "circulation" for him again. He never forgot Bremen and its people, even though others soon followed their example and invited him.

The Bühlerhöhe resort, a creation of the Jugendstil architect Wilhelm Kreis, lies high above Baden-Baden and the Bühler valley in the mountains north of the Black Forest; it was "a monument never used before, a matter of luxury far too excessive for a sports institute." This was Gerhard Stroomann's description of the castlelike building of red sandstone into which he, a clinician from Munich with a bright future, moved in 1920. It was his personal ambition "to go to the vacant, completely unknown and unformed Bühlerhöhe, with my medicine, as a human being, serving the spirit," in order to establish in a short time something that would be more than merely a respectable institution of medical care. "Bühlerhöhe has become known worldwide not only as a medical concept with closer and closer ties to science, but also as a human isle destined to bring people together again internationally." When Stroomann—remembered as the "physician from Bühlerhöhe"—used such expressions, he did not do so only in view of his attempt to create on his "mountain" a place for wholesome intellectual exchange that would contribute to the knowledge of "what is happening today" through lectures and discussion. In the words of Max Weber, he also put himself at the disposal of "the endeavors concerned with the creative spirit, limited to the quietest and most private relations," which at the same time aimed at a broader impact.

Max Kommerell, who in the late autumn of 1943 came to Bühlerhöhe to restore his very poor health, offered (in a letter to Rudolf Bultmann) a keenly ironic description of the physician and the situation: "The medical superintendent, Dr. Stroomann, has something like a timid soul, which he hides under the cautiousness of a man of the world capable of settling everything. He likes to nibble on poetry and would prefer to observe quite noiselessly, in their privacy and intimacy, all kinds of poets and writers. *Ex officio* he is strongly psychological and has been influenced by psychology in his earlier development. He has healed a whole string of important contemporaries, or rather their broken-down nerves; among them are bankers, technological geniuses, and scientists."

If Stroomann had had his way, the poetic and literary dimension would probably have prevailed. But politicians of the time, like Tschitscherin, Stresemann, or Chancellor of the Reich Hermann Müller, came to him too. Ernst Toller was one of his patients, and so was Heinrich Mann. After he survived (more or less unscathed) the Third Reich and the subsequent difficult days of the French occupation, a new element emerged at the forefront of his efforts, with which he hoped to achieve the objective of his innermost endeavors and desires. In 1949, after the withdrawal of the occupation forces, he organized the "Wednesday Evenings," lectures, which continued as his favorite creation until his death in 1957. Before a growing audience, these lectures articulated various topics that dealt with important intellectual questions of the day in contemporary criticism, philosophy, language, poetry, fine art, music, and psychology. Important scholars, artists, and people active professionally spoke in their field and were accessible for discussion in the round *Kuppelsaal*. Names like Carl Orff, Friedrich Sieburg, Emil Preetorius, Karl Kérenyi, Max Bill, Beda Allemann, Kurt Bauch, Georg Schmidt (from Basel), and Hans Kienle indicate the class of these speakers. Martin Heidegger joined them on 25 and 26 March 1950, repeating the lectures he had given in Bremen.

There is a report in Stroomann's sketches, called *From My Red Notebooks*, about this and other evenings with Heidegger later on. The report is written in the physician's pathetic-expressionistic style, which echoed the style of his favorite poets from his generation: "Heidegger spoke four times in Bühlerhöhe, and each time an exceptional excitement dominated his entire presentation and his appearance before the lectern, as with no other contemporary. . . . But who can close himself off to the emerging power of his thinking and knowledge, which is manifest and newly created in every word, and which indicates that there are still undiscovered sources? How much we owe him in our 'Wednesday Evenings'!"

Stroomann, who was responsible for these arrangements, presumably knew well that, despite the well-intentioned exuberance, something was missing in these meetings with the philosopher. In another passage in his written records, he says that it is always "like a celebration or an inspiration. People are speechless. But when discussion begins, it contains the greatest responsibility and the ultimate danger. Practice is often lacking. One has to stay with the point . . . even if it is only a question."

What Bühlerhöhe lacked was an appropriate audience. In the urbane atmosphere of this resort, real dialogue that aimed at the topics under discussion was hardly possible. The resort guests from the nearby sanitarium, the prominent pensioners from Baden-Baden and from the wealthy West German industrialists, and the large number of merely curious people—attracted by the "big names" that were announced—were all mixed together in the auditorium. The few students from Freiburg or Heidelberg who participated did not alter the view of these gatherings as highly social and fashionable. This audience was clearly interested more in a stylish kind of entertainment than in rigorous mental work—an intellectual attitude that Nietzsche, in a letter to Lou Salomé, rebuked as "taking knowledge as a pleasure alongside other pleasures." Bühlerhöhe was not suitable soil for a seed that might be able to prepare seriously a new intellectual future.

It cannot be denied that in Bühlerhöhe there were individual evenings that were very fruitful for the audience, especially when there were none of those paltry discussions with no preparations. Some examples from notes on the "Wednesday Evenings" may clarify the pros and cons. A skilled and well-educated speaker like Emil Preetorius knew how, after his lecture "Abstract Art," to draw not only the Afghan minister of culture into discussion, but also, in the end, Heidegger. In a very engaging discussion, in which Heidegger expressed his views on the relation of abstract art to modern technology, he characterized abstract art as "a tool that unfolds the being of technology" and as something that is entirely different from art, something that would misunderstand itself if it took itself to be "art." Technology completes the European spirit in terms of its character and scope. When the Greeks characterized art as *techne,* they meant neither today's machine technology nor what we call art, but rather a manner of revealing the emergence of the world.

However, only by hearing Heidegger's speech on technology a year later in Munich could one grasp entirely the relations he indicated that evening in Bühlerhöhe. Here, as in so many other discussions, Heidegger could merely indicate certain things that many in the audience grasped only in fragments—which, therefore, promoted misunderstanding. How regrettable the level of discussion was may be seen from a couple of comments taken down during Allemann's lecture "On the Poetical" (Über das Dichterische). He had indicated that a poem must be understood mainly in terms of rhythm and that there are instances of words that have a rhythmical and not an absolute meaning in a context. Here Heidegger remarked that rhythm must be understood in terms of *Geschichte* and not in terms of history—that is, in terms of a "from where" (*Woher*) and an "in the direction of" (*Wozu*).[6] The question is whether rhythm in nature comes close to what Allemann has in mind. "What do we mean by rhythm?" Here someone from the audience interjects, "Why do we want to explain everything?" To which Heidegger responds: "This is an error. We do not want to explain, but to clarify."

In the course of the discussion, Allemann's statement is clarified to mean that the poetical is a bringing forth into a *Gestalt* (Hölderlin's *Ges-*

talt der Himmlischen). Does Allemann mean by this a *Gestalt* in language? In the meditative silence someone interjects, "To liven things up, may a woman say something?" After a long pause Stroomann's secretary says there is an Indian saying that goes, "Whoever understands the secret of vibration understands everything." Another woman speaks, stating that the poet cannot bring forth the divine *Gestalt*, but instead one that can be sensed as if through a wonderful veil. Allemann responds decisively, "No. What is astonishing in a work of art is precisely that this veil is *not* there. Rhythm works through the word." Discussion becomes more lively. "Can we exist without art at all?" Allemann denies this, and a woman points out that there are many people who have a great aversion to poetry. People laugh. Someone says, "I can easily live without works of art." Another interjection: "The inventing of and getting into the rhythm" smacks of dadaism. There all we need to do is babble."

The auditorium resembles a dissatisfied and rebellious class in school. Finally Heidegger says, "I am really amazed at how you 'philosophize' here. I have not encountered such problems for a long time. Our intention was to meditate on the poetic debate with poesie. Is this debate perhaps no longer an issue for the historian of literature? Poetic dialogue between poets? Or perhaps something more? What form does the dialogue between poets take?" Allemann responds, "Entirely inevitably—with each word."

This deplorable level of discussion, inadequate and at times shameful, must have been a great disappointment to the philosopher Heidegger—a disappointment that could not be mitigated by the two or three pertinent comments. The few encounters he had with his significant contemporaries that were productive, in human terms and in terms of issues discussed, could not make up for those experiences. And even here there were disappointments—as in the case of Ortega, where the encounter brought neither an encouraging agreement nor a genuine debate. Basically, the whole atmosphere at Bühlerhöhe worked against this. With its hotel looking after business (and functioning irreproachably) and with the pressure of daily guests, it was the very opposite of the Platonic Academy. And as soon as Gustaf Gründgens, together with Elisabeth Flickenschildt and Antje Weisgerber, appeared at the lectern with a somewhat silly talk, with gestures, about the stage and modern art, the recently evoked spirit of the poets and thinkers departed; and Heidegger left the auditorium without being recognized by the great pretenders.

Stroomann wanted the "Wednesday Evenings" to contribute to the knowledge of "what is happening today," to be something like a taking stock of our time from various points of view, analyzing things broadly and from all sides. It was a reckoning, however, that only at first glance seemed to correspond to Heidegger's attempt with "Einblick in das, was ist." Because Heidegger held a high opinion of Stroomann as a human being and as a physician, he withdrew only slowly from this venture in Bühlerhöhe. Heidegger did not want to hurt Stroomann's feelings and disillusion him. Nonetheless, he soon realized that nothing could grow at Bühlerhöhe. Stroomann's early death saved him from the disappointment that would have inevitably come upon him one day. It is to Stroomann's credit as a physician and friend that he stood up for Heidegger in the early 1950s. Friedrich Sieburg, in the obituary he published for Stroomann in the *Frankfurter Zeitung,* said, "One can appropriately say, without any exaggeration, that he was a true supporter of the philosopher Heidegger."

The Munich Academy

Not caring for the atmosphere that I presumed to prevail at Bühlerhöhe, I did not go there for Heidegger's lecture in March 1950. I still remembered the impressions from Bremen. But soon thereafter, in the second half of April, Count Clemens von Podewils phoned me in Icking. He was the general secretary of the Bavarian Academy of Fine Arts in Munich, which was founded after the war and whose president was Emil Preetorius. Podewils told me that they had succeeded in getting Heidegger to accept an invitation to give a talk before the Academy in early June. Since he had heard that I knew Heidegger rather well, he wanted to discuss the details with me.

I wrote to Freiburg without delay, to find out Heidegger's intentions. I added an invitation to stay in Icking, so that he could see the place my father had chosen for his retirement—a place that might have become a refuge for Heidegger during the war and where his manuscripts were still well protected. Because he assumed that I was involved with an important project, he apparently delayed his response for several weeks, presuming that in the meantime Podewils had informed me about everything. Finally, he let me know that it went without saying that on the planned visit to Munich he and his wife would never ignore Icking: "Simply out of remembrance for your parents this must not happen, not to mention your own active participation in what I am undertaking during these months in terms of the public. This remains an ambiguous issue and an inescapable tribute to *Ge-stell.*"

Preparations for the lecture in Munich during the following weeks led me to a closer relationship with Count Podewils. This allowed me to become acquainted with his noble, discerning, and straightforward way of thinking, which was to be tested in all the difficulties that appeared then and later. Podewils, who did not know Heidegger personally, inquired a great deal about the philosopher and soon realized that his appearance in Munich would not be entirely without problems. While Heidegger withdrew to Messkirch to write the new lecture, its theme was intensely discussed in the beautiful rooms where the Academy convened in Munich's Prinz-Carl-Palais. I kept Heidegger informed by letter. In mid-May he simultaneously informed Podewils and me that the final formulation of the theme of the talk would be "Über das Ding" (On the Thing), without any elaboration.

There were still some matters to be attended to in which I became involved, as Podewils's representative. For as soon as the rumor spread that the philosopher with a "political past"—and with his alleged "existentialism"—would speak in Munich, there were both requests and opposition. Everyone wanted to take part somehow in this sensational visit. Former students and old friends, like Father Lotz (who taught metaphysics at the Jesuit college in Pullach) and Schelling scholar Manfred Schröter, tried to arrange meetings with Heidegger for their circles. Also, with the legitimate claim of a host, Count Podewils wanted to take Heidegger to his country residence in Haarsee. According to Heidegger's explicit request, Romano Guardini, his old schoolmate, was not to be forgotten in all this. After doing a great deal of persuading, I was finally able to head off a reception for the prominent people of Munich that the Academy was planning. In this connection Frau Heidegger wrote, "My husband will be sufficiently shocked that something like this was even planned." And Heidegger added, "This will go on and on. I shudder at the whole thing." In the end a schedule was prepared omitting as much of the "official" as possible and making room for, among other things, a visit to Icking, as a respite from the likely strenuous days in Munich.

Thus, under the joint direction of the intelligent Count Podewils and myself, everything would have moved forward nicely had it not been for the fact that public resistance to the mere announcement of a Heidegger lecture provided seeds of discontent of all kinds. It was already a time of unrest in the Bavarian capital because the legislature was dealing with stormy arguments about banning Werner Egk's Abraxas Ballet, allegedly immoral and condemned as a Black Mass. The city hall experienced a similar stormy scene when a standard-bearer for Minister Hundhammer recommended cutting off electricity to *Csárdásfürstin,* a play allegedly staged in accordance with Nazi tastes. In the same breath he disparaged the philosopher Heidegger, who "as a former support of the Nazi regime" dared to speak publicly in the Bavarian Academy of Fine Arts.

These were days in which intellectual standards on the Isar were threatened. Whereas President of the Republic Heuss attended the Passion play in Oberammergau, the Bavarian minister of culture could not in good conscience do the same, because the actor who played Christ had been categorized as a party member by the denazification authorities. It is difficult to describe what went on behind the scenes. The culture bureaucracy and the circles behind it engaged in stubborn opposition, intrigues, distortion—even threats—in order to stop Heidegger from lecturing. A close examination of those who participated in this process would probably have shown that hardly any one of them had ever read any of Heidegger's writings or even grasped a single sentence of his. Who knew what was really at issue in Heidegger's rectoral address? Who knew that after 1936 he had been allowed neither to publish nor to travel without the Gestapo's permission?

This unrelenting opposition meant that, at the very least, the philosopher's appearance in Munich would occur in an adverse and unfriendly atmosphere. At the same time, however, a noteworthy thing happened that revealed that the opposition was in no way unified. A gap separated those in favor of Heidegger's appearance from those against it. Heidegger's name worked like *aqua fortis,* separating clergymen from clergymen, poets from poets, philosophers from philosophers, and students from students. While clergy of the strictest observance talked of the devil, the brightest minds among the Benedictines and the Jesuits supported Heidegger. While some students from the University of Vienna—stamping their feet all day—sat out to hear Heidegger speak at least once in their lives, the Kant Society, apparently concerned with the good of its members, announced a counterlecture for the same evening.

Before the heat of the battle and the waves of pros and cons had reached their apex, I received a telegram from Heidegger's residence in Zähringen, on the afternoon of 26 May, which completely upset me. The message read, "Today canceled speech irrevocably. Explanation follows. Heidegger." Since I could not reach Podewils that evening, I was confronted with a riddle, which took more and more distorted forms under the influence of "nighttime ghosts." What had happened? The following day I received another telegram from Heidegger reiterating the rejection but indicating that he was "willing to give the speech in a private circle."

Finally, illumination arrived by mail. What Heidegger wrote me at that time deserves to be kept in view. The way he reacted to an insult (as he perceived it) shows the overly strained and, indeed, deeply wounded condition into which he had been put by all the injustice, reproach, invective, and meanness of the past five years—along with the ensuing strains on his personal situation.

He wrote, "I have nearly had my fill. On 24 May in Messkirch I received a telegram from the board of directors of the Academy demanding a style of presentation and, additionally, a subtitle that would be acceptable to the Academy. I have now irrevocably canceled the talk. I don't believe that Count Podewils has anything to do with this. But three months ago I agreed to give a talk, with no honorarium, with the precisely formulated title 'Über das Ding.' Now, fourteen days before the talk, I am asked for something more. Setting aside all the particulars of this behavior, it seems to me that they do not trust me to be capable of presenting something perhaps very essential to this Academy. Nothing like this happened to me during the entire Hitler period. I deeply regret the whole thing. All of this, and whatever else is added to it, pains me very much. Two days ago, on my mother's name day, I went to her grave. Since that moment, the rest of my way has finally been clear to me. It is very regrettable that young people are being deprived of opportunities that could be for them hints to something beyond those opportunities. That is finally finished. I must decline the responsibility for the failure of this possible assistance and must place it on the university, the government, and other responsible authorities."

He concluded by indicating how painful it was to him that my friendly efforts, which had taken so much time and energy, led to nothing and that he would not be able to visit Icking. The prospect of sharing a few days with me, which would also have been refreshing and exciting for his wife, was now gone. He also said that he would decline invitations from various student organizations at Heidelberg, Tübingen, Marburg, and Bonn—especially because his situation in Freiburg was still as scandalous as before. "But let's be done with it. Something else is at stake. I only hope that the energy for work is sustained and inner and outer peace is preserved. I thank you cordially for all your wasted efforts and send you my greetings in good friendship."

This letter deeply shocked all who were involved—including Count Podewils, whom I had contacted immediately. First of all, it was incomprehensible that the board of directors of the Academy could request a "style" of presentation that would reflect the character of the Academy.

Neither Podewils nor Preetorius would be capable of doing something like that. That Heidegger would reject such a demand, however, (which now lay in black and white before him), was something to be anticipated.

Clarification followed immediately. On 28 May a third telegram reached me in response to two perplexed and helpless letters: "We will come to the house in Icking." Hastening to Freiburg as a messenger and peacemaker after Heidegger's cancellation, Countess Sophie Podewils was received coolly; however, she brought light to the matter. It turned out that the Academy's telegram had been garbled. Instead of "style of presentation" (*Vortragsstil*), it should have read "title of the talk" (*Vortrags-Titel*). Basically a matter of formality, the request made in the telegram was for a title that would somehow reflect the nature of the Academy as an institution of fine arts. Apart from the fact that Heidegger had clearly articulated the title of his talk much earlier and that the additional request was a pedantic one (no one knew who had actually made it), what was now left was the awkwardness of the telegram, about which Countess Podewils could do nothing. As Frau Heidegger wrote me the same day, this alone would never have induced Heidegger to cancel the lecture so mercilessly: "Please help to smooth out the waves of shock and confusion." A few days later Heidegger wrote to say that the incident was completely settled and that for the sake of the work itself he had moved beyond the petty; and he added, "I am pleased to make myself available to the young people."

What this undertaking in Munich had almost ruined never became visible to the outside. Because of the excitement at the Academy, both invited and uninvited guests filled the seats—the result being that only a few students were admitted. The situation reached its culmination on the evening of the lecture, when a large number of people, driven by curiosity, simply stormed the lecture hall of the Academy. People pushed their way onto the steps and chairs and into the corners and aisles of the lecture hall, wedging themselves between the audience members who had tickets and were already seated. Finally, Heidegger was able to begin his lecture—which was an essential expansion of the first part of "Einblick." Here again he spoke of earth and sky, mortals and divinities, in whose fourfold the world appears, and of the mirror-play of the gathering four, wherein thing becomes thing and world worlds. Partly following and partly resisting, the audience was so absorbed by what was said that it did not notice that the secretary of state left the hall at this point. The obvious insult was hardly observed. Then Heidegger quoted Rilke's dedication to Picard, in which the word mirror-play (*Spiegelspiel*) appears; but he went far beyond what the poet had in view. This speech was an appeal to humans who—not as "living things," but as "mortals"—make the world as world their dwelling place.

Were these statements—which some did not want to take seriously, considering them a rather poetic arabesque—appropriate for an audience that did not expect anything more than so-called stimulations, even from philosophical lectures? In this respect a large portion of the audience at the Academy was not any different from the audiences at Bühlerhöhe. On the other hand, there were a large number of people in the audience who took Heidegger seriously and had real discussions with him on this occasion, as well as on his other visits to Munich. It was especially in the Podewils's circle of friends that Heidegger found a lively echo. The circle included the Count himself, with whom Heidegger soon became friends, and members of the Academy—poets, artists, writers, musicians, and linguists. Among these were Carl Orff, Ernst Jünger, Friedrich Georg Jünger, Richard Harder, Ilse Aichinger, Günther Eich, Preetorius, Guardini, Georgiades, von Weizsäcker, and Heisenberg. Clemens Münster, a television director, provided Heidegger with information about radio and television that was interesting to him in connection with the elucidation of the emergence and unfolding of technology.

The contact with young people that meant so much to Heidegger did not materialize here to any large extent. An exception was the repetition of the lecture "The Thing" in Icking on 10 June. Here there were only young people gathered, including students from Vienna and Freiburg. Hardly more than two dozen people gathered around Heidegger for a whole day; but the joy of following him on his pathway of thinking, a rigorous practice, was quite noticeable. Two hours of discussion in the afternoon, after a long discussion break in the garden, showed—to Heidegger's delight—that his talk had not been given in vain. The conversation about the "fourfold" took up Lao-tzu, about whom a young woman made an essential contribution. In the end the guests who were invited to the lecture and to the colloquium had perhaps some inkling of what would occur once the calculative, systematizing, contemporary philosophizing could turn into a mindful thinking. For many participants the encounter with Heidegger became a hint.

The exertion of uninterrupted discussions and debates with many people, of whom he knew only a few, was too much for Heidegger. The next day he became ill. There was no question of traveling back to Freiburg, and we were all terrified. But the physician who was called in quickly quieted our fears. The patient, indeed, needed complete rest and quiet so that he could overcome, with a little help from medication, the effects of the apparent overexertion. After a day of great weakness, Heidegger recovered quickly. Actually, I liked the idea of his staying longer than expected at the house in Icking. I had some good and memorable discussions with the convalescing patient on the terrace and on the bench near the forest. Sitting behind the peasant table from Worpswede, he wrote the two poems "Der Tod" and "Die Fluh," which he gave me as a gift in memory of my mother. He wrote in the guest book, "Nur was aus Welt gering / wird einmal Ding (Only what is wrought from the world / will one day become a thing), 10–13 June 1950. Martin and Elfride Heidegger."

In his letter that arrived a few days later from Freiburg, Heidegger thanked me "for the hospitality that comes from real friendship and that radiates again and again in your parents' house." This letter brought those days to a close, reminding me again of everything they had brought. Heidegger wrote, "Staying at your house in Icking felt like the first and second visits in Bremen—but these days were so crammed and too unfamiliar after a long seclusion. But this does not need elaborate discussion. You live in a lovely place, and I wish you well in your work during the next few weeks. The name Icking is now full of significance for me, and we can relate to its various meanings." Heidegger closed with cordial thanks to our housekeeper, Käthe Heidelck, for the "Bremenian consideration and care" with which she looked after Heidegger and his wife.

Over the next two years, during which I remained in Icking, Heidegger registered his name in the guest book several times—once, on 27 April 1952, with specific reference to Sophocles' *Antigone,* which he had experienced in Hölderlin's translation put to Orff's music. His visits at that time were especially devoted to the Academy's great series of lectures, in which he himself also spoke. Clemens von Podewils reported on these lectures in his memoirs on Heidegger. At one point I took part in one of those "internal preparatory sessions," in which Heidegger presented "Was heisst Denken?" (What Calls Thinking Forth?). However, I could no longer practice "the neighborly attendance" to Podewils and Richard Harder that Heidegger had suggested to me for the sake of encouraging discussion, because by the late summer of 1952 I had given up the residence in Icking and had moved to Freiburg.

I took part (as a guest in Munich, in 1953) in only the first memorable conference of the Academy, which was also its most productive and successful one. The conference, "The Arts in the Epoch of Technology," included the following lectures: "Man's Situation" by Romano Guardini, "Modern Physics' Image of the World" by Heisenberg, "The Question concerning Technology" by Heidegger, "Plastic Art" by Preetorius, "Language" by Friedrich Georg Jünger, "Music" by Walter Riezler, and, finally, "The Balance of Technology" by Manfred Schröter. This time the students gained admittance almost by force. On the evening Heidegger spoke, the entire intellectual community of Munich in the 1950s—including Hans Carossa, Heisenberg, Ernst Jünger, and Ortega y Gasset—was gathered together with the youth and the very young from all the faculties. It seemed as if this lecture would receive the greatest attention, even though Heidegger's movements in thinking were more difficult to follow, especially for the uninitiated, than was Heisenberg's presentation the evening before. In commemorating both men, Carl Friedrich von Weizsäcker elucidated the intellectual dialogue that took place at that time between the scientist and the thinker and contrasted this dialogue with the one between Plato and Aristotle, which also was never completed. I mention this because, in the tension of those evenings, an attentive audience could have noticed the dimension in which the debate occurred.

When Heidegger concluded his lecture with the celebrated words "For questioning is the piety of thinking," there was an ovation like a storm breaking from a thousand throats that did not want to cease. I had the feeling that the suspicion and hatred that had encircled this master and friend had finally broken up. This was perhaps Heidegger's greatest public success.

In the winter semester of 1951–52, Heidegger again held lectures at the University of Freiburg. Because his own chair had long ago been taken over by a replacement, a special "legal designation" had to be found. By getting emeritus status, he was officially rehabilitated. The almost boisterous pressure of the crowd—which at times necessitated transmitting his lectures over the loudspeaker to other lecture halls, since the large auditorium was inadequate—did not deceive him for a minute about the totally altered situation at the university. Certainly, he could see from the faces of his audience how sincere the desire to understand him was. But he felt—and learned from contact in isolated discussions—that "communication no longer took place—or not yet."

After this first winter of renewed academic activity, in the early spring of 1952, he returned once again to the theme that he had set out to deal with in the framework of the Academy in Munich: "Discussions in Munich make it increasingly clear to me that in all fields the task lies in the hands of *your* generation. It does not lie in the hands of the old ones, who do not grasp anything, nor in the hands of the younger ones, who cannot make it without the *next* older generation—even if one could assist them immediately (which cannot be done because of institutions and their democratized decline). As an individual, one appears nowadays as a comic figure in the university. I am not at all deceived by overfilled lecture halls, after observing for a semester the failure of a larger seminar."

In retrospect, Bremen, Bühlerhöhe, and Munich retained their significance as places where the isolation that was imposed on the thinker's free expression was shattered. Their significance lay also in openings to those larger audiences, with whom Heidegger had had hardly any contact earlier. But in all this Heidegger quickly recognized the disadvantages and dark sides. It was inappropriate to charge him with ambition. In the fifties he had already drawn conclusions from his insights, even if on occasion he had to disappoint a well-meaning patronage that liked to decorate itself with his name. He also limited the lectures in the University of Freiburg and in the end gave them up entirely.

The generation on which he had placed his hopes was destroyed by having lost its very best in the war. A name like Felix Hartlaub may represent them. That those who survived could realize only a little of what Heidegger considered to be their actual task is a case of negligence and failure—including, painfully, my own. Did we miss a historical moment here? What remains to be done is written at the end of Heidegger's *Letter on Humanism:* "What is needed in the present world crisis is less philosophy and more attentiveness in thinking; less literature and more cultivation of the letter. . . . With its saying, thinking lays inconspicuous furrows in language. They are even more inconspicuous than the furrows that the farmer, with slow steps, draws through the field." [7]

4

Dialogues

Notes from the Fifties

Throughout the five decades in which I knew Heidegger—first in a pleasant acquaintance while I was a student and finally in a cordial friendship—there were occasional conversations and mutual communications, but there were also numerous dialogues that explicitly deserve to be called such. These were dialogues that could not all be kept in memory, but rather could only be transmitted occasionally—as Goethe put it, "with one single, important word." One of those failures that can never be corrected is my failure to write down these dialogues, some of which seemed unforgettable. More or less accidentally, however, some of the notes I took render more than mere summary catchwords. Some of these dialogues took place in Icking and Munich, some in Freiburg at a later time. Because these notes were taken for the most part right after I was together with Heidegger and because they seemed significant in some respect—an impression that still remains today—I reproduce them here, revising them slightly from a stylistic point of view and inserting some explanations.[1] (There are notes on other dialogues with Heidegger in chapters 6 and 7.) Heidegger himself never saw these notes and did not know that they existed. Personal and private matters have been excluded.

24 February 1952
(At the end of the first winter semester in which Heidegger lectured again at the University of Freiburg, during a visit to either Icking or Munich)

Asked questions about his lecture course. Heidegger responded that it was problematical. He found the attention of the audience good, and some members were apparently deeply impressed. But more disappointing was the seminar; it was too difficult and needed guidance. In his words: "The students are no longer capable of anything. None of my own students is sent to this seminar. Generally it amounted to nothing.

One would have to lecture on 'interpretations' again. Theoretically I could stop lecturing at any time, but the lecture course is announced and will be carried out."

Question: How will it go from here? "A seminar in Todtnauberg is also no solution. This should not be turned into a 'school of wisdom' à la Keyserling."

Question: Who should participate in the seminar? Heidegger's response is that the idea of a "list" of invited participants, as Vietta proposes, is not practical—Vietta overlooks the fact that there will be other participants besides just those whom Vietta has in mind. (Thus it became clear that Vietta did not have a "lease" on Heidegger, although he thought he did.)

A suggestion for a compromise: Lecture in one semester and not in the other. Heidegger argues that the summer should be kept free for his own work, which would give more coherence to the winter semester and make it more suitable for lecturing.

Heidegger: "One cannot say everything in a lecture course. What is most important remains in silence." (Remember Jacob Burckhardt: even "Köbi" kept silent.) "Burckhardt had his city lectures. But many people who attended those lectures were only curious. I cannot give lectures as a 'secondary' activity, although a former student of mine, who is now a teacher, suggested that holding lectures would take little effort. (And that pertained to the seminar!)" Heidegger seemed to like my remark that in lecturing he is always totally "present" (*da*).

Then we spoke about books and about a work on "space in antiquity." Heidegger: "That will be a fair absurdity, because antiquity did not know anything like *the space*, but only *places*." We mentioned Erik Wolf's *Frühgriechische Rechtsdenker* (Early Greek Thinkers in Jurisprudence) and Boehringer's book on Stefan George, and then Beissner's edition of Hölderlin. Heidegger: This edition should be judged critically; in part it contains inadequate interpretations. For instance, it is a highly daring move to patch up "Wie wenn am Feiertage"—in Heidegger's view, an indefensible move.

Then we talked about Barlach's *Ratzeburg*, which was performed in Darmstadt. Heidegger: "This won't work. Young people do not listen. Vietta deceives himself, and Sellner—despite recognition of his intellectual accomplishment—is dragged into the 'current operation' (*Betrieb*)." The conclusion to which one resigns oneself is, "This whole thing does not make sense." Finally we spoke about music and recent records.

"Beautiful Pachelbel's Canon. Orff must like it." And Haydn's "Cassation," which shows again that Haydn is not a "grandfather."

At the end we spoke about Friedrich Georg Jünger's *Dalmatinische Nacht*. I told of the impression this novel had had on Gertrud Eysoldt. When I recently visited her in Ohlstadt, she re-created all the events of the book as a sequence of dramatic scenes—seen with the eyes of a great actress.

27 April 1952
(In Icking, on the occasion of the reproduction of *Antigone*)

At the dinner table Heidegger is in high spirits and, in view of what was offered, praises the good Bremen tradition that Fräulein Heidelck maintains. When I ask him what he "thinks" about having a cup of coffee after the meal, he responds very seriously, "I do not *think* at all." I correct myself and say, "What do you hold of drinking a cup of coffee?" To which Heidegger responds, smiling slyly, "In that case, please let me have one."

Conversation about the university as a "business operation" and the format of teaching in seminars. Heidegger talks about Rickert, who restricted participation in a seminar to a select few. Since Rickert's agoraphobia forced him to hold his seminars only at home, he (Heidegger) sat next to Guardini (who was then already a chaplain) in the adjoining room at the very end of the table. In order to hold his lectures in the old building of the University of Freiburg, Rickert used to be transported by car and then tricked into sitting at the desk that was quite close to the entrance of the auditorium.

Like Rickert, Husserl was given to monologue: nothing but phenomenology throughout the semester. When Heidegger was Husserl's assistant, he managed once to bring up a different topic. Husserl let him finish the first sentence, but then interrupted the presentation—and from then on spoke on the old topic throughout the semester, whereby, of course, some magnificent things were discussed. After such a seminar session, in which no one interrupted Husserl with a single word and everyone listened to him, Husserl said to Heidegger, "Didn't you also have the impression that today's participation was especially intense?"

Husserl's special style is shown in another anecdote. Husserl had been invited to Amsterdam to hold three lectures, and Frau Malvine Husserl took care of everything. "The old man worked up to the last hour before departure. Even on the way to the train station, he spoke of nothing but absolute consciousness on the one hand and nature on the other." On the platform, where the train coming from Basel could be heard, Heidegger finally says to Husserl, "Well, Herr Geheimrat,[2] what about history?" Taken aback, Husserl taps Heidegger on the shoulder and says, "History? Oh yes, I forgot about it." With that, he got on the train for Holland.

24 April 1953

(In Zähringen)

Heidegger is quite nervous; there are shadows of irritability. He feels depressed because of the continuing ugly attacks against him and the occasional lack of understanding on the part of those who are close to him. He speaks with bitterness about journalism. How was his trip to Munich? He says that he spoke with Podewils, Guardini, and Ludwig von Ficker.

I talk about a newspaper report that describes Heidegger's participation in a conference about television sponsored by the Bavarian Radio. I mention the "well-meaning" anecdote in that report according to which Heidegger, the "absent-minded" professor, mistakes a television technician for a famous writer and makes positive comments on his latest work. Heidegger is horrified. He says he listened for an hour and a half to the introductory paper by Clemens Münster, which addressed the *technical* requirements: "I was interested in learning something about the technical procedures, given that we must still submit ourselves to all that." Beforehand he did ask Münster not to announce that he (Heidegger) was attending the conference. "One can no longer make a move in public without being noticed—not even half a move." Of course, the newspaper's anecdote and the participation in the three-day conference is all made up. Now the three-dimensional film is still to come: things become more shocking, and we are far from the end of these sorts of things.

We speak after that about Orff's *Trionfi.*[3] Heidegger heard *Carmina Burana* on the radio and intends to buy the record. He likes Joachim's interpretation very much. Have I seen the performance? I say no and talk about Frau Stroomann's negative impression of it, especially of *Trionfo di Afrodite,*[4] which she finds impossible: "Everything in Greek, that's all." At the end a huge Aphrodite is projected against the back wall of the auditorium. Heidegger shudders and inquires whether Orff was satisfied

with all this. I know nothing about Orff's reaction. Heidegger heard similar things from Walter Riezler (who after many invitations refused to go
to Stuttgart). In summer Heidegger would like to see the reproductions in
Munich.

Then we talk about Sartre's visit to Freiburg: "He sat there, in the
chair where you sit now. We spoke for an hour and a half. As Albert
Schweitzer's nephew, he speaks German well. It was a good conversation.
I am pleased that Sartre was here."

It is worth mentioning how Sartre heard about Heidegger for the first
time. In Marburg Heidegger had a Japanese student, Count Kuki, who
subsequently went to Paris and was introduced to the situation of modern
French philosophy by a young man from the École normale. The young
man was Sartre—whom Kuki frequently told about a German philosophy professor who was nearing his forties and who had published a book
called *Being and Time*. That is how Sartre found Heidegger and arrived
at existentialism. . . . (Heidegger then takes his copy of *L'Être et le néant*
from the shelf and shows it to me.) Sartre told him that Count Kuki had
died recently.

We talk about events in Munich. Countess Podewils wrote to tell Heidegger about Barrault and the deep impression his lecture at the Academy
made—a lecture I had heard. Can I say something about this lecture? I
try a brief summary and describe what Barrault looks like. Heidegger
demands a precise description of the scene about silence, where the "nar-
rated" silence suddenly becomes present. "A great actor—a great one."
But how far removed all this is from what is essential—what theater
could, perhaps, still give us!

Then we speak about books. I show him the Rilke-Gide correspondence I have brought along. He opens the book, and the first thing he
finds is the letter in which Rilke announces the gift to Gide of an edition
of Hölderlin's works. Heidegger is moved. "Gide—I have not yet read
anything by this man. Please bring me something by him."

In mentioning the Gide-Claudel correspondence and the issue of the
situation of Christianity today, Heidegger talks about Gabriel Marcel,
Sartre's antagonist: "A zero who is puffed up by Catholic circles. Marcel
is extremely angry because I do not respond to his nonsense. Now he has
written a book, no, a play about me." Puzzled, I ask whether he (Heidegger) appears in it. "Yes. There is a philosopher in the play who lives in a
hut which he considers the center of the world. He reigns there, exuding
philosophical mysticism. Until he gets entangled in language and gets lost

in it. . . . The play must be terrible, but it exists. The German title is *Die Wacht am Sein* (The Watch over Being)."

Heidegger gets agitated because this touches again on what is most dear to him. Finally, I change the subject to his upcoming visit to Bremen and ask what he will talk about. He says, "About a theme that you wanted so much: Who is Zarathustra? Unfortunately I am a bit out of contact with Nietzsche at present. This will be a considerable amount of work for me. However, I already know how the theme will unfold, which is especially important to me. I shall be dealing with Nietzsche's thinking about revenge—with which you are somewhat familiar—with his thinking about the eternal recurrence of the same, and with the notion of the overman. After Gottfried Benn's terrible platitudes in his recently published essay on Nietzsche, it is perhaps necessary to do this. Let me interject a question, Petzet: Has Benn become senile? Or—as I almost suspect—has he always been like this with respect to these sorts of things?"

Later, on a walk to the Zähringer Burg, we speak more about Benn. Heidegger is bewildered and deeply annoyed by what Vietta has said and written about Benn: "I do not understand this inept praising. We all agree that as a poet Benn wrote many splendid poems inspired by expressionism and that these poems will last. Even today he may produce something like that. But Benn's books! Nowadays people think that when they have read *Ptolemäer* or *Probleme der Lyrik*, they have come closer to the riddles of the universe. What views! Incidentally, it is typical of people today that they think they have to explain their poetry. That smacks of arrogance vis-à-vis things. Take Benn's *Probleme der Lyrik;* if you are sincere, you will admit that it is badly written and wholly marginal. What emerges from poesie in this book? As I said before, many of Benn's poems will last. However, Benn never freed himself from expressionism and never went beyond it. Think about this from the perspective of painting.

"And now one gets angry when somebody like Heidegger suddenly writes about Trakl and meddles with the work of poetry. You will admit that what we were able to work out about Trakl in Bühlerhöhe is a world removed from Benn's 'thinking' on poems. The result is that Benn, to whom I never did the slightest harm, begins to express himself about me in an uncouth and caustic fashion. He never forgave me for my *Hölderlin.* Something like that would never fit into Benn's cynicism and his misunderstood views on art, even when he still believes he understands Nietzsche."

Heidegger, who knew how much I was touched by Benn's poetry, did not say these things maliciously, but rather in a sad tone.

14 April 1959
(Freiburg)

An appointment to meet Heidegger in the Buchhandlung Albert.[5] From there we go to the Berthold-Weinstuben and have a glass of red Italian wine. We speak about physicians, and Stroomann's name comes up. Heidegger asks about my work on the editing of Stroomann's literary remains. From a folder I pull out a note by Stroomann that prompts a discussion. It is a small piece of paper on which Stroomann had recorded a newspaper report from 1948: Sartre visits with Jaspers and to his astonishment meets a typical German professor, instead of a man who maintains a broad openness to the world. Jaspers is "painstakingly accurate, highly reflective, and instructive." And here Stroomann remarks, "I imagine Jaspers to be an unhappy man and not favored by the muse (*nicht musisch*). He was a psychiatrist, which ruins one anyway." For a moment Heidegger looks at me perplexedly and then slowly says, "Exactly! That is exactly the case! Nothing can describe Jaspers better than this 'not favored by the muse, unhappy.'" He goes on to say that he was with Jaspers near the end of December 1926, when the news of Rilke's death arrived. This deeply affected Heidegger, but Jaspers began to disparage Rilke as an impossible human being and a terrible spectacle. "Jaspers did not have even a spark of poetic ingenuity. This is basically sad."

I ask him whether I should include this passage that I found in Stroomann's book. He insists that I should. I suggest that something like this is a necessary correction of distortions. Suddenly Heidegger looks at me penetratingly and says, "Distortions? Apparently something terrible has been published. Do you know about it? Rainer Marten wrote to tell me that I should not read it at all, and I am not going to. But you tell me about it. It is better if I hear it from you."

Heidegger could only have meant Paul Hühnerfeld's book. I picked out at random a couple of those "facts" that Hühnerfeld alludes to and mentioned them to Heidegger as considerately as I could. Hühnerfeld writes that Heidegger indeed did not *avoid* the war, but that the examination committee had found him too weak for active service—and consequently the weak philosopher could hibernate in the security of the backcountry. Apart from Hühnerfeld's failure to mention the fact that Heidegger *was* called to military service in the West, during the last years of the war,[6] he was furious about the sarcastic remark concerning his weakness: "Do you know why I was too weak? Because I went hungry for months in order to finish the *Habilitation*[7]—for months and months.

I wonder whether Herr Hühnerfeld knows what hunger is all about when there is no way out and no one is there to help."

The "anecdotes" mentioned in the book seem for the most part invented. Heidegger says he will talk to me at another time about his meeting with the theologians of the Evangelical Academy of Geismar. At any rate, it was not he but the Spiritual Board that was highly embarrassed, because he (Heidegger) knew the Bible better. But when I quote the most wicked statement of Hühnerfeld's malicious booklet ("Poor philosopher. He was never touched by faith and never affected by the divine rays"), then Heidegger's face darkens; he becomes silent and looks at me with the eyes of one deeply wounded.

Hühnerfeld mentions that on Heidegger's writing desk (the desk of the "hopelessly provincial" philosopher) there were pictures of Dostoyevsky and Pascal. For a moment Heidegger gets angry, but then regains his composure and says quietly, "This must come from Szilasi. Who could otherwise know about all this? *He* was in Marburg and not Herr Hühnerfeld!" I try to intercede, saying that I cannot imagine Szilasi's doing something like this out of malice. "No," Heidegger says, "not out of malice; not for one moment do I believe that Szilasi did that out of malice. But he allows himself to be manipulated by this scribbler, who approaches him in a charming way and then turns things around." But what can be done? "There is nothing to be done, Petzet. Even when one defends oneself, one comes too late and appears stupid. They want to humiliate me—or, worse, they want to topple thinking. But they will not succeed. Look, this fellow Hühnerfeld wrote me six months ago on behalf of a good publisher in Berlin, one who publishes monographs on 'twentieth-century minds'—Stravinsky, Picasso, etc. He wanted to know if I would meet with him and give him biographical materials. I responded by saying that in my opinion it was high time to instruct the reader less about what is biographically interesting than about *at last* thinking through *the* issue with which I have troubled myself for forty years. My life is totally uninteresting." In response, Hühnerfeld sent him a boorish letter loaded with impudent threats, saying that he would get revenge. And now we have his "revenge," put together in four months.

It is almost seven o'clock, and Heidegger must go to the train station to pick up his wife. He would actually like to tell me a bit about Tübingen and Stuttgart, where for the first time he held in his hands the original manuscripts of Hölderlin. He says that I cannot at all imagine how stirring this is. "Now I understand what Norbert von Hellingrath wanted to do; out of these pages the 'present' speaks to us. What the philologists have done with these manuscripts is simply not accurate. These manuscripts also at first pull the rug out from under my own lecture. Consider Hölderlin's letter to his mother from Bordeaux—it does not let one alone."

Heidegger tells me that his lecture in Munich (where there is a growing obscurantist opposition) will be the last one. There, he said, he will state everything; "after that they can chew on this for leftovers." Later on, in Bremen, in a very intimate setting, he will be saying what is specifically his, as he did recently. But in Munich he would like to be surrounded once again by those who are loyal to him. The old Residenz Theater is, of course, too small to hold students in addition to the large number of members of the Hölderlin Society and those who are officially invited. In light of this, the official advisor to the university, who is a Catholic, has indicated to the president of the Hölderlin Society that the large auditorium of the university will be put at its disposal, with the condition that Heidegger does not speak there. "Yes, Petzet, that's the way it is."

At the train station Heidegger wants to know when I will be finished reading the galley proofs. Perhaps Thursday? In that case I should bring them at three o'clock. "After that we will go to the Jägerhäusle for a glass of wine!"

16 April 1959

I return to Zähringen with the bundle of corrected galley proofs. Guzzoni, a doctoral student of Fink's, joins us. He too has read galleys. Finally Heidegger returns from his walk, having forgotten that he had an appointment with me. A smiling Frau Elfride Heidegger says, "Ah, Herr Petzet, you know what happens if I do not write everything down." Heidegger asks me to wait. Half an hour later he asks me to come upstairs. Can I possibly come tomorrow morning? Then he can speak longer with me; today he must pursue an important thought and cannot afford a longer break in between. I agree without delay, but as I am about to go Heidegger says, "Perhaps we can quickly go through the galleys, then tomorrow we will be free for other things."

As we go through the galleys, it is clear that Heidegger accepted all the minor changes I proposed. This time I found almost nothing, but Guzzoni had detected a number of mistakes that I had overlooked. I am somewhat ashamed; but Heidegger is kind and says that sometimes he, too, finds almost no mistakes, because his reading gets sidetracked by the issue—and that is presumably what happened to me. A passage near the end of the lecture deals with *Ereignis*.[8] His wife had found an important omission here, which Heidegger shows me. The statement reads, "There is nothing to which *Ereignis* goes back and nothing that can in any way (*gar*) explain *Ereignis*." But instead of "goes back" (*zurückführt*), it should be "may be led back" (*zurückgeführt*). I read this sentence, then the entire passage; finally I say, "In my opinion this sentence must be as it appears in the galleys." In that case, says Heidegger, "in any way" (*gar*) makes no sense. I respond, "But it does indeed. For at this point *Ereignis* gets illuminated in two directions." Heidegger is troubled. He looks back at the manuscript; there he finds *zurückgeführt*. Then I say, "In that case you must stay with your text." Heidegger: "Why? I am going to think this over very carefully. It could be that *you* are right." Chuckling, he adds, "A typical Heideggerian passage, don't you think?" I reply, "I did not want to say it, but I thought so all the time"; and we laugh.

As I am leaving he gives me a present—the Norwegian translation of "Der Feldweg"—and says, "Did you know that Hölderlin's friend Böhlendorf was in Bremen and was a friend of your Mayor Smidt? At some point you should write an essay entitled 'Hölderlin and Bremen.' "

<h2 style="text-align:center">17 April 1959</h2>

We walk up the Eichhalde toward the Jägerhäusle. I take up the remark that Heidegger had made yesterday about Böhlendorf: "When I looked through the biography of Smidt this morning, I did not find anything about Böhlendorf. But Friedrich Wilmans, Hölderlin's bookseller in Frankfurt, was in Bremen earlier; and Smidt often mentions him. He also mentions that in 1813–14 he (Smidt) was in Freiburg for a long time and stayed with his relatives. In those days Jacob Grimm was a young lieutenant in the Hanoverian staff. Smidt also became acquainted with Wilhelm von Humboldt and visited Hebel in Karlsruhe. He sent the *Hausfreund*[9] to his daughter in Bremen, referring her especially to the chapter entitled 'Hauptplaneten'." Heidegger is astonished and stops. He is completely delighted: "What relations, what connections! We have no idea at all how people in those days related to one another and lived with one another. What you discovered is very beautiful. Please continue to track down Smidt; see if he was in Schiller's audience, or was a friend of Fichte, or knew Goethe. And how about Napoleon?" I tell him that Smidt, as a young man in Milan on his way to Brera, encountered Napoleon and was greatly impressed by his appearance and presence. Later on, Napoleon twice received Smidt as a senator in Paris, as well as the less well known mayor of Bremen, Gröning. Smidt had been described to Napoleon as "a most dangerous man." Heidegger: "You should investigate what Smidt said about Napoleon between 1799 and 1800, that is, before Lunéville, when Smidt had connections with Wilmans and through him, certainly, with Böhlendorf. Everything these people said and wrote about Napoleon in those days is important in view of Hölderlin's *Friedensfeier* (1801). We have not yet determined at all what the best people of that time really thought about Bonaparte and do not know how he appeared to the world."

Naturally, I am reminded of Beethoven and Goethe; I say, "I found Allemann's interpretation of *Friedensfeier* totally accessible from the first moment, even obvious. From my dissertation director Elze, I learned something very different about Bonaparte from what our Prussian nationalistic historiography wanted us to believe, since this historiography distorted the essentials." Heidegger: "It is regrettable that people still want to perpetuate these views by drawing upon Hitler's stupid comparison of himself with Napoleon." As the conversation progresses, I mention Berthold Vallentin's works on Napoleon, which reflect Stefan George's view that in Napoleon's case a semidivine kind of incarnation took place—and George thus prepares the basis for understanding *Friedensfeier* as a hymn to Napoleon.

Coming back to Heidegger's lecture on language, I asked him, "What did you decide to do with that typical Heideggerian passage?" Heidegger: "I opted for the version you preferred, namely, "goes back" (*zurückführt*), for I find this ambiguity just right. Especially when you read the passage in the context of '*Es gibt*' (It gives)." When I remark that this is perhaps a point where language is smarter than the author, Heidegger laughs: "Yes, Petzet, that is exactly so." I take this opportunity to bring up something that has preoccupied me for days—namely, that what is said in *Being and Time* on language shows itself in another way in the lecture on language, as though we were just dealing with another version of the same thing: "What you speak about here as the 'having-already-heard' that occurs prior to all 'speaking'—isn't this the same as the 'being-always-already-along-with' mentioned in *Being and Time,* that is, in the existential constitution, the sudden recognition of which came over me in a flash thirty years ago?" Heidegger stops walking, turns to me, and says, "It is splendid that you say this. We don't even need to talk about it, since you have noticed it. Basically it is no different from what I tried to show forty years ago. But who pays attention? Read section 34

of *Being and Time!*" I respond, "But what about the young people, between the ages of twenty and thirty, who are still themselves and have not
sold out to prevailing standards, as happened to me at that age?" Heidegger: "Yes, I am aware of that. But now, when I speak for the last time on
Hölderlin, where will the young people be? *Outside. . . .*"

When we arrive at the almost-empty Jägerhäusle, Heidegger picks
the table next to the big window in the middle of the large room. Then he
says that he must quickly phone Podewils, who is anxiously awaiting the
manuscript. "And while I am on the telephone, think about how *Sage* can
be translated into French.[10] I have found something for this rendition."
Of course, I did not find anything. After a while Heidegger comes back
from the telephone and says, "I did not expect that you would." He goes
on to say that his wife had mentioned casually that the French do not
have a word for *Märchen* (fable). This prompted him to think on La Fontaine's fables: "*fabula—phasis—*φῶς, then the whole golden thread to
the Greek language was there; the French *fable* = *Sage*." We toast each
other with *Wasenweiler Spätburgunder*.

As soon as we have drunk the wine (a *Viertele*), Heidegger orders
once more: "In good brotherly style, we are going to drink yet an *Achtele*,
all right?" At first I do not understand what he means by "brotherly" and
ask if he has in mind his brother in Messkirch. "He was the one who
discovered that Swabian is related to Greek: *To no-ein te kai ein-ai*, which
naturally means 'another one and . . .' (*Noch ein und . . .*). You see,
Petzet, this is the whole of the Messkirchian wisdom of the *Achtele*."
When the wine arrives, Heidegger toasts his brother Fritz, who has just
retired. "If only I had the time, I would go and help him. This first day of
May, how is he going to get over it? But I must prepare the Hölderlin
lecture, and time is short."

The day before, he had shown me photocopies of Hölderlin's poems,
which had a stunning effect on me. He was not surprised, believing that
just looking at those pages and holding them in one's hands is something
tremendous. They make Hölderlin simply "present." Only now, he says,
can he understand what Norbert von Hellingrath encountered.

Then I recall a distant and long-forgotten event. I tell Heidegger that
twenty-five years ago in Berlin, right at the beginning of the Third Reich,
I knew a young Jewish assessor and expert in international law, whom I
had met in Erich Kaufmann's seminar. We liked each other, began a conversation, and became friends. Once, in wintertime, he invited me to his
magnificent residence on the Thielplatz in Dahlem, and we spent half a
day drinking whiskey (which was unusual for me). That night he showed

me a small, used edition of Plato dating from the end of the eighteenth century. This set had belonged to Hölderlin, and its margins were covered in many places with his handwritten notes. Heidegger is electrified. He pounds on the table with excitement and says, "You saw *that*, Petzet? That set exists?" I admit that then, in 1935, I had no idea what that set meant; I vaguely recall that, in my drunken state, Heidegger's name had flashed through my mind like lightning. But who was the owner of these volumes? I had forgotten his name long ago. I had met him only once or twice and very soon lost sight of him—hopefully, he had gone abroad. Heidegger feverishly took note of what I told him, saying that it had to be reported to the Hölderlin Archive that such an edition existed. Even that much had not been known until now. "Hölderlin used to work with books exactly as you describe it."

Then he returns to the lecture on language and mentions that Podewils told him recently on the phone how, with the translation of the lecture into French (a task to be undertaken by Beaufret), he (Podewils) sees how far removed Romance languages are from our own language and how close ours is to Greek. "This is good. At least people are beginning to notice this, one by one. What has actually taken place in the transformation of the Greek by the Roman language—and its total change—is so *fundamental* that it is not yet understood at all. And people nonetheless speak so readily about antiquity."

Finally, I find the opportunity to tell Heidegger about Walter Schulz's lecture in Tübingen on the occasion of Schulz's refusing the call to assume Heidegger's chair. The newspaper report of the lecture (I had already sent the clip to Heidegger) is distorted in that a significant passage of the lecture is omitted. To the students who congratulated him for staying at the University of Tübingen (and who arranged a torchlight procession for him), Schulz said explicitly that the work of the young philosophical generation—wherever teacher and student come together—can be fruitful only under the aspects indicated by Heidegger. That is why Schulz carries out his entire work in the light of Heidegger's thinking.

Heidegger finds the omission horrifying, whatever the reason may be. "It is gradually becoming uncanny." He cannot understand it. And, finally, "Good that you told me this. It changes many things."

On the way home we discuss the question of publishers. Not the least of the complaints is about how, if at all, to unify the realm of business efficiency with intellectual matters or with a sense for what is at stake. For a moment Heidegger becomes vehement and says, "Worse than bad. What can one do?"

I say good-bye to him in front of the house at Rötebuck 47. Once again he expresses his wish to see those who are loyal to him in Munich, especially in view of the growing opposition there. "However, I am going to offer the opposition something heathenish, which they will think about for a long time!"

Reflections on the *Spiegel* Interview of 1966

From the moment Heidegger reappeared in public in Germany and began publishing new books and essays, the return of one who carried the blemish of having supported national socialism aroused the suspicion of the press and brought on the protests of old opponents who believed that he had been put out of commission. That Heidegger, whom Hühnerfeld considered a "hopelessly provincial" man, dared to load the cargo of his burdensome thought into the fragile ship of postwar hopes was something that the functionaries of culture did not exactly welcome. They would have preferred to get rid of him before his thinking could begin to take root in the new generation and create unrest there. A smoldering hatred directed against Heidegger's unpopular demand for rethinking and returning to a new beginning became noticeable in numerous attacks, misinterpretations, and even personal humiliations aimed at the philosopher in the fifties and even in the sixties—a hatred that spared not even his honor. What always provoked this animosity anew was Heidegger's silence. One could not get statements out of him that one would have been able to control (cf. *T&G*, p. 40). An objective discussion in such an atmosphere was as good as impossible. Such a discussion began only as the storms finally subsided—and also as people began to be ashamed before the admirers of the philosopher abroad. Even the loudest cry fails to have any effect against one who is silent.

It has often been found puzzling that, apart from a brief justification in *Der Spiegel*, Heidegger never defended himself. His best friends suffered from the fact that they could respond only with their own counterarguments, not with corrections that came from the person under attack. Frequently, Heidegger was implored and pressured to take a stand against insinuations that those in the know recognized as lacking all foundation. I myself experienced how a reputable newspaper abroad refused to publish an objectively secured response to a mean attack against Heidegger, justifying the refusal on the ground that they knew better. Nevertheless, Heidegger never managed to express himself in such a hostile public, so that for a long time he appeared to be in the wrong.

He was convinced, however, that it would be stupid to enter this field where he would always arrive too late. Although he did not read all of the bad things that were propagated about him, he somehow heard of them or was told about them by his friends. Although he would seem calm on the outside, these sorts of things hurt and pained him immensely. On the occasion of a television program to honor him, the eighty-year-old Heidegger said to Richard Wisser, "People have not treated me well." In the end, no one knows how much Heidegger suffered from what was done to him over the years. As I said before, he was not an insensitive man. An irrelevant or even personal reproach hurt him in a way that no one can measure.

What especially affected him were insinuations about his alleged behavior toward his former Jewish students. These innuendoes were aimed at labeling him an anti-Semite. It was thus understandable when he got angry at some of the statements and occurrences related to Karl Löwith's call to the University of Heidelberg after the war. I had brought to his attention an article in *Neue Zeitung* entitled "Heidegger-German," along with a critical essay against him in *Neue Rundschau,* not anticipating the outbreak of anger I would cause. Heidegger's response (from his sickbed) showed all his bitterness: "I am not surprised that a fifty-five-year-old man who, from 1919 on, took my courses and seminars for nine whole years and almost every other day in Marburg dashed into our house in order to squeeze something out of me can report on some things and thereby *appear* to many uninformed people to be in the know. *Neue Rundschau* and *Neue Zeitung* do not report that the same author, while an immigrant in the United States (having come there from Switzerland and Paris), spread the most outrageous lies about me. What is painful to me is the terrible abuse of the essential word *Kehre* (turning).

"In 1929, when Löwith was an extreme Marxist (today he has turned Christian and occupies the chair of philosophy in Heidelberg), he wrote about *Being and Time,* saying that it was a 'concealed theology.' Later on he changed that to 'atheism'—as one uses that term. Löwith does not inform his readers that the genuine *Kehre* is communicated for the first time in 1930 in the lecture "Vom Wesen der Wahrheit." At that time Herr Löwith himself heard the lecture and received a typescript of it. He is silent about this, as well as the fact that in the lecture course of 1927 (the year *Being and Time* was published), I dealt with the question of being and not subjectivity for four hours every week.

"But I have already written too much, because what is at stake is another matter altogether. Now, as I enter public life again, they have found the right man for the right job, one who can very subtly undermine everything beforehand. Herr Fischer's magazine now tells what is going on with Heidegger, and *Neue Zeitung* and its backers provide the necessary assistance. People do not want to deal with genuine questions and experiences; rather, they want to retain or regain the upper hand in the sphere of public debate.

"I keep asking myself *why,* if these gentlemen know so exactly (and apparently better than I) what my thinking is all about, do they not produce the facts themselves, raising and settling the issues? It will not be long before the Greek thinkers are put on trial because they thought 'only' Greek thoughts—not Egyptian or Hebraic or everything else mixed up.

"You yourself have noticed that these people are only rattling off clever talk. The writer who will now unfold his own influence in Germany orchestrates, with the help of people like himself, the business of literature. Now, when such figures appear in the questionable universities of West Germany, one should no longer set foot in any such lecture hall; I am carefully considering this and other matters. . . ."

This letter demonstrates the bitterness that threatened to get the better of Heidegger in the fifties, despite his experience that young people were again turning toward him. In the end he swallowed the slogan "Thinker in Needy Times" (invented by Löwith), strengthened in the deep skepticism expressed in his already-quoted statement regarding those students of his who were doing work in universities: "It amounted to nothing." I do not know whether Heidegger had discussions with Löwith later on that smoothed things out (he traveled regularly to the meetings of the Academy in Heidelberg). The fact that Löwith later took part (with a large contribution) in wishing Heidegger well on the occasion of his eightieth birthday was—despite all the homage paid to him—hardly enough to obliterate what had happened earlier. For years the hunters the press sent after him continued their persecution. "The chase is far from having reached its culmination—that is, its depth," Heidegger wrote me once as the awkward gossip about him continued.

What he called the "business of literature" in the letter quoted above was repugnant to him not only with respect to his own person. Because his thinking after the war had turned increasingly toward language—giving poetry a wide berth—he often had conflicts with philologists. It is understandable that philologists who worked in ancient and modern languages were opposed to him, since Heidegger was frequently opposed to their science. As early as 1949 he wrote to me that the methods used in some journal articles were cheap. "It seems, however, that the literary person is the necessary counterpart to technology. In the 1880s Nietzsche said all that needs to be said about the literary person: one who is actually nothing but represents almost everything, who plays the role of and 'represents' the expert, and who with all humility takes it upon himself to be paid, honored, and celebrated in place of the expert."

On occasion he stated that etymology would be an obstacle to thinking as long as it was given priority vis-à-vis the emergence and unfolding (*Wesen*) of language and was considered the voice of the absolute. He offended the specialists with this sort of statement. But it is not surprising that, according to Heidegger, not only the "professional language," but also the whole of the impoverished and abstract modern way of speaking—all the way to literature—is determined by the rule of *Ge-stell*'s unfolding. This was made clear often enough in our conversations, which were permeated by a concern for a humanity that conjures all this up but cannot manage to handle it. Heidegger did not stop there with his critique of the Western mind in its self-certainty and self-complacency. In September 1961 he wrote to me from Todtnauberg, saying that the whole hollowed-out being of the West has now come to light. Yet no one takes note of this. The process of becoming generally ever more stupid will continue in Germany. No one grasps yet that, in the epoch of *Ge-stell*, human beings are required to transform all their ways of existence. Thinking, as Heidegger understood it, is not a convenient cure-all, and neither are these the conclusions that human beings should draw from it.

Frequently, we spoke about the awkward and disgraceful situation of the philosopher in his own university and department, even beyond his retirement. He was of the opinion that a "system" was working behind this—everything happening so as to undermine not only him but also thinking. It is an illusion to believe that such scribbling has no effect beyond momentary confusion. Of course, in the long run this whole thing will collapse: "They have hardly understood *Being and Time;* what can they manage to do with the later works?"

That is why it was so difficult for Heidegger to get readers and listeners to have the necessary perseverance and care. He was always the teacher who was concerned with genuine communication but who was so often disappointed. Still, he could not ignore the fact that the attempts he was making then in Germany, in his speaking and writing, often had more far-reaching consequences and were more fruitful than "we ourselves are capable of seeing."

Over the years, the more a generation found itself ready to listen to

Heidegger and began to turn to him (especially abroad—for example, in France), the stronger became the demand of those close to him that he free himself once and for all from the burden of repeated reproaches by means of a kind of public "confession." Heidegger was vehemently against doing something like this. He had a clear conscience in regard to both himself and the matter of his thinking. He found no reason to commit a "Canossa-Gang" [11] in order to excuse *post factum* his earlier action and especially his thinking—and *post festum* do injustice to both. In any event, he himself was of the opinion that his resignation of the chancellorship in February 1934 and his whole intellectual posture (which emerges from numerous statements that were well understood by his students) had made it abundantly clear that he was not a National Socialist, and no further steps were needed (cf. *T&G*, p. 29).

But it was not only a proud, perhaps obstinate, persistence in a stand of conscience that was at work here; something more prevented him from taking such a step. He knew only too well what kind of storm such a gesture would create. Fierce arguments would flare up, awakening what had long ago subsided. He feared, presumably with justification, that such a gesture would destroy the beginnings that were being made for his work to have a renewed and productive impact. The work that he had resumed in 1949 would then be in vain. And it was with this work, whose fruits were attained with difficulty, that he was primarily concerned in his old age. Apart from the fact that each new storm would not only damage but also, under certain circumstances, paralyze his capacity for work, Heidegger believed that he would serve no one by stirring up the public anew and by returning to occurrences that lay deep in the past. A young generation that had experienced the Third Reich as children and was now entering the university would be irritated and would put his books aside with suspicion. This meant that he would be forced to see threatened the seeds that he had spread in the furrows of his thinking.

In the mid-sixties one could only assume that Heidegger would never publicly take a stand on the questions, claims, insults, or attempts made to exonerate him—issues that were much too much talked about and that became confused through argument and counterargument. At the most, it was thought, it would be only after his death that we would learn what these things were really all about.

In the end, this assumption proved to be right. A few days after the death of the philosopher, the German weekly newsmagazine *Der Spiegel* published a detailed interview with Heidegger conducted by its editor Rudolf Augstein. As the editorial note indicated, this interview had been taped ten years earlier, on 23 September 1966, in Heidegger's home in Freiburg. Heidegger's only inviolable condition for granting the interview was that it should be published only after his death. The magazine respected this condition and saw to it that the existence of the interview did not become public knowledge, although the secret does not seem to have been kept completely. In any case, the publication of the interview on 31 May 1976 produced considerable excitement among those who had no inkling of its existence. The explosive power of the "bomb" was by no means diminished by the fact that the interview had been preserved for ten years in the files of the magazine, and *Der Spiegel* accomplished one of the greatest surprises in its history—a history that did not suffer from lack of sensations.

The account of what happened prior to the interview is complicated and hardly worth being given in detail. For those who knew Heidegger even a little, it was astonishing that, once he decided to take the step of communicating with the world about certain issues after his death, he should choose *Der Spiegel*. For the journalism that *Der Spiegel* practiced and represented in an exemplary fashion was something that he basically disliked. On the other hand, he knew only too well that *Der Spiegel* (which he used to read regularly) attracted the public's attention and reached a wider circle of people than any other newsmagazine. He was sure that here the philosopher's posthumous words to the public would reach, in addition to those who were genuinely concerned with these issues, those opposing and contradicting him, as well as the merely curious or indifferent.

I (who was taken into confidence relatively early and at first vehemently protested against such an interview) no longer remember everything that occurred during the preparations. There were complications, aggravations on both sides, new arrangements, and, finally, the terms of the procedure—the day of the interview and the already-mentioned condition. Heidegger asked me to be present, like a "second," because there would be two interviewers. I remember a visit I paid to the editorial office of *Der Spiegel* in Hamburg in order to be introduced to Georg Wolf (who was the other participant in the interview and who had philosophical training) and to discuss some questions. I met Rudolf Augstein only on the morning of the interview when I went to the Colombi Hotel in Freiburg to meet the gentlemen and bring them to Zähringen. That Augstein (whom I presumed at first to be an "inquiring executioner," wanting to go for the master's throat) won my full sympathy in no time was due to his cordial admission of a "Heiden-Angst" in having to confront the "famous thinker."

There were six of us: Augstein, Wolf, the photographer, a stenographer, a technician, and myself. Frau Heidegger received us at the entrance to the house and indicated that I should guide the small group to Heidegger's study above, where he awaited us at the door. I was a bit shocked when I looked at him and noticed how excessively tense he was. Pictures taken during these long morning hours—the interview began shortly after ten o'clock and ended around one—show clearly this heightened tension. The veins on Heidegger's temples and forehead were swollen, and his eyes bulged a bit in excitement—somewhat menacing signs that in the course of the interview became milder and eventually disappeared. The photographer, Frau Digne Meller-Marcovic, published most of the pictures she took in a beautiful volume that gives astonishing testimony to her ability to capture the nuances of expression, gesture, and important moments in speaking. That we completely forgot the presence of Frau Meller-Marcovic and did not in the slightest feel bothered by the camera is excellent proof for the human sense of measure in the merciless service of technology.

I do not want to retrace here the exciting course of the conversation between Augstein and Heidegger, which moved those of us who were listening; nor Augstein's way of increasing the tempo from question to question, from response to response, a tempo that hardly let up; nor the intensification and culmination of the interview. It is accessible as a document checked by both sides and, according to Heidegger's wishes, amended at some points. I would like only to say a few words here about my impression of the whole interview; this impression emerges neither from the text nor from the most expressive pictures, but it continues to have an effect on those still living who participated in the interview.

Because the interview began to address the issue right away, without any preliminaries, Heidegger's initial tension led me to fear an outbreak of anger by the seventy-six-year-old man at the moment when, after a long reticence and barely appeased annoyance, he was called upon to speak out for the first time in front of strangers. (Was he constantly aware that it was not only a few people in that room who were listening to him, but a worldwide audience?) However, he kept his composure completely. Only the rumbling tone of some of his sentences would convey—especially to those who knew Heidegger and were aware of what was still hidden behind these sentences—that here something broke through that

Bürgerschule Messkirch 1901/2. Martin Heidegger in the
second row, left

Pencil drawing of MH by Ernst Riess, 19.

MH at the five-hundredth anniversary of the founding of the
University of Freiburg

Clara Rilke

MH in Munich, 1953

MH receiving honorary citizenship from the city of
Messkirch. Left to right: Bernhard Welte, Elfride
Heidegger, MH, Jutta Heidegger

Erhart Kästner inducting MH into the Berlin Academy

MH with Elfride Heidegger and Bernhard Welte

Left to right: Heinrich Wiegand Petzet, MH, Elfride
Heidegger, and Fritz Heidegger

MH with Petzet at the Hebel conference

MH with Werner Heisenberg

MH with Ernst Beyeler in front of Kandinsky's
Improvisation No. 10

MH with Andrei Voznesensky

MH with Eduardo Chillida, 1969

MH with Jean Beaufret

MH in Le Thor, 1970

MH near the hut

MH with his brother

MH with his brother on Feldweg

MH with Jean Beaufret in front of Camus's house

The Messkirch town hall and market square fountain

Paul Klee, *Ein Tor*, 1939

Paul Cézanne, the gardener Vallier, 1906

MH looking at the St. Victoire mountain, September 1968

had been blocked for many years. All the while he avoided any digression into what was not essential or what would appear like a private feud. In a very few instances he retracted what he had said. As the political kinds of pettiness and personally colored reproaches disappeared from Augstein's discreetly formulated questions (Augstein, obviously, felt in the course of the interview that such things were inessential and that the moment demanded that he get to the point), the more Heidegger began to feel unconstrained in his responses and, without noticing it, to take charge of the interview. When the interview reached its climax with Heidegger's famous words, "Only a god can save us," an atmosphere was established between interviewer and interviewee that went beyond the moment and that could not suffer from the minor debate that ensued on the expressibility of modern art. When Augstein finally pronounced *Der Spiegel*'s famous standard concluding sentence, "Herr Professor, we thank you for this interview" (which Augstein would have forgotten had I not whispered it in his ear), everyone breathed easily. This was not just a flowery phrase. Finally, toasts were exchanged with a Markgräfler wine served in old rummers; and then the door opened to admit Frau Heidegger, who had been anxiously waiting for the past three hours.

She remained with the small group, which now—minus the stenographer and the technician—accepted Heidegger's invitation and set out for Todtnauberg in order to see the hut, the philosopher's other place of work that had become as important to him as the hermitage in his brother's place in Messkirch. This trip, which was favored with mild and sunny September weather, was also captured by the photographer's camera. (Later, without being burdened by her official mission, she returned to Todtnauberg to take a large number of especially successful pictures of life in and around the hut.) First Heidegger showed his study to his guests, who were obviously a bit shocked by its complete austerity. At that time not even the picture of the aged Schelling hung on the wall. No one had expected such an icy cell. However, they soon found themselves in an unusual atmosphere. We sat around the table near the window in the corner of the large room—a room that had heard quite a number of discussions at different "altitudes"—for a modest luncheon. One could see that Heidegger had rid himself of a heavy burden. His look told me that—me, who had known this burden for a long time. He was in such a good mood that he reached for the volume of Hebel's poems and read some of it to us—as though he had to do something good for his visitors in terms of the *genius loci* (genius of the place). The return trip to Freiburg began in a relaxed mood in the late afternoon.

The publication of the *Der Spiegel* interview after Heidegger's death had a clarifying effect without being able to silence entirely the accusations that had been brought for many years. Many did not take any notice of the interview. Since then, the philosopher's unspoken hope that hostility might be transformed into an objective opposition has hardly been fulfilled. *It is to be hoped that in the future things will change somewhat in this respect, particularly in regard to Heidegger's explanations of the entire complex issue of his chancellorship—explanations that were held back for a long time (till 1983) and to which I have already frequently referred* (cf. *T&G*, p. 21ff.).

Not everyone had the courage of Rudolf Krämer-Badoni, the writer, who decisively rejected Heidegger's conception of art but did not hesitate to acknowledge publicly Heidegger's philosophical posture and humane attitude. As a postscript to the book that rejected Heidegger's theses, he wrote (in 1980) that he did not want to be misunderstood as joining Heidegger's various opponents or perhaps enemies: "I personally declare that I consider Martin Heidegger to be the most significant contemporary philosopher. But in regard to Heidegger the citizen, I suggest that his almost immediate turning away from a brief political engagement should be taken for what it was: bravery in the face of a dictator."

5

The Encounters

In the years after the end of the Second World War, many important people sought a connection with Heidegger and met with him: philosophers, theologians, scholars from various disciplines, artists, and poets. The changes that took place from time to time in his relation to the public, his frequent participation in events outside of the university (which he mostly disliked), his membership in academies in Heidelberg and Berlin, his appearances as a lecturer (especially in Bremen and Munich), his occasional appearances in others cities in Germany and elsewhere (Paris and Athens), and, finally, the seminars he gave abroad (France)—all this contributed to his meeting many men and women from outside the old academic realm. Basically, most of these contacts meant little to him, and in the last decade and a half of his life he began gradually to avoid the mindless activity (*Betriebsamkeit*) that often stemmed from curiosity about him. On the other hand, these years also brought him into contact with people who became important and valuable to him, so that he in turn looked forward to associating with them. Thus his circle of friends widened, and this filled the gap caused by the loss of friends who had died or who had become estranged from him because of political or intellectual misunderstandings. Of course, he never entirely got over the loss of those old friends with whom he once traveled a stretch of the way. Broken loyalties, however they came about, hurt him more than anything else.

Not every meeting in those years really deserves to be called an "encounter," even if it involved a well-known name. After Heidegger's death, those who had real encounters often gave personal testimony to them: the physician Medard Boss and the broker Clemens von Podewils and his circle, not to mention those who were close to Heidegger for a long time, like Hans-Georg Gadamer or Walter Biemel. This is not the place to discuss them, although I was often an eye- and ear-witness to their meetings with Heidegger. Here I would like only to talk about what I experienced and what impressed itself upon my memory, that is, about those encounters with people whose association with Heidegger also became an event for me.

Egon Vietta

Heidegger's reappearance in the intellectual life of Europe in the early postwar years is connected by many threads to a man whose name is nowadays hardly mentioned, Egon Vietta. Born in Brühl in 1903, he was a lawyer of half-Italian descent, dark and lively. He attended Heidegger's lectures in the late twenties in Freiburg and was so decisively moved by Heidegger's thinking that he established personal contact with him. Having given up the legal profession after the war, he devoted himself entirely to the philosopher, whom he admired and energetically stood up for whenever he could. His little book *Die Seinsfrage* (The Question of Being), published in 1950, is still today an often-cited testimony to this relationship.

In this polemical pamphlet, whose wording and style betray the experienced lawyer, Vietta proceeds from the assumption that late European civilization is a civilization without philosophy and no longer knows where to look for the roots of its own emptiness. The dread of philosophy on the one hand and the exploitation of nature and humanity on the other are the bases for Vietta's large-scale critique of technology, a critique that he complements with a penetrating exposition of Heidegger's lectures in Bremen, "Einblick in das, was ist." These ideas had remained fresh in his memory (from 1949), and he was able to enhance them from his own written notes. The pamphlet contains something of the flavor of the discussion that occurred in the intimate circle of Bremen, so that it offers an especially vivid view of those days that were so important for Heidegger—especially in terms of nineteenth-century poetry (George, Ungaretti, Mallarmé, and Benn), which appears to Vietta as an unconscious "escape" from total scientism. The destruction of the idea of humanity as a center, the necessity of an essential, large-scale transformation, and the inescapable question of death constitute the other main points of this work, which—despite its truncated and occasionally fanciful features—offers a comprehensive introduction to Heidegger's problems.

When, twenty years earlier, Vietta was working toward publishing a presentation of the philosophizing of *Being and Time*, Heidegger had indicated that a genuine appropriation of what he (Heidegger) had said would mean that what he has said in his books "have only a single task, namely, to let the being that we ourselves are become a real distress and a real liberation. Only when books and sentences have disappeared by fulfilling their function, only then will understanding be attained." Heidegger is thus not to be confused with book-knowledge! And Vietta, as he pointed out in another place, was clearly aware that spreading a philosophy through propaganda empties that philosophy of any significance and reduces it to mere prattle, as happened to humanistic education. The passion with which Vietta supported the philosopher did not always protect Vietta from the semblance of propaganda on his part, causing opponents to blame him and friends to leave him.

Because Vietta was a writer, he had a fine sense for the poetic bearings of philosophy (Heidegger attended his moving play about the war called *Monte Cassino,* which was performed for the first time on 1 December 1949, in Essen, with Willi Baumeister's decor). He was also very familiar with Rilke.

The evening when we were all together in Bremen is unforgettable. After the discussion that followed the lecture "Einblick in das, was ist" in the Senate house—where we discussed the "fourfold," or mirroring of earth and sky, mortals and divinities—Vietta, who had been silent for a long time, entered the discussion by saying that he had something to contribute of which Heidegger was perhaps not yet aware. Then he read aloud from a newly published volume of Rilke's poems, the fragment that talks about "Ballspiel für Götter / Spiegelspiel" (Ballgame for the gods / mirror-play). Heidegger was visibly surprised, because here the poet had anticipated what the philosopher, guided by the matter of his thinking, might have believed as a neologism (*Neuschöpfung*). Vietta succeeded in unearthing many treasures along these lines. He wrote a number of aphorisms ("On Heidegger") which have not yet been published. In one of these he says that one cannot understand Heidegger using the usual method developed for understanding a philosopher, according to a Western formation of "logos." Using such a method means "falling back into the stance of a thinking that is traditional and rationally determined," that is, falling back on a thinking whose "mere play of intellectual wit" is under attack in Heidegger.

Because he realized that Heidegger's thinking was world-historical, Vietta brought it beyond Europe. Once when, on one of his numerous journeys, he arrived in the United States for a longer stay, he was received by an American university president who was interested in European philosophy. After a long wait, Vietta is finally led in to the president. The powerful man slaps Vietta on the shoulder with the usual joviality and, looking at his watch, says to his puzzled guest, "Now, Mr. Vietta, tell me all about Mr. Heidegger—in five minutes!" [1] The small circle in Stuttgart to whom Vietta related his American experiences burst out laughing.

Heidegger himself was somewhat amused by the story—but suddenly looked serious again and said that, after listening to an account of the fascinating world of America, he would like to pose a single question, the response to which was more important to him than all the praise of the technological perfection of life in America. The question was the following: "How do Americans comport themselves toward death?"

For a moment even the eloquent Vietta was speechless. But then he described the repulsive customs for dying and burial that are common in America (common, anyway, among those who are to some extent well-off)—rituals with corpses that are painted, embalmed, and arranged in desired positions, as Evelyn Waugh later described in his macabre novel *The Loved One*. Heidegger listened to all this in silence and then stood up from the table. Without discussing what had just been said, everyone knew that Vietta's report had revealed to Heidegger the American attitude toward death, which was to him at the same time a revelation of American life.

Egon and Dory Vietta visited me at my house in Icking during the Academy Conferences in Munich in the late winter of 1951. Dory Vietta, a highly intellectual and passionate woman, enthusiastically supported the revered philosopher—almost more vociferously than her husband—and would not allow anything said against him. That afternoon in February stretched out in a conversation in which we mutually assured one another about the matter that meant so much to each of us in his or her own way. Vietta wrote in my guest book, "In memory of the leisure of this afternoon, in which we confirmed one another in a dialogue that has taken us from the leisureless world around us and a bit deeper into the future." For himself he permitted little leisure. For a while he worked as a producer with Sellner in Darmstadt for the important Barlach performances. Later on he gave up this position and took to traveling. By bringing together Buddhism and Heidegger's thought, he wanted to bring to literary fruition his knowledge of and experiences in India and the Far East. But he did not make it. After his wife's death in 1959, he died suddenly in the same year, at age fifty-six, while preparing a modern exhibition in Baden-Baden.

One of Vietta's aphorisms reads, "If Heidegger's thinking were understood, then the technological age in which we live would come to an end." If Vietta had written only this sentence and communicated only this insight, then he—who in his inner restlessness always appeared to me to be unhappy—would deserve a grateful commemoration.

Erhart Kästner

It was a midsummer day in the late fifties at the main train station in Hanover. Everywhere there was the noisy excitement of vacationers, and mountains of luggage stood on the platform for trains heading abroad—where in a few minutes the southbound train from Hamburg would arrive. People pressed, yelled, and argued. Everyone was looking for the best place to board the train. In this chaotic back-and-forth, I almost collided with a traveler who stood quietly in the midst of the general commotion. But words of pardon froze on my lips, and I simply had to laugh as I suddenly found myself looking on the cheerful face of Erhart Kästner. Fair and free, bareheaded, his curly hair a little disheveled, he was standing right in front of me all by himself, accompanied only by his big blue linensack, which like a sheepdog seemed to watch that he did not board the wrong train. When I inquired where he was heading, he responded happily, "To Crete."

How old I felt next to this young-looking world-wanderer, who in truth was six years older than I! It seemed that he had put Wolfenbüttel—with its library, where for years he attended to the office that was held by both Leibniz and Lessing and to which he brought new glory—in a kind of deep vacation slumber and was hurrying nonstop to his beloved island. In those days, however, this island was not yet a destination praised in advertising brochures. Those who traveled to Crete still entered the realm of distant adventure, with all its severity and bliss, away from every "American way of life." [2] That afternoon I traveled with Erhart Kästner a very short way in the direction of Crete, but I had to get off the train in Göttingen. I felt sorry that I had to leave him because we were just having a good conversation about Heidegger.

This unexpected meeting on the platform, down to its smallest detail, now appears to me typical of Erhart Kästner. None of those who were waiting for the train, moving excitedly under the compulsion of their insignificant plans; none of those who had plunged from domestic concerns into vacation worries, planning out the standard course of their vacation weeks—none of them indeed possessed the freedom and unconcern of Kästner as he traveled to Crete. It was this inner freedom that gave him the lightness that surrounded him like an aura, a clarity and immediacy that animated his surroundings and challenged others. As is the case with such human beings, Kästner was completely unconventional, despite all his suppleness in good manners.

That evening I could not stop thinking about the man who had been my travel companion for a short time. It was either in Munich or in Bühlerhöhe that I had gotten to know him through Heidegger. Everything that touched me in this brief new encounter suggested features that Heidegger must have esteemed in Kästner: that human freedom which neither fears nor is limited by offices and institutions.

As an appointed official in Dresden and later in Wolfenbüttel, Kästner never deviated from loyalty to his innermost vocation, being, as Gundolf put it, "an observer of the affairs of the world." He knew that there was something in life besides big and small positions that degrade human beings in a society that has stagnated through bondage to the pursuit of affluence. Didn't he once write that one must pay attention wherever there is freshness at work, on earth or in people? He himself possessed this precious gift of freshness that is, as he put it, "borrowed from the morning of creation." And like a rivulet in a mountain, often bursting forth wildly, stopping at what is hard, then sweeping on and flowing again, reaching for things, as if the task were not only to bring gems effortlessly forth, but also to bring forth what is light, like a bird, as gentle to the touch as down feathers—that is how Kästner's language emerged. His style of writing is characterized by conciseness; Jean Paul's words apply: "Conciseness of language grants vastness to thinking."

With that, my reflections that evening returned to Heidegger. Erhart Kästner was one of the very few who, in his own way, responded to the thinker. He understood—or, better, heard deeply—what the thinker thought, appropriated it in his own way, and said it in a manner that was completely his own without altering its core. In his few speeches (for example, on the occasion of conferring the *Bremer Literaturpreis* on Celan or in his address to the Academy in Munich), Kästner talks seriously and emphatically about the "modern way of completely calculating the world"; where else could such ideas grow than in the ground prepared by Heidegger's thinking? It was this same ground that gave rise to Kästner's lament on the death of things, killed by modern sciences, and to much more, that he stated in his short speeches and in his *Beschreibungen und Bewunderungen* (Descriptions and Admirations).[3]

He considered himself indebted to Heidegger. For this reason he stood up for Heidegger and, when it came down to it, did not shy away from openly confessing his adherence to him. When Günter Grass was elected to the Academy in Berlin, Kästner resigned from it because he did not want to belong to the same institution as a man who had disparaged Heidegger (in the novel *Hundejahre* [Dog Years]). And Kästner knew exactly what he meant when he told Heidegger on the occasion of his seventieth birth, "We need you."

By "we" he meant the artists. The dialogue was about art, not least about modern (contemporary) art. They spoke of Bissier, with whom Heidegger had had friendly relations in his early Freiburg years and whom Kästner now visited in Hagnau. When I picked Kästner up one evening from the train station in Freiburg, he spoke with delight about Bissier's *Miniatures* and about his (now destroyed) *Garten am Bodensee* (Garden on the Bodensee), which is, as Kästner put it, "a single poem." They spoke of Mark Tobey—whom Heidegger once visited in Basel (after Kästner encouraged him to do so), looking to follow a little the traces of Klee in the high old house in the suburb of St. Alban. Heidegger went from room to room, all filled with pictures, engravings, large and small sketches. As amazed as he looked, he was quietly absorbed in what he was seeing; the venerable Tobey, who spoke as little German as his guest spoke English, followed Heidegger with examining and inquiring eyes.

Above all, Heidegger and Kästner spoke about the Greeks. Their common ground was the Greece of antiquity—which Kästner had experienced concretely—even though Heidegger could not always follow his friend's excursions in modern art. I was aware of this and at times did not speak about my new "treasures," like Altenbourg, whom Kästner and I loved in the same way. But Hellas! That was different. Heidegger esteemed Kästner's books highly and loved them as paraphrases of the great theme of Greece. Here the two men followed closely related paths. At one point they wanted to make—and even planned—a trip together to Greece. I discussed this trip with Kästner, down to the smallest detail, and was saddened when—for reasons I do not know—these plans did not materialize in the end. Was it because it was a bit daring, even bold in terms of everyday practicality—that is, did this trip quietly instill in Heidegger (who was at the time over seventy years old) the fear that he would not be able to manage it? For both Heidegger and Kästner, Greece remained a great love.

From this description, some may get the impression that Kästner was a "go-getter" who lived only for his own goals. But this impression would be wrong. In his relationship to Heidegger, he was very considerate, even tender, as befits a man of intellect and heart in such a friendship. There was a deep seriousness about life behind all this. The state of the world, which all of us so easily denied, concerned Kästner painfully. And it was exactly in this concern with the state of the world—which is different from politics—that he met Heidegger, a meeting needing few words:

"How everyone managed to live in the foreign land of modernity, with its absurd shadowy affairs and under a terror that is no longer awkward enough to be bloody."[4] Both Heidegger and Kästner took to their graves the answer to this question—a question that at some point will also be put to us.

Only those who were very close to Kästner knew that he suffered from a grave disease that would keep him from living to enjoy a long and leisurely retirement in his home in Staufen im Breisgau. At the beginning of his last book, which contains his notes and views on Byzantium, we read the strange exhortation not to become too old. His much too early death, shortly before his seventieth birthday, confirmed this exhortation.

But it would be inappropriate to conclude memories of Erhart Kästner on a sad note. Recalling his encounter with Heidegger, we hear a different note. What made being together with Kästner so unforgettable was a tone that evoked something of that powerful, bright voice that disperses all tribulation with the warm undertone of an affectionate humor. It was a rainy day in September 1959 when the chancellor and the dean from the University of Freiburg came to Zähringen to congratulate Heidegger on his seventieth birthday. On the same day, in the evening, the people of his home town of Messkirch were also to have their share in the pleasure of honoring Heidegger. In a heavy rain, with as much volume as the instruments could deliver, the *Feuerwehrkapelle* (fire-department orchestra), blared marches and native tunes in front of Heidegger's brother's house, until Heidegger himself came out in the intense thunderstorm and expressed his gratitude. But he was delighted above all by Kästner's presence. What a surprise this was for Heidegger! The evening at the Adler restaurant, turned into a happy party, during which Kästner found in Fritz Heidegger his master in repartee.

The next day, in a celebration in the city hall that was free of any false dignity, Kästner of all the speakers chose the best words when, in the name of the Academy of Berlin, he said, "In the Academy you are not only admired but also loved, as you are loved in Messkirch." Only Erhart Kästner in his freedom could articulate such words of friendship, with a reverence for Heidegger that he never relinquished.

Ludwig von Ficker

On the occasion of a lecture in Bühlerhöhe by Ludwig von Ficker, onetime editor of *Brenner* and mentor of Georg Trakl—a lecture in which he evoked the true character and poetry of the poet, who died in 1914—

a reviewer for a German newspaper wrote that Ludwig von Ficker had kindled a flame of love for his deceased friend. The audience in the lecture hall sensed that this was someone who had actually felt and experienced the suffering and the loneliness of the poet. That evening it was not so much a lecture as an oration, a human exhortation, from which Trakl emerged in a deeply touching way. It brought to light a unique relationship that bound the poet to his friend, protector, and benefactor—one who dedicated his entire life to this relationship. What Ludwig von Ficker—already an old and frail man—said then was not the detached observational contribution to the discipline of Germanic scholarship that the specialists who heard him repeat the lecture later in Freiburg might have expected it to be. It was a confession of truth. Who could forget how von Ficker's simple sentences revealed the last years, days, and hours of the poet's life, and how he, the friend, talked about their sad farewell? Who could forget how he read, with a trembling voice, as if it all was happening at that very moment, the account of the farm boy who was Trakl's loyal companion: the irrevocable burdened with the whole weight of an inhuman and inverted world. What Ludwig von Ficker presented quivered with the memory of what he had experienced; and he summed it up at the end by reciting the poem "Grodek," since his own words threatened to fail him. An experiencing of certain things that withdraw from a rational touch was manifest in what he said and how he read.

This encounter with Ludwig von Ficker must have meant a great deal to Heidegger, who since his early days had been familiar with Trakl's poetry. For here, in an unexpectedly lively manner, he came close to a poetry that was as important to him as that of Rilke. In the *Kuppelsaal* at Bühlerhöhe stood Heidegger and von Ficker, one over against the other, more moved than words can describe. I was then introduced and very amiably included in the personal relation just established. It is not to my credit that our relationship remained amiable. But it was tacitly confirmed when I approached von Ficker on the occasion of a talk he gave before the Student Association of the University of Freiburg, in order to excuse Heidegger's absence because of illness. How cordial and expressive even a brief encounter can be in terms of looks and words when they come from the heart, as was the case that evening in the Auditorium Maximum, shortly before von Ficker stood before the lectern! I did not belong to the group of Germanists[5] who later seized upon him.

The two encounters with Ludwig von Ficker, in Bühlerhöhe and in Freiburg, gave me the courage to ask him a question that on the surface appeared inessential but that touched upon deeper issues. In connection

with Heidegger's upcoming seventieth birthday, I had been invited to contribute to one of the Festschriften. The brief reflection that emerged at
that time basically remained a fragment because I had not thoroughly
thought it through. After Heidegger had read the piece, he said, "Apparently you do not know at all what you have touched upon here!" I had
wanted to show how one work of art is mirrored in another work of
art—a painting in a poem, for example; this was something that Goethe
once spoke about. As an example I had chosen a still life by Juan Gris
from the Museum of Fine Art in Basel and Trakl's "Rondell." This led to
my writing to von Ficker about the formation of that poem by Trakl. His
response, which came promptly, at first disappointed me a little. On the
other hand, it confirmed basically what I had already guessed. He simply
said, "Usually, in the evening, when I returned home and entered my
room, Trakl would be sitting near the window, looking out onto the landscape, still lost deeply in thought about the poem on which he had just
been working. After I turned the light on, he would rise; and, if he needed
to read to me what he had written down, it would be enough for him
simply to ask me whether I liked the poem. That was all." Thus the mood
and the time of day in which Trakl could have given him the short poem
"Rondell" came back to his friend's memory. He also felt that it was not
possible for the poet "with his taciturn nature" to have accompanied "the
delivery of the poem with some kind of explanation about its particular-
ity." The poem needed no explanation, since each stanza carried completely and purely in itself what it had to say.

When I read this letter, I thought immediately of Heidegger, who
more than once had expressed to me his consternation that some modern
poets found it necessary to "explain" their poems. The response from
Innsbruck[6] shed a small but significant light on Trakl's poetizing and
therefore deserves to be mentioned here.

On Ludwig von Ficker's eightieth birthday, Heidegger went to the
celebration organized by von Ficker's Austrian friends. In the morning,
when I took him to the train station and asked him to greet von Ficker
for me, I could see how much he was looking forward to that day. And
he was not disappointed. Animated by the spirit of the day and the place,
he ignored what he had prepared for the banquet and gave that beautiful
and spontaneous speech in which he used the image of towers, of Saint-
Exupéry's "beacons in the desert," as a way of congratulating the jubilar-
ian. When he returned from Innsbruck, he wrote me to say that the celebration had been very nice, not too extensive, but a unified whole: "Herr
von Ficker was revived. We visited some of the places where Trakl had

stayed or wandered about. The trip in the old Austrian cars was sometimes a bit difficult." Heidegger took quite seriously the places that he
visited in connection with the memory of a poet or a thinker. He was
aware of the power of such places. He could, quite unexpectedly, ask
questions that showed what connections such occasions had for him and
how their significance moved him. On a trip to the Valois, Beaufret told
me that at one point on the return trip from Normandy to Paris Heidegger had suddenly asked, "Are we here in Nerval's country, in Sylvie?" The
road at that point had just reached the Valois, and there was still enough
time to turn toward Abbaye de Châalis—which reminds one so impressively of Gérard de Nerval, the first French translator of Goethe's *Faust*
and the author of the exquisite story "Sylvie."

Later I could confirm Heidegger's impressions of Tirol, after I myself
had visited the high-lying village cemetery in Mühlau where Trakl is buried. That quiet place looks a little like the Messkirch cemetery—which
looks out on the Swabian-Alemannian countryside—where Heidegger
himself is buried.

Clara Rilke

Rilke's significance for Heidegger became known after the philosopher
gave a speech to a closed circle of friends on the twentieth anniversary of
Rilke's death, "Dichter in dürftiger Zeit" (Poets in Needy Times).[7] In
those days my own work was guided strongly by Rilke's star. Thus it is
understandable that Rilke is frequently mentioned in our correspondence
of the years 1947–48, in which Heidegger put the poet into the larger
historical context. As he noted, it is important to relive the basic experiences of Nietzsche and Rilke and to take seriously their views of the contemporary epoch. Although even Rilke had to touch upon and pass
through experiences of a technologically controlled psychology (already
turned into psychoanalysis), in the final version of his poetry he still experiences and articulates something else. In another letter Heidegger
spoke of Rilke's relationship to Rodin: "Everybody says that Rilke
learned how to work from Rodin. But no one notices that this pertains
principally to speaking and writing about poetry."

Because of my preliminary work on a book about Rilke and Paula
Becker-Modersohn—whose profound relationship had not yet been entirely illuminated—I wanted more and more to seek reliable information
where it could be found, by turning to the only survivor of a past that
was decades distant from me—to Frau Clara Rilke. As a child I had met

the sculptor once, at my parents' house in Bremen, when she came for a visit. With the help of some photographs, she was making preparations for a bust of my grandfather, Heinrich Wiegand. This work was to be added to a series of medallions of meritorious citizens of Bremen in the big hall of Börse. At that time Clara Rilke wanted not only to talk to Wiegand's daughter, but also to see the grandson.

I returned to this "encounter with a child" many decades later when, early in 1948, I inquired in Fischerhude whether Frau Rilke would receive me for a conversation about her friend Paula Becker-Modersohn. One day in March, we had a long, happy, and fruitful visit, which led first to correspondence and later to further visits and a continuing discussion that culminated in the first edition of Rilke's *Briefe über Cézanne* (Letters on Cézanne), published by Insel. In addition, we continued to exchange ideas about Paula Becker-Modersohn.

I immediately wrote Heidegger a detailed letter and described Frau Rilke's rustic old residence in Bredenau, in whose garden the wide and quiet Wümme flows, flooding all the farm fields in early spring, and I also told him about the many little treasures that Frau Rilke showed me: a well-thumbed Reclam edition of *Niels Lyhne,* in which Paula had drawn small spring blossoms and which she gave to her friend right at the beginning of their common period in Worpswede, and the small silver icon that Rilke had brought back from Russia. Heidegger was delighted with this letter and suggested that it made Clara Rilke's residence quite vivid, adding, "The early encounter of Paula Becker-Modersohn with Jacobsen and later with Cézanne is amazing" (20 March 1948).

I gladly conveyed Heidegger's greeting to Frau Rilke. It was obvious, however, that Heidegger wanted to get to know her himself and to discuss further the topics I had touched upon, not the least of which concerned Cézanne. But he was not primarily interested in Frau Rilke the artist, with whose work he was not yet familiar. Rather, he wanted to meet the wife of the poet, which she remained whether she was near or far. The days of December 1949 in Bremen, taken up with lectures and discussions about "Einblick in das, was ist," in fact left him no time to pay a visit to Fischerhude. It was only on a short excursion to Worpswede that he seemed suddenly to think of Rilke and of "the two sisters, the blond and the dark one," as Rilke used to call Paula and Clara when he first met them. During the visit he paid in "Schluh"[8] to Vogeler's daughters and to Hans-Hermann Rief, executor of Vogeler's estate, much was said about Clara Rilke and her life since leaving Worpswede a long time ago.

It was Heidegger's next visit to Bremen, on the occasion of his "Logos" lecture in the early spring of 1951, that brought the realization of the desired and carefully orchestrated visit with Frau Rilke. I was a little worried as we began the drive to Fischerhude on a beautiful morning in May. Would everything go as planned? Would the two entirely different human beings manage to get along with each other? Each of them had his or her own specific characteristics: northern and southern Germans would be facing each other. But I thought that, since Heidegger liked the Bremenians, he would also like the businessman's daughter Clara Westhoff, who had in her so much that was Bremenian—although life had carried her around a great deal and did not treat her gently. She used to alienate some people at first by her "masculine" appearance, by the awkwardness of her elongated gestures—motions that had their parallel in the long and powerful strokes of her handwriting, which even in a brief communication took up a whole page. Such peculiarities, coupled with a powerful, tough appearance and large, strong facial characteristics, concealed from those who did not know her the treasure of an inexhaustible and simple goodness that always prompted her to presuppose the very best in her fellow human beings. Her exquisite brown eyes occasionally betrayed a slight melancholy that was usually concealed behind her capacity for joy, a trait that made dealing with Clara Rilke often such a cheerful affair. But how would she meet the philosopher from Todtnauberg, who in those days was called an existentialist? I tried to allay my concerns with the thought that, beyond remembering Rilke, their humor would perhaps bring them close to each other.

In the meantime we pulled up in front of the house in Bredenau. The car returned to Bremen, and I pulled the old-fashioned doorbell. The door opened and Frau Rilke, dressed in white, stood under the lintel made of a beam—as she is seen in the pictures that show her together with her friend Paula. She held in her hand the inevitable handkerchief, which she was said never to let go of. At first there was a moment of confusion, which betrayed that each of them had imagined the other one differently. We went to the small library with the coffee table, near the studio, where the guests would be able to warm up after the cool morning drive. Heidegger noticed the old edition of Kierkegaard's works on the shelf, and the conversation turned immediately to the years in Paris. Frau Rilke said that, in their first period in Paris, she and Rainer Maria read together the works of the Danish writer; and she mentioned a poem of her husband's that belonged to those days—a poem that she had recently shown to a lady but now could not find. Heidegger took one of the small volumes, opened it—and the sheet of paper with the handwritten poem fell out! There was surprise, amazement, and happiness: "Professor, you brought me luck." Frau Rilke's initial reserve was gone, and I had the feeling that I was now superfluous as a mediator. The hostess and the guest understood each other so well and found so much common ground that it was as if they had known each other for a long time.

We moved to the large studio. At first Frau Rilke, who had begun painting again after the war, wanted to call attention to her paintings— which Heidegger indeed liked. But he also had come to see the works of a lady who used to be a student of Rodin—works about which I had already talked to him a bit. Thus Frau Rilke showed him some of her best works. These were sculptures that bore witness to Frau Rilke's great talent in creating form, as well as to her handicraft and emotional empathy as an artist. They included a bust of Paula Becker-Modersohn (passionate but controlled), Rilke's and Heinrich Vogeler's images in bronze (Vogeler's impressed Heidegger extraordinarily), and the noble head of Alfred Schuler—works that all radiated spiritual greatness. The small model of a boy in action, just finished and captured in clay, stood on the disk. Frau Clara subjected it to a couple of quick and sure strokes, which Heidegger followed with admiration.

The conversations in the studio and a walk through the garden down to the river made the morning pass quickly, and noon soon arrived. We considered going to Fischerhude and eating in the restaurant so we could return in the afternoon. However, Heidegger accepted with pleasure Frau Rilke's spontaneous offer to have a very simple lunch in the kitchen. He was pleased to have a meal in the style of the countryside and in surroundings that made him visibly happy. Thus we sat around the well-scrubbed wooden table and had pancakes and canned fruit. Later Frau Rilke called me aside and told me how nice it was to have a guest with whom she could talk about everything, about people and things that the younger generation knew hardly anything about: "Heidegger knows all the people in Paris that we knew; he knows about the old days." Now she needed to question Heidegger and to talk to him about so many things that teatime would hardly suffice. Not knowing how well she would get along with Heidegger, she had invited a fellow painter to tea, so that she would have someone to talk with; but now he would probably disturb the whole thing. She wondered what she should do, since she could not rescind the invitation now. So she asked me to engage this painter in all kinds of discussions on art, so that he would have little opportunity for talking with Heidegger; she wanted to do plenty of that herself!

With a small conspiratorial smile, I was sent upstairs to her living room, where a comfortable couch was set up for Heidegger to take his usual afternoon nap. She withdrew for a while to her bedroom. But before the time was up, she knocked at the door upstairs, where I was watching over Heidegger's siesta; and in a few minutes she was conversing with him not only about mutual acquaintances, but also about Rodin, Maillol, and Paula's art. As they were talking, Frau Rilke was moving back and forth in her emotional manner; and while putting the tea table in order, she knocked over the sugar bowl. Unfazed by this small incident, she put on the pot filled with rainwater, which, as her friends knew, made the tea so tasteful.

By the time her fellow painter arrived, the little party was in full swing. Joining us as the fourth person of the group, he must have been a little astonished at how lively and familiar the words exchanged between the philosopher and the sculptor were. Remembering my own assignment, I tried to carry on a profound conversation about abstract art—which in those days was just emerging—and listened with one ear to the other two. Soon I had to give this up and finally provide the fellow—who had been cheated out of his own interests—with the opportunity to put his questions to Heidegger. But, if I remember correctly, he succeeded in doing this only occasionally, because the main actors both continued to navigate in their common waters. Finally, much too early, the doorbell rang; Dory Vietta had arrived to take us back to Bremen in her car.

It was already dusk. Heidegger would have gladly stayed longer. But the discussion on the previous day's lecture had to take place in Bremen and, despite Frau Rilke's reticent requests, could not be canceled. She accompanied us to the garden gate. One more time the elderly lady bent deeply in order to see into the car and cordially bid farewell to her departing guest. Heidegger looked back as long as she could still be seen, then he turned to me and said, "Petzet, *this* woman I could also have married!"

Three years later she died. When Heidegger held his lecture "Wissenschaft und Besinnung" (Science and Reflection) in the golden hall of Bremen's Schütting a few weeks after her death, he began with the following words: "Today I speak in memory of Clara Rilke. . . ."

Hertha Koenig

One of Picasso's world-famous paintings is *Saltimbanques*, or *Family of Rope Dancers*, painted in Paris in 1905. This painting is one of the significant examples of the brotherhood of fine arts with poetry. For Picasso's painting is reflected in Rilke's Fifth Duino Elegy, which for this reason is often called the *Saltimbanques* elegy. This much one who is interested in artistic or literary matters can find in books. But today we have a little trouble with the dedication accompanying this elegy (an elegy that originated suddenly, "in a radiating rush"); it reads, "To Frau Hertha Koenig." It seems that no one knows who she was. Was she one of those numerous "female friends" of Rilke whom one likes to ridicule? Or was there something special about this woman to whom Rilke dedicated a crucial piece of his poetry?

As numerous pictures still testify, she was one of the most beautiful women of her time. Born in 1884 in Westphalia into a family with ancestors from Russia (her grandfather was one of the intimate confidants of the last czar), she lived in Paris and Moscow as a young girl. After a short marriage to the classical philologist Roman Woerner, she withdrew to her ancestral property in Westphalia with its old Wasserschloss Böckel. The inhabitants of the neighboring villages, whom she accepted in the old patriarchal style but with an alert social consciousness, never guessed that the lady proprietor wrote sonnets that Rilke once found to be better than his own. Her poetic work is almost as forgotten as she herself, although there are a few things among her poems (not only her "flower sonnets") and in her prose work that are still worth reading today (for example, a novel about her Swabian great-grandfather Nikolaus Lenau). She had a rapport with many important intellectual figures of her time and was a welcome guest in Gerhart Hauptmann's circle. She admired the poet Otto von Taube and frequented the house of Princess Cantacuzène (Elsa Bruckmann) in Munich, where Hertha Koenig owned an apartment on the Isar quay of Widenmayerstrasse. It was there that after 1914 she got to know Rainer Maria Rilke.

Poetic handicraft played a special role in this relationship, which soon turned into a delicate and reliable friendship. Rilke's high opinion of her poetry strengthened the profound human understanding that united them for many years. Hertha Koenig's active role in Rilke's oppressed life, and her concern for the poet himself and for his work—even beyond his death—have never become public knowledge. This would have been contrary to the noble and highly discreet character of this woman.

But how did it come about that Rilke dedicated the "Fifth Duino Elegy" to her? From early on, Hertha Koenig had not only loved the old

paintings and carved woodwork in her ancestral castle, but had also developed a liking for the art of her own time. With an infallible taste and
sensitivity, she collected various works of art—paintings by Hodler and
Vogeler (who sketched illustrations for her volume of poetry) as well as
by Nolde and Klee. What appeared from the outside to be without coherence attained its unity in that the various works all embodied the spirit of
their owner. On the spur of the moment, the young woman bought three
paintings by Picasso in an art gallery in Munich because they impressed
her in human terms. There were paintings from his blue and pink periods,
and among these was *Saltimbanques.* The latter hung above her desk in a
large room in her Munich apartment. During one of her long absences,
she put this apartment at Rilke's disposal when the poet was helpless and
homeless during the First World War. That is how in 1915 the poet came
to find himself sitting at work under Picasso's painting; and in those days
he added to his signature the expression "guard of Picasso's paintings."

Two years later, in a more difficult period of Rilke's life, Hertha
Koenig invited him to her estate in Westphalia. There he spent the late
summer months and the autumn of 1917 in an old room high in one of
the castle's towers (made livable for the guest with a few pieces of furniture), in her company as well as that of her friend Augusta Hartmann.
With its austere and simple aspect, this "Rilke tower," as the villagers
called it, reminded one a little of the tower in Muzot.[9] Here, too, Rilke
was and remained a stranger, one of "these acrobats, even a little more
fleeting than we ourselves." [10] When he wrote these words in Muzot four
years later, he remembered his sentry duty for Picasso's *Saltimbanques*
and placed the name of his poet friend Hertha Koenig above the elegy,
thus forever bringing together the painting, the name, and the poem.

When I told Heidegger at one point that while Rilke was staying in
Böckel, he used to pass by a baroque statue of Orpheus when walking
down to the garden every morning, Heidegger finally decided to pay a
visit to Frau Koenig and thus to Rilke's castle in Böckel. Because I not
only had described to him my impressions from Böckel, but had also
talked to Frau Koenig about Heidegger during various visits to her estate,
it was not difficult to obtain an invitation. The occasion was the philosopher's last visit to Bremen, for the *Schaffermahlzeit,*[11] in 1962. After
breakfast on the fourth day of this visit, we were all together with an old
student of Heidegger's from the Freiburg period—in order to say good-
bye. Then the big automobile that Frau Koenig had sent for us from
Böckel arrived. In a few hours we reached our destination, driven safely

by Herr Gustav. We drove to the land of the poetess Droste-Hülshoff—to meet another poetess.

After the hectic days in Bremen, we were surrounded with peace and quiet in the Böckel house (Frau Koenig never spoke of a "castle"). Outside, the February day was radiant and shone through the huge windows, making the drawing room with its dark decor appear friendlier. Without delay we sat down at the table. As we took our places the hostess said, "Today we have the *Bundespräsident*'s[12] soup, but without dumplings," thus hinting at Theodor Heuss's visit the week before. The president had wanted to meet the former inhabitant of the Hammerschmidt Villa, which he now occupied as his official residence. Hertha Koenig, whose father owned the villa, had spent part of her youth there. She talked about the visit while that soup was being served. Attentively examining the unfamiliar surroundings of the small room with its old, darkened pictures of the Italian countryside, Heidegger was more silent than the hostess would have expected. I was familiar with this silence, which did not indicate impoliteness. But Frau Koenig worried that it indicated a failure to establish contact with Heidegger. In her little book *Die Mutter Rilkes* (Rilke's Mother), she noted, "Uneasy luncheons are not my strong point."

At this point she rang the bell to have the main course served. Then a hidden door opened, and a ghostly apparition entered exactly like the one Frau Koenig describes in her above-mentioned book. In that scene, during luncheon in a hotel in Munich, "everyone turned toward a mysterious event. A black figure, wearing an overcoat, a hat, and a long veil, walked with difficulty but with head held high through the rows. Her hands were trembling, and her glittering eyes were looking for something. . . . If instead of noon it had been midnight, then one would have supposed that this figure brought back a time long past—a figure that was the only living and acting being among the shadows who were silently taking their meal."

We, too, were sitting mutely. What kind of ghost comes through a hidden door? Our bewilderment ended only when our hostess broke into a cordial laughter. Her well-staged joke was successful. It was Maria, her confidante and loyal aide from the countryside for more than half a century, who had performed the macabre scene. Realizing that both guests had recognized her, she curtsied with a courtierlike grace and vanished through the secret door. This was and was not Maria! She had appeared wearing the hat and overcoat of Rilke's deceased mother—things that Phia Rilke had bequeathed to her because she had devoted herself wholly to the old lady after the death of the latter's beloved René—a death she never quite overcame. The sequined shawl and veil that hung from the rather pert little black hat, the long dress that covered her figure in a fashion long past—all these things seemed, as Maria moved in them, to have been made for her. As the old lady, she had evoked an entire epoch. Here in Hertha Koenig's presence a spell was broken again, just as ten years earlier at Fischerhude with Clara Rilke. And what followed was by no means an "uneasy luncheon."

After a midday rest, Frau Koenig showed us her works of art. As we went from room to room looking at things and asking questions about them—Rilke's former room especially interested Heidegger—it became dark outside, earlier than would have been normal. A dark rain front approached from the west, strong winds came up, and it quickly turned into a storm, causing the planned walk through the garden to be put off until the next day. Heidegger took me aside. I noticed how much he liked his hostess as he asked me, "Do you think I should recite something after tea?" Before I could respond, Frau Koenig approached us and said, turning to Heidegger, "Professor, would you please recite something after tea? I shall meet you then in the library." She probably had in mind a text by Heidegger himself. However, she wholeheartedly approved when Heidegger proposed reading something from Adalbert Stifter and asked permission to look for the volume. As we sat down to tea, Heidegger took his place under the bust of Alfred Schuler by Clara Rilke; and he opened *Die bunten Steine*. Frau Koenig asked permission to invite Maria to listen. She said that Maria was no longer illiterate and participated in everything intellectual. Thus Maria, the Bavarian farm girl, joined us as an attentive listener. While the storm outside rattled the high windowpanes, Heidegger began to read Stifter's story "Kalkstein" to us.

The choice of this story remained unforgettable for one particular reason. The next day it was reported that the gale and high water in Hamburg and the coastal areas had caused a serious flood disaster; Stifter's story culminates in the poor priest's concern for the schoolchildren, who are frequently threatened by flooding and must often cross an overflowing stream after bad weather. A strange coincidence! After these events, Stifter's words attained another, graver significance. To the happier side of the evening belongs the question that Heidegger quietly put to me before dinner, namely, whether Maria was Catholic. When I answered affirmatively, he was relieved that he had chosen the proper version of "Kalkstein," in which the clergyman is Catholic—since there is a version in which the clergyman is Protestant and married. This second version would have bothered Maria and made her unhappy. This was a good choice, and Böckel turned out to be wonderful! The next day we went to the garden, where the storm had wreaked much havoc. Heidegger was shown Rilke's favorite pathways and the places where he liked to sit. When the wind subsided and again allowed the innocent sunshine of early spring to come through, Frau Koenig proposed a drive through the countryside. In a small village near the Wiehen Mountains, we passed many farmsteads with proverbs written in powerful strokes on their entrances. My friend Martin Nagel came from there; Heidegger knew him well. He frequently conversed with Nagel (while Nagel was working in Freiburg's surgical clinic) and saw clearly that this young physician was concerned not only with "good handicraft," but also with what makes up a conscientious physician—with what Saint-Exupéry called "to be permitted to help the living." In his parents' rustic home we found an improvised lunch; and on the way back Heidegger remarked with pleasure, "Now I know where Nagel comes from." To know this about a human being whom he esteemed was not an indifferent matter to him, especially when such an origin pointed to a realm that he himself knew well—as it did in Nagel's or Beaufret's case.

The afternoon and evening in Böckel were devoted to a conversation that started with Schuler—whom Hertha Koenig knew well in the last years of his life and who died in her arms—and then turned to the poets who had crossed her path in the almost eighty years of her life. She told us of evenings in the Bruckmann house and mentioned historical figures such as Ludendorff (whom Rilke did not like) and Hitler, whom Elsa Bruckmann patronized and whom Frau Koenig once met while with the admirable ladies from Munich. Finally, conversation turned again to the poets—Schuler, Max Picard, and Rilke—whose letters were preserved by the tall old secretary in the window recess of the library. We spoke a great deal about Regina Ullmann and the verses she wrote on Picasso's *Saltimbanques.*

Heidegger inquired about *Saltimbanques,* and Frau Koenig mentioned that before the First World War she once visited Picasso in his studio in Paris. She wanted to thank him for all the pleasure she had received from the three paintings of his that she owned (besides *Saltimbanques,* she owned *Näherin* and *Tod des Pierrot*). But the monosyllabic Picasso did not react at all to her expression of gratitude. Moreover, she did not understand the paintings she saw in his studio; and, somewhat disappointed, she left. She could not really explain the reason for Picasso's denying, so to speak, his own work. I suggested that perhaps in those years Picasso had been so occupied by completely different problems—like his adventure with cubism—that, as Frau Koenig herself saw, he had lost his relationship with the products of his most recent blue and pink periods and presumably did not want to be reminded of them. Frau Koenig accepted this view, and I had the sense that she had lost her ill feeling about the painter's rejection of her and regained her old admiration for his genius. Segments in the unending conversation were Picasso, Paris, Rilke, and his wife, who had been a friend of Frau Koenig. Later we listened to old music, to records of Pergolesi and other forgotten Italians. It must have been almost midnight when we went to bed.

The next day Herr Gustav drove Heidegger (who was unwilling to bid farewell) to Bielefeld, where he wanted to visit a relative before returning to Freiburg. I decided to stay in order to keep the elderly lady company and to talk to her about the fullness of the past days. The big table where the three of us had dined (and in front of which "Mother Rilke" had made her appearance), as well as the library with its commemoration of Stifter, hardly seemed empty. I had a feeling similar to the one that permeates the end of Mörike's Mozart story. In the evening Hertha Koenig dedicated one of her most beautiful poems to me in Heidegger's memory. (Later on she received from him, as a token of his gratitude, his own handwritten poems, bound in a blue leather cover—a volume that disappeared from her possession, like so many other things.) That poem is called "Genius Loci":

Here the dead walk around.
Here words remained fixed
To a heavy weight,
Words still valid.
Out of the paintings on the wall
A smile slides mutely
And changes with the light.
Those who once procured a hearing
Have said everything.—
to the pewter in the cupboard
Only the evening light reaches out.
Never before was it held
More tenderly, by any hand.
Outside a bird
Asks imploringly. Asks once again,
Does not quiet down,

Who knows what it is looking for?
From the fissures of the tower
An owl escapes quietly,
With wings wide open toward the woods.
Heavy mist draws
Over the meadows. The woods turn pale.
Who knows what is happening?
Already the pond trembles.

Andrei Voznesensky

For a long time a picture of Dostoyevsky sat on Heidegger's desk as an homage to the literary genius of Russia. He was familiar with Russian literature. Tolstoy's "The Death of Ivan Ilich" is mentioned at a crucial juncture of *Being and Time*. He liked Goncharov's *Oblomov* and spoke with pleasure of its cheerful aspects, even as one sensed how seriously Heidegger took the anxiety about the world that was concealed in this fictional character.

The possibility of Heidegger's having a living contact with the real Russia had to be something special. As he was approaching eighty, he experienced such an event, which turned out for him to be a gratefully acknowledged confirmation.

Andrei Voznesensky, who along with his friend Yevtushenko was the most famous and, in Germany, the most widely read lyricist of the younger generation, came to the Federal Republic in 1967. This poet, who was educated as an architect in Moscow, had visited the United States for awhile seven years earlier. He had experienced the American way of life, critically evaluated it, and later traveled to Italy and France. Being a member of the Bavarian Academy of Fine Arts, he was invited to Munich to recite some of his poems. Clemens and Sophie von Podewils subsequently invited him to their estate in Haarsee, where in the course of conversation he ascertained that Heidegger was also a member of the Academy. To meet Heidegger was his only wish, if the short time of his stay in Germany would allow it.

But it was hard to know what to do. It was necessary to speak with the philosopher immediately and to make the arrangements, if he would agree at all. But how? Up to that point the Heideggers had had no telephone, because they wanted to avoid the inevitable disturbances associated with it. But Count Podewils found a solution. He called me in Freiburg to see whether I knew where Heidegger was and whether I could communicate the poet's wish to him, adding that there was a great hurry. Although I knew that Rötebuck 47 had acquired a telephone connection a short time ago, I did not mention this, since Heidegger's telephone number was to be kept strictly a secret. As a consequence of the phone call I made to Heidegger, however, the secret was revealed. For, pleased about the announced visit—which he never could have anticipated—Heidegger contacted Haarsee.

Early the next morning, Podewils, Voznesensky, and Kaempfe, his interpreter, arrived by car in Zähringen. As the photographs of the meeting in Heidegger's study show, there was a harmonious accord between the two men from the beginning. Although the language barrier could not be removed (they tried to communicate through French and English), their conversation soon went beyond the topic of translation and "became anchored in deeper ground," as Count Podewils later wrote. Everything he saw in this room—the sketch of Hölderlin that showed him lost in thought, the small photograph of Heidegger's mother on the desk, the serious-looking walls of books all around, and especially the countenance, the gaze, and the friendly posture of the aging thinker—all these told the young poet enough, certainly more than he could commit to the vehicle of words transmitted by a foreign boatman.

The university's Department of German Literature and the Division of Russian Language quickly improvised and arranged for Voznesensky to give a lecture that evening—an arrangement that could have used more advertising. Nevertheless, the news that one of the most famous contemporary lyricists of the Soviet Union would be reading his own poems traveled with lightning speed; and in the evening one of the largest halls of the university was filled to capacity. Voznesensky—who appeared to be a little shy, though unconstrained—talked about his public readings in his native Russia (while Kaempfe skillfully translated what he said). These readings were attended by thousands of people, who would listen spellbound to the words. But how would the small group in Freiburg compare with performances bigger than any soccer game? Such performances repeatedly proved the interest that the whole nation took in its poets and what they produced. Voznesensky, however, must have noticed the audience's attention and readiness, which seemed to encourage him more and more. Even those who did not grasp the language—and most did not—were soon fascinated, especially in the poems he read, by the now melodic and musical, now keenly evocative way of reciting, as well as by the élan and gentleness manifest in the poet's presentation:

I—a Kaluga lad,
Clearly didn't blunder
In a prickly jersey clad,
With a crackling diploma.[13]

These verses concerned not only the Russians, but all of us:

Who are we—pokerchips or giants?
Genius in the bloodstream of the planets.
No "physicists," no "lyricists" exist—
Just pygmies or poets![14]

The openness with which the poet from Moscow confessed perhaps astonished some people:

An artist firstborn—
Is always a tribune.
In him the spirit of overturning,
And rebellion—eternally.[15]

As Pushkin put it, "Here was a pathos for freedom that could hardly be surpassed." This was a poet without metaphysical embellishing, but with a strong humanness:

There is no secret in my vocation.
My destiny convinces me entirely
I am going to be more than music:
Warmth and bread for people.

Much too quickly, the reading came to an end. After that we sat together in the bar of the hotel where Voznesensky was staying. Now Heidegger was the host and the one who expressed gratitude. In the midst of a large group of admirers (mostly young people), who had noticed with astonishment that he had been sitting in the first row, Heidegger took the other center of the ellipse—alongside the hero of the evening—in whose festive space they again and again caught sight of and toasted each other. I rarely saw Heidegger so happy and lively. When I took him to his taxi at the end of the evening, he struck me as being very happy. Earlier, in saying good-bye to Voznesensky, Heidegger had proposed that on the following day I should show the poet around the old section of Freiburg. Accordingly, we made an appointment.

When I picked Voznesensky up the next day, he looked a little fatigued after the exertions of the previous day. But he soon woke up, especially since two beautiful female students who were learning Russian accompanied us. Voznesensky looked at the shop windows in the streets of the old city and was fascinated by a gun shop's display. He purchased a pistol. Then we moved on to another realm altogether, looking at the cathedral and the splendor of its colorful windows. When we returned to the wide square, with its colorful stands of eggs, sausages, bunches of mimosa, and Swabian straw shoes, all bathed in the brightness of the late-winter light, Voznesensky suddenly stopped and said that now he had one special desire: He would like to see the Schwabentor. I was certainly surprised that he knew about the edifice. However, since we had enough time and the old gate of the city was quite close, I took him there. "Look, that's the Schwabentor,"[16] I said. But Voznesensky shook his head and said that that wasn't it. I emphasized that this *was* the Schwabentor—there was no other. But the poet said no, that can't be it, because one would see St. George and the dragon on the Schwabentor. Now I knew what he wanted: the fresco of the saint, the protector of old Russia, that is painted larger than life on the other side of the gate. I showed it to him, and Voznesensky glowed with happiness. When I pressed him to tell me how he knew about this painting, he said, "Akhmatova composed a poem about it. She was once in Freiburg." Thus he stood on the spot where the great Russian poetess was reminded of her country and expressed this in verse.

An hour later Voznesensky returned to Russia. But I met him one more time, and that deserves to be mentioned. It was in Frankfurt in 1975, on the occasion of the celebration of Rilke's one hundredth birthday. He sat at one end of a phalanx of fourteen poets, adjacent to the stage. He drew attention to himself by the focused and relaxed posture that he kept throughout the two-hour presentation, although he could hardly understand a word. Finally Voznesensky, the last one to go to the podium, read a poem of Rilke's in Russian, with such controlled pathos that it brought the applause and ovation of the thousand people present—almost as in Moscow. As we were leaving, I looked for him at the exit. He recognized me immediately, asking how Heidegger was doing and whether I had found Akhmatova's poem. A few days later, when I communicated his greetings to the eighty-six-year-old Heidegger in Freiburg, we spoke about the poet who wrote

Courageous in a certain way
everyone strives toward his own truth:
The warm through the crack,
humans on the course of a parable.

Heidegger and Voznesensky: This was an encounter that was one of those actions Hans Bender hoped for in his "Letter to Russia," in which "a very complicated coexistence" between two nations came to pass.

The Clergyman from St. Alban: Paul Hassler

In the Basel suburb of St. Alban, opposite the house that Jacob Burckhardt used to rent and where the view stretches beyond the old trees to the Rhine River—there, behind a high garden wall away from the street, is the vicarage of St. Alban's Church. That house has a long history, going back to the Middle Ages and the period of the huge earthquake in Basel. With its original foundation and renovations around 1500, the house has remained almost unchanged up to our own time—if we ignore the insignificant alterations that changing times impose on a building always serving the same purpose. The conservative attitude of the people of Basel may have contributed to that, at least until a few years ago. Here, in the small, modest rooms of this house—with its paneling dark from age, its timbered ceilings, and its simple stairway of heavy oak—Calvin lived after his flight from Paris and, as a twenty-six-year-old theologian, wrote his *Religionis Christianae Institutio* in 1536. There was both protection and great scope in this quiet chamber, with its corner window that looks beyond the river to the faraway mountains of the Black Forest. The colorful birds and flowers of the large garden took part in the growth of and concentration on great thoughts. After visiting the vicarage, Hans Jantzen, that unforgettable interpreter of Gothic cathedrals, said that if he were to come back to the world again, he would like only to be the pastor of St. Alban's and to live there.

However, the thinking of the vicar about whom we now speak had hardly any similarity to the thinking of Calvin. This vicar's thinking was far removed from any fanatical narrowness, and he disliked everything priestlike and life-negating. While he attended to his office here—he came as a preacher to St. Alban's Church from the community of Graubünder of Zizer in the diocese of Basel—one could feel the genuine "freedom of a Christian" enveloping him and his work. Art and music found a home in him. Paul Hassler came from a family in which music was, so to speak, hereditary. Among his great-grandfathers he counted Hans Leo Hassler, the grand master of German music around 1600, whom Kaiser Rudolf II knighted and gave the title of "von Rosenegg." But however well this title fit Paul Hassler—he loved flowers and attended to his roses by the old, decaying walls—he no longer used it.

Paul Hassler took seriously the question put to Christianity by modern times. He occupied himself with Bultmann and Barth and was a friend of Barth's successor, Heinrich Ott. He also realized an ecumenical way of thinking. That this man was himself a questioning human being was perhaps the real reason that his first encounter with Heidegger developed quickly into a genuine friendship. The immediate occasion had nothing to do with his religious profession but, strange as it may sound, with modern art. Among his closest friends were Ernst and Hildy Beyeler, who were known well beyond Basel as the owners of an art gallery that today enjoys international fame. After moving to Basel, Hassler, himself a fine and sensitive connoisseur of art, gradually became an "amateur art expert." Because of his continuous association with the Beyelers' gallery in the Bäumleingasse and the object lessons he received there, he entered this field as an occasional interpreter. Soon the vicarage turned into a treasury of modern art. This treasury was made up of borrowings from the Beyelers' gallery that produced that often-fruitful tension between past and present—a tension that arises not when the arbitrariness of fashion obtrudes, but when the high claim of quality is preserved.

The large Klee collection from Pittsburgh (which Beyeler later sold in Düsseldorf) initially hung for months in the old aristocrat's house at the edge of the rectory's property and was accessible there to the friends of the Beyeler gallery. It was natural to bring Heidegger to the neighboring clergyman's home so that the old gentleman could rest there after he had looked at the collection. But this interlude in one of the rooms on the upper floor—which presumably was Calvin's bedroom and later was called the "Heidegger room," because the philosopher frequently spent the night there—turned into a prolonged coffee break; and conversation went on much longer, until Heidegger finally was driven back to Freiburg. This conversation was often continued, but it did not at all center only on art.

For Heidegger found in Paul Hassler a dialogue partner with whom he could discuss philosophical and theological matters equally seriously. We can read in and between the lines of their letters so many things that indicate the content of these thoughtful discussions. Bultmann's theology is often in the background. If Heidegger had been present at a meeting of the "Old Marburgers," he would report on it. Occasionally Heidegger would ask Pastor Hassler for something especially important—for example, Hassler's theses for an upcoming dialogue in the vicarage, because the dialogue needed careful preparation. Heidegger saw clearly the important tasks that Heinrich Ott faced in his university profession as successor to Karl Barth; and Heidegger wished for Ott that the friends from Basel would keep him good company. All the letters Heidegger sent to the vicarage or to Riehen, where the Beyelers lived, include greetings to Ott.

Once Heidegger had a long and serious dialogue with Heinrich Ott and Paul Hassler in the study overlooking the Rhine. It took so long that it was almost dark before the friendly battle could be brought to an end. Hildy Beyeler finally opened the door and said, "Do you have to keep on babbling? The dumplings are about to burn." Nevertheless, they tasted good because the hostess knew how to take superb care of her guests. But she liked best of all to listen to the conversation herself, participating inwardly in the dispute of the minds.

Heidegger also frequently visited the Beyelers in Riehen and, among paintings by Kandinsky and Klee, read aloud to his friends from Basel. Professor Ott recalls that Heidegger once played there the tape of the speech he gave on Hebel's anniversary—the speech at the end of which Heidegger quotes Hebel's poem ending with "un s'git noch sache ehnedra." [17] While explaining this, Heidegger commented, "Indeed, this is the ontological difference put in Todtnaubergish!" [18] Another time, when thanking Hildy Beyeler for a visit, Heidegger sent her a postcard from Messkirch and wrote, "This postcard shows a view of the upper Danube valley, near Messkirch, through which Hölderlin wandered. In his hymn *Der Ister* (Istros: The Greek name for the Danube), he presented this landscape in lasting words. When I come to visit you again, I shall read you the hymn, along with the commentary." And this did happen.

An unforgettable event was a drive in Paul Hassler's car to Messkirch to hear Heidegger's speech as part of the celebration of the seven hundredth anniversary of the city. Late in the evening, after the speech and festivities were over, we were strolling through the old narrow streets of Messkirch; and we thought we saw in the display window of the bookstore, brightly lit in the moon light, a picture of "the one and only brother," [19] whom we had been with earlier. But as we looked closer, the picture turned out to be that of Abraham a Sancta Clara. We had to laugh, because Abraham a Sancta Clara was also one of Heidegger's relations—from the distant past. The next day Heidegger was especially intent on showing us the exhibition of the works of the master from Messkirch that had been put together by Altgraf Salm in the city hall. This was a justifiably admired presentation of the great painter, of whom today there is only one single painting in St. Martin's Church in Messkirch and whose other works are scattered in museums throughout the world—in Donaueschingen, Basel, the Louvre, and America.

Better than any attempt at describing the relationship of the aging Heidegger to Paul Hassler is to consider their correspondence, which shows how close the two men became in the few years that they knew each other. When Hassler became seriously ill in the early spring of 1967, Heidegger wrote to him, "I often remember the conversation we had one evening about the present situation of the world. This conversation was a gathered meditation that took place in your quiet and hospitable vicarage above the Rhine. In the meantime illness has overtaken you. It is part of your vocation to bring consolation in such situations. When you yourself are in need of consolation, this is sometimes more difficult, sometimes easier. A friendly word however, always brings a little help. That is what these lines would like to offer you, along with the wish that recovery may proceed well and thoroughly and may take away from you everything that is oppressive. . . . When I had jaundice five years ago, I found out how illness can unexpectedly affect people like us. That's why during your recovery I wish you the power of a concentrated mind, to which everything—even the most ordinary things and relations—can appear like new if the proper insight is granted. Above all I wish that, in this period of recovery undisguised nature addresses you and that through it you are claimed by what never ceases to claim human beings. In one of Hölderlin's poems, composed a year before his death, we read, 'Das Glänzen der Natur ist höheres Erscheinen' (Nature's shining is a higher appearing). In view of these words, the talk about Hölderlin's madness becomes puzzling."

When on 8 December 1969 Heidegger thanked Paul Hassler for the latter's congratulations on Heidegger's eightieth birthday, he wrote, "Your friendly greetings on my eightieth birthday were devoted theologically and philosophically to the ontological difference, which has troubled my thinking for decades. Thus your greetings aimed at the very heart of my thinking and released a corresponding happiness. For that, I thank you wholeheartedly. On this occasion, I would also like to thank you and Herr and Frau Beyeler for the friendly disposition all of you showed toward me—both from near (the city in which you so effectively work) and from far (our beloved Greece). For the years of my old age, I had expected undisturbed peace for an earnest meditation. But so far it has been different, since there have been increasing claims on me from the outside. I do not say this to complain, but mention it as the reason that I

was hindered from continuing to have meetings with my friends in
Basel. . . .
"What is essential remains, however: the lasting remembrance and
gratitude."
Three months later, on 9 March 1970, Paul Hassler died.

Jean Beaufret

On his last visit to Freiburg, Jean Beaufret wrote his traditional words in
the guest book, "Toujours de passage," but added " . . . mais fidèlement
de retour" (Always to go away . . . but faithfully to come back). These
words vouched for the abiding quality of his friendship. However, the
promise of his return remained a hope—for his "being on the way" soon
led him to a land from which no one returns. That makes it even more
important to record whatever I can remember about the appearance and
character of this excellent man—not least of all with reference to Martin
Heidegger. Beaufret must certainly be regarded as the most loyal and
most understanding friend that Heidegger had in his later years. If ever
anyone crossed Heidegger's path who was his equal, it was Jean Beaufret.

It was with pleasure that Heidegger told of their first meeting, which
sounded like a cheerful fable from a gloomy time. In the autumn of 1947,
a French occupation army jeep appeared in Todtnauberg, and an officer
decorated with a medal of the Resistance got out. The person approaching Heidegger was the forty-year-old Beaufret, who, a year and a half
after the end of the war, determinedly overcame great difficulties and
crossed numerous borders to get to Todtnauberg. And this in order to
reach a goal he had long sought—to make the personal acquaintance of
the philosopher with whom he had corresponded since 1946.

In addition to a few desirable things that he brought along to still
hunger, Beaufret brought above all openness and unpretentiousness of
spirit. They immediately took a liking to each other which, supported by
mutual respect and growing commitment, soon turned into an affectionate friendship that remained unchanged until Heidegger's death. What
was important to this friendship was only one thing, to which both had
committed their lives: the matter for thinking.

Their meeting, however, did not happen by accident. As early as
April 1945, in newly liberated Paris, Beaufret held a lecture course at the
École normale supérieure with the topic "À propos de l'existentialisme—
Martin Heidegger" (On Existentialism—Martin Heidegger). Called to
various lycées in France, active for a while in Alexandria, Egypt, and hav-

ing written a book on Fichte's philosophy of right (after a longer stay in Berlin in 1931), the young lecturer had long ago proven himself a brilliant philosophical mind. He was captured in the war but escaped from the German guards. He joined the Resistance in Maquis, and as a bold fighter he barely escaped the claws of the Gestapo. After the liberation of Paris, he soon became active as a teacher and was intensively involved with the intellectual foundations of existentialism, which was growing at that time. It was his greatest wish then to communicate and converse with a man who was considered all over Europe to be the leader of this intellectual movement. What was fashionable was not what mattered to him. For this reason, he obtained permission to go to Todtnauberg, though he had to struggle against a number of military and civil obstacles. Following that memorable first meeting in December 1947, the outcome of this dialogue appeared in Bern in the form of a letter to Beaufret: the significant philosophical treatise that under the title *Letter on Humanism* is, besides *Being and Time,* perhaps Heidegger's most famous work.

In correspondence as well as in conversation, the communicability of this energetic and rich mind was highly engaging and a sheer pleasure to everyone who associated with him—whether on human, artistic, or literary problems. Whenever he philosophized, he willingly switched to German, because he was of the opinion that things can be expressed better and more precisely in German than in French. In matters of elucidation and interpretation, he was an unsurpassable master. One evening in Freiburg, over a bottle of wine, Martin Nagel asked Beaufret to indicate the essentials of Heidegger's philsopohy. At first I was alarmed, remembering the American fellow who wanted to be informed about Heidegger in five minutes. But Beaufret did not avoid the question; in a little less than half an hour, he offered such a wonderful insight into the basic issues of Heidegger's philosophy that we, his fascinated and amazed audience, felt we knew clearly for the first time what this philosophy was all about.

Conversations with Beaufret! When one was with him, something soon took shape that was characteristic of neither mere entertainment nor rigorous discussion. An atmosphere emerged that enveloped both the speaker and the listener, cheering and animating them. Conversation with him was always spiced with that cheerfulness that radiated from Beaufret's whole being and surrounded him like a bright aura. This was certainly far removed from the buffoonery often called humor in Germany. Those who knew him will never forget his smile, which prompted Marcel Jouhandeau to say, "Son sourire, c'est tout lui" (His smiling, that is all he). But he was also a dreamer who could forget the reality of his immediate surroundings, even lecturing before an audience of hundreds. And had not the university janitor turned off the lights to remind him unkindly of the time limit that he had already surpassed, Beaufret's enthusiasm for the topic of Heidegger would easily have carried him beyond midnight—which was in any case the time for him to become fully awake and experience the pleasure of thinking. This sometimes led to small difficulties when he came to Zähringen from Paris with his younger associates François Vezin and François Fédier (this happened at least once a year into the seventies). Then Heidegger's house would be transformed into a kind of Platonic Academy where dialogues never ceased; and at times it became difficult to put an end to the ardent discussions so that Heidegger could get his night's rest. Often I had to intervene and take the three Frenchmen to my apartment or to the Zur Traube tavern, where the discussion would then be energetically continued. In this way, those friends in Freiburg who did not participate in the rigorous philosophical discussions in the inner circle of Zähringen experienced some of the best and most penetrating dialogues, whose center was always Beaufret.

I especially remember Beaufret's participation in the seminar session in Bremen in 1960. He already knew many people from that circle; and at the end he became our spokesman for the presentation of the gift to the host, which he accompanied with an exquisite address in French. A picture of him and Heidegger taken at that time beautifully shows their unique relationship. In his dealings with Heidegger, Beaufret—for all his profound admiration of the master—always kept a delicate distance and showed an affection that did not overlook small weaknesses. And when the rest of those sitting around were virtually out of their element with the old gentleman, reacting to him with reservation or awkwardness, Beaufret would freely express himself, without ever overstepping his self-imposed limit. His three-volume work entitled *Dialogue avec Heidegger* is a beautiful testimony to his inexhaustible and intensive lifelong support for the revered master.

The connection with Beaufret was not broken after Heidegger's death in 1976, but was deepened every time Beaufret came to Germany. He used to travel to Zähringen on anniversaries in order to pay a visit to Frau Heidegger, after which he would go to Messkirch to visit Heidegger's grave and to see Heidegger's brother, with whom he always felt an intimate bond. He went there for the last time in 1980, for the funeral of Heidegger's brother. In Paris, he was in turn an unforgettable friend and host. He awaited us at the Gare du Nord and saw us off there, as if it were Heidegger himself who was being honored. We had unforgettable days and evenings in Paris; we had cheerful and serious conversations amid the bookshelves of the study; and we had long drives out into the country, among the castles and gardens where Paula Becker-Modersohn once lived. And finally we went to the abbey of Châalis, in whose ruins the roses smelled so exuberantly sweet.

At the beginning of May 1982, Beaufret once again came to Freiburg in order to give a lecture entitled "On the Way with Heidegger"—in Heidegger's old lecture hall, before a new generation that thronged around him and thanked him with applause. The next day he visited me together with a couple of old friends, energetically participating in everything. This was the same old Beaufret. It seemed as if he had overcome the disease that had attacked him. That is what we all too readily believed. Three months later, however, he died a difficult death in Paris. One of his friends wrote, "At the end he no longer laughed." He was buried in his rural homeland, the highland of Creuse.

But in remembering Jean Beaufret, something else must also be said that gives special weight to his relation with Heidegger and to what he did for him. For Heidegger, Beaufret was not only what one casually calls a sympathetic dialogue partner; he was also one who understood Heidegger deeply and, in a brotherly fashion, thought along with him. He understood why Heidegger wanted to go to Provence. The many trips that Heidegger made to France in his old age did not represent an attitude that could be mistaken for "cultural tourism." Except for his first trip to France to participate in the philosophical discussions at Cérisy-la-Salle, all of Heidegger's trips had one goal: to see Cézanne's country. It is to Beaufret's lasting credit that he gave Heidegger access to that country. There among people who were openly sympathetic to him, both in thinking and in human terms, Heidegger found that simple and rich life that must have sometimes reminded him of Socratic gatherings. The *boule* games in the village square under the shadows of sycamore trees were part of these gatherings, as were the walks with the poet René Char, who lived close by. These were days in which everyone had his own dignity and happiness. These were especially days of "companionable meditation," of the "proper hours of dialogue . . . trimmed hard to the wind of the matter of thinking," as Heidegger had put it years earlier in *Aus der Erfahrung des Denkens*. An almost Hölderlin-like radiance shines from the minutes of the seminars at Le Thor, which were quite different from a university seminar.

There was, however, more to these days—days that were without a schedule, without pretension, and yet claimed by the highest claims.

Beaufret gets perhaps the most credit for opening Heidegger's view to the St. Victoire Mountains. In his old age, Heidegger frequently said that Cézanne's path was his own path—a statement whose full significance has not yet been grasped; he thanked Beaufret wholeheartedly for having been led to this path. We shall see later what this means. But a commemoration of his friend from France would have been incomplete without explicitly pointing to this contribution here. Jean Beaufret's name will always be associated with Martin Heidegger's in the light of Cézanne's, in the presence of the "holy mountain."

6
Heidegger's Association with Art

Art and Artists

Heidegger considered it an honor and a duty to belong to the philosoph-ical-historical group of the Heidelberg Academy. He went to their meet-ings in Heidelberg when at all possible. It is less comprehensible at first glance why the Bavarian Academy of Fine Arts (founded after the war) named Heidegger a member. Are we not accustomed in our tradition to lining philosophy up with the sciences?[1] How does a philosopher fit in with artists? In dealing with this question, Carl Friedrich von Weizsäcker, in his memorial address for Heidegger and Heisenberg in Munich, comes to the conclusion that neither was a member because of any artistic tal-ents he might have had. Rather, they were members of the Academy—and rightfully so—because of "the essential conjoining of the beautiful and the true"; it was a question of the common origin of knowledge and art—a relation that has been thematic in philosophy ever since Plato. Perhaps one should add that Heidegger's association with artists has a particular justification, because he was the one who freed philosophy and thinking from the grip of the sciences.

What was his attitude, not only to the artists and their works, but to art itself? How did this attitude appear to one who grew up and was educated within very firmly traditional conceptions? From early on, my own experience of art was characterized by a concept of art that revered something like a perfect ornamentation of life in its works. In everyday life, with the stresses of work and career, the work of art—whether it belonged to the domain of the perfectly "beautiful" or the merely "pleas-ing"—was a *super-additum,* as it were, something added to the everyday, a thing of more profound character, which brought joy and edification and without which life would certainly have been more impoverished. But if need be, it could have been absent—although one would not have willingly given up this "abundance" of beauty once one had participated in it.

Over against this, what Heidegger said about art appeared to be almost scandalous. What one usually learned and took for granted without thinking received a push from Heidegger such that it collapsed as soon as one tried seriously to follow the path of his thinking and to appropriate his insights into one's own thinking. The three lectures under the title "Vom Ursprung des Kunstwerks"—given in the Free German Seminary in Frankfurt a few years after the Bremen lecture "Vom Wesen der Wahrheit"—were not allowed to be published at that time. The thoughts in them were only sporadically disseminated in transcripts. They deviated too much from the official ideology of art that Goebbels and Rosenberg had proclaimed as National Socialist dogma. Only in 1950 were these lectures made public, in *Holzwege*.[2]

Among Heidegger's attempts at thinking that are revealed in *Holzwege*, not the least important was the requirement found in "The Origin of the Work of Art" (and which Heidegger had already intimated in Bremen in 1930): that it is not a question of revision, but rather of a complete break. Conventional aesthetics did not work anymore. This failure began with the dethroning of the conventional ideas of matter and form in the work of art—ideas that were taken for granted, without thinking, and which were presented as a serviceable "tool" that properly occupied a middle position between thing and work. The work through which Heidegger illustrated his thoughts was a painting by van Gogh entitled *Peasant Shoes*, whose various versions each show the same thing in a compelling way. The philosopher says that here a being comes to stand in the light of its being and that art's way of being unfolds as "the establishing-itself-in-the-work of the truth of beings." He says further, "The work of art in its way opens up the being of beings." "The appearing jointed in the work is the beautiful." "Beauty is one manner in which truth unfolds essentially as non-concealment." Then art is "a becoming and happening of truth."

As von Weizsäcker said in his memorial address, all of these statements are enigmas at first—enigmas that still today can arouse many people to indignant protest, people who are imprisoned in the traditional representation of traditional aesthetics that is no longer thought through—but these protests do not refute or invalidate the thought of Heidegger. Most of the time people were too quick to call such a thinking "mythical." I cannot elaborate here to what extent this misses the point; Heidegger's statements are given here merely to indicate the direction of his thinking on the question of art and to provoke the reader to think deliberately by thinking with him. In so doing, one should not leave unheeded a statement by Hegel, one that is extremely revolutionary for an unprepared reader. It appears in his lectures on aesthetics: "For us art is no longer the highest way in which truth provides existence in itself. . . . One can easily hope that art will climb ever higher and reach completion, but its form has ceased to be spirit's highest need."

In encounters and conversations with Heidegger, art played a significant, even decisive, role from the beginning—first as he viewed (many times) the paintings of Paula Becker-Modersohn in Bremen and Worpswede, later as he looked at van Gogh's works during a visit to Holland. Meanwhile, Cézanne's significance for Heidegger was already increasing; he had come to know Cézanne through a series of important originals in the Beyeler gallery in Basel, in the Swiss museums, and in France. There Picasso and Braque were added. But Cézanne remained the star toward which Heidegger's way was moving—the chief witness for a new transformation of art, which was being prepared through this master. It was Paul Klee in whom Heidegger finally saw this transformation really accomplished: the Klee collection of David Thompson of Pittsburgh (exhibited in Basel in 1959) conveyed this insight by Heidegger. One should also not forget the decisive impressions from the realm of sculpture, which his close relationship with the Erker gallery in St. Gallen and its director Franz Larese gave him: besides Zadkine and Heiliger, there was contact above all with the art of Eduardo Chillida. The versatile Larese, in his work as publisher of the Erker Press, cultivated exciting contacts with modern poets—a fact whose importance for Heidegger should not be underestimated. It suffices to say that Franz Larese belonged to the intimate group of those who were invited to Le Thor.

In the following pages I attempt to show some of Heidegger's steps— a presentation drawn from the memory of our "art trips" together, from notes on our conversations, and from letters. Perhaps thereby it will become clearer why, in the course of time, the worlds of Cézanne and of Klee took the place of the world of van Gogh (which has become an extremely well worn example in the Heidegger literature, because of *Peasant Shoes*).

Since the poetic character of every work of art should never disappear from the observer's field of vision, let me here remind the reader of what Heidegger—in his interpretation of Mörike's poem "On a Lamp"—called the manner of root-unfolding of the work of art: "The work of art in its true character is itself the epiphany of the world, which is lit up by the work of art and preserved in it."

"The Great Painter": Paula Becker-Modersohn

The focus of Heidegger's first visit to Worpswede in 1930 was *not* the "Worpswedeans," those five painters who had once made the moorland village famous and on whom the art market of their followers still thrives, a hundred years after their discovery. It was to commemorate the painter Paula Becker-Modersohn. Heidegger wanted to visit her grave and to get to know her paintings.

Up to that point Heidegger had known her work only from some prints; he had never before seen an original of hers. That is why it was so much more moving for him now to be shown a whole series of paintings—in Philine Vogeler's gallery and in the Worpswede Art Exhibition, where the Roselius Collection used to show some of the works of hers that it possessed. They were mostly paintings from her early years as an artist—pictures from the rural surroundings of Worpswede, pictures of old women ravaged by heavy work, pictures of people in the poorhouse, on whose faces lay the dull weight of a used-up life. Then there were the pictures of children, which—here as well as later, in the Böttcherstrasse in Bremen—delighted Heidegger the most, maybe even enthralled him: the little girl on the farmer's stool with straw plaiting, the little girl on the red-checkered pillow, or the blind little brother. Later he wrote me about the first of these: "The little one is the *reticent amazement of shyness* itself—an excellent example for the work of art as truth's taking shape in the image." In Worpswede he acquired a color reproduction of *Elsbeth* (Paula's stepdaughter), which Paula had painted in 1903. The pensiveness and the total childlike character of the little girl in the polka-dot dress, with a crown on her head, standing next to a foxglove plant every bit as tall as she—Heidegger liked very much this child's delight, with the symbolism of a youthful bursting into bloom.

For Heidegger, yet another name was intimately related to Worpswede and inseparably linked to the painters: Rilke. Although the poet lived in Worpswede for only a short time, he was received there not just by a "gracious stranger," but by "the first homeland in which I saw human beings living"—not to mention that the second part of the *Book of Hours*[3] was written in Worpswede. After his departure this experience stayed with Rilke—and thereby also the continuing bond with a few of these people: Clara Westhoff (who later became his wife), Paula Becker-Modersohn, and Heinrich Vogeler. It was particularly the poet's association with the two friends Clara and Paula that occupied Heidegger's thoughts: what endures of such encounters, what is granted and what denied. He liked it when I would show him pictures of this time. I once sent him a photograph of the Rilkes as a young couple; he thanked me cordially "for the letter with the fascinating picture! Now I must always remember that the *Letters on Cézanne* are suspended between these two people and that their friend Paula is also in this suspension."

It was not until after the war, during a visit to the Roselius Collection in the Böttcherstrasse, that Heidegger saw the portrait of Rilke that Paula Becker-Modersohn had painted in Paris in 1906. We had already spoken about this painting, and now Heidegger gave it the greatest attention. It is not saying too much to say that it shocked him. For he immediately sensed the true significance of this work—a significance that lies far from the qualities that art historians ponder, a significance that prohibits one from discussing it (as has so often happened) merely as an unfinished, even "ugly" portrait. Oskar Kokoschka had a similar response ten years later. He also was supposed to have painted a portrait of Rilke at one time. On the basis of Paula Becker-Modersohn's portraits (of Rilke and of Lee Hoetger, as well as a self-portrait), he confessed in Bremen that in his judgment she was the greatest female painter of all times. Heidegger agreed totally with the opinion that in her portrait of Rilke the poet shows himself in a way that could not have been seen by his contemporaries—because it was revealed only in the poems of his later period. The view of the painter, full of presentiment, knew in advance the poet who at that time was in no way mature enough to do so. And in her painting she placed the poet before himself in a way that must have affected him almost like a violent demand. He spoke of this often, admiring the power of this great woman—a power that went way beyond her own time.

As might be expected, in this connection the "Requiem for a Friend" came up in conversation. When I asked Heidegger whether he considered the poem to be a genuine poem of Rilke, he answered that he could make such a judgment only with qualifications, but that in any case "Requiem" was more than merely a stage on the poet's way. Contrary to many critics, who take Rilke's stanzas as exaggerated lamentation in majestic words and consider them awkward, Heidegger took the poem very seriously. For Heidegger saw the tragedy that overshadowed the painter's last year alive: that fatal tension—even split—between a total devotion to her existence as a woman and the call to an art with which she had already set out to enter the circle of the great artists of her age. She wanted both of these, each in its fullness, but only one of them could be fully achieved.

In front of the portrait of Rilke, about which the painter herself wrote to a friend that it was not yet completely finished, the question of "completion" came up. Heidegger's response was that regardless of how the experts dealt with the question or critically analyzed it, their answer had to do with the technical aspect only—the "producing" of the painting—and had nothing to do with the essential statement. In one of his last conversations with me, Heidegger broached the question once again, this time taking it up in general terms. It was on 8 February 1976, the one hundredth birthday of Paula Becker-Modersohn; Heidegger called me in the evening, to say that we should remember the day together and "each drink a glass of wine in honor of the great, *great* paintress." It seemed to me that he wanted to hark back again to the time, almost fifty years earlier, when we had stood for the first time in front of her paintings and then at her grave in the cemetery in Worpswede. At the age of thirty-one, after a "rapidly mounting work" (Rilke), she had to leave behind the whole future of her art, undone "Completion?" asked the trusted but now somewhat tired voice on the telephone. Heidegger himself was in the middle of his ninth decade. "Completion?" Maybe in the end the uncompleted is more effective than the completed? Completion: finished, settled . . . Completed and effective certainly do not mean the same. After all, "incomplete means staying open—for a further way—to where? We should take that up together sometime."

That conversation was never to take place. It remained incomplete. Heidegger died in May of the same year.

Heinrich Vogeler

Of all the painters in the Worpswede group at the end of the nineteenth century, Heinrich Vogeler, along with his whole character as an artist, was the most alien to Heidegger's sensibility. Thus he knew hardly anything of Vogeler's until he heard that I was planning a larger publication on this artist. Vogeler had been known to me since my childhood in Bremen through his *Jugendstil* works; his etchings were the first pictures imprinted on my mind as I grew up. My desire to give full due for once to this artist—who had enchanted his own youth with his *Fairy Tale of the Frog King* and *Dream of Love,* but who had come to such a tragic end—had become for me an inner necessity over the years. Even so, it was clear to me that, in contrast to Paula Becker-Modersohn, Vogeler was not a "great" artist.

Heidegger knew that, too. Therefore only seldom did we speak of this artist's work, though he brought to it his full appreciation. He saw some of Vogeler's best paintings in Worpswede and in Böckel Castle; and from time to time he received detailed reports on the painter's last years, his most difficult. So it was more than simply a polite gesture when I invited him to the festive presentation that the publisher had arranged for the finished book, an evening in the *Kunsthalle* (art gallery) in Bremen— even though I knew Heidegger would not come. At the same time I sent him a prepublication copy just off the press. Thus it was even more surprising that a letter came on the evening before my departure for Bremen—one of the most detailed letters that I ever got from him.

I want to present the letter here in unabridged form. For it is an example of the span of his vision, the precision of his view, the depth of his empathy, and the undeterrable artistic taste of his judgment. It is at the same time a fine example of the human gift of real friendship. The letter of 17 May 1972 reads:

Dear Herr Petzet,

I would like to say a few things prior to the preview of your book, the biography of Heinrich Vogeler, in order thereby to be present in a certain way at the celebration—which will be something like a homecoming for you.

The way in which your book unfolds—right down to the style of language of each section—shows an amazing correspondence to the particular character of each historical period of the individual epochs in the artist's life. I would surmise that this remarkable correspondence emerges not so much from a premeditated and explicit method as simply from the fact that you were able to let yourself be claimed and led by the character of the matter to be presented.

This brings into the style a peculiar transformation and development, beginning with the time of wild financial speculation in Germany [after 1871] and continuing all the way up to the turbulent years before the First World War, to the Russian revolution, and finally to Hitler's invasion of Russia.

To connect this more clearly to the biography of the artist, it means that the more alone fate forced him to be, the simpler your presentation becomes—right up to the final gathering of your whole text into three pages of "recollection," which you clearly distinguish from mere remembering.

Whoever notices and ponders this—in view of Clara Westhoff's bust of Vogeler—will be shocked by the vicarious fate of this artist. The title *From Worpswede to Moscow* is historically correct. But considered in terms of the essential unfolding of events, it is not true enough: It does not reveal the hidden destiny

(*Geschick*)[4] of the artist, that is, the poet.[5] He does not find the proper place for his art; nor is his art able to determine this new place, either for it or for the one that is to come after.

What takes place behind your presentation is not accessible to art history or to biographical interest.

This artist and the attempt he made with his work follow the essential destiny (*Geschick*) in which great art is no longer the necessary form for the presentation of the absolute—as Hegel saw it—and is therefore without a place. Its refuge today is the babbling turmoil in the dilapidated shack called "society." In a superficial sense, this artist is driven to communism by "love for humans." But in truth it is terror, hidden even from himself, in the face of the end of art that was to found a world, in the era in which metaphysics is dissolved in a universal technology. Heinrich Vogeler's love for humans wanders around worldlessly in an age of a will to power that breaks out to extremes.[6]

One could ask, Why was this artist not overturned by van Gogh and Cézanne? Why was he dislodged from the path of art? Or was there neither path nor way?

I wish for your book only one thing: that it provoke reflective thinking in a time that talks a lot about "models for thinking" and "pause for thinking," but that really only calculates.

Heartiest thanks and greetings, and from my wife as well.

Yours,
Martin Heidegger

Van Gogh and Cézanne

With the question why Vogeler was not fundamentally overturned by van Gogh and Cézanne, Heidegger was pointing to two basic thrusts in art—brought together and exemplified in these two painters—that had come to the fore at the end of the last century and that for a long time determined our epoch. We once had a conversation about this—how in the work of van Gogh, on the one hand, the power of "expression" had exploded all traditional notions regarding form as well as color; and how, on the other hand, that "saying from out of the matter itself," to which Rilke calls attention in Cézanne, leads to the loss of every justification with regard to the question of "beautiful" or "ugly," because in the work of art "being *as* being" appears. Both stances, which can be called stances concerning the world, received their literary expression in 1907, independently of each other, in letters by poets: in letters on color, in the cycle

Letters of One Who Has Returned by Hofmannsthal; and in *Letter on Cézanne* by Rilke.

We learned of Heidegger's being decisively moved by a van Gogh painting through "The Origin of the Work of Art"—the three lectures he gave at the Free German Seminary in Frankfurt in 1936. There he referred to van Gogh's *Peasant Shoes* (painted more than once) as an example to illustrate the tool-character of the tool, in order to ask in connection with it about the thing-character of the thing and finally the work-character of the work. It was a painting from the realm of simple life, like so many of the paintings—often dark and heavy like the earth— from van Gogh's early period. Twenty years later, when we traveled to Holland with friends from Bremen and could show Heidegger the new Kröller-Müller Museum in the Hoghe Veluwe, he saw other van Gogh paintings: some from the Paris period and, above all, the works from Provence, magnificent testimonials to the painter's decisive period. In addition to the general impression of the light that, with color, makes all things new, it was individual paintings that especially occupied him. There was one originating in the month of Heidegger's birth (September 1889) of a radiant wheatfield, a painting that spoke to him; and he lingered a long time in front of *Hospital Garden of St.-Rémy*. We spoke of the onset of illness in van Gogh and in Nietzsche—strangely, occurring at the same time—and of the stunning similarity between Nietzsche's poem on crows ("Solitary") and the flock of crows in the *Wheatfield* that van Gogh had still managed to paint in Auvers.

During this visit to Holland, Heidegger was moved by the works of van Gogh (which he had known up to that time mostly through reproductions) and was pleased with the wonderful art foundation of the Kröller-Müller family—but to the same extent he disliked the unattractive landscape, especially the Zuidersee. We had to end an excursion into a mammoth, newly diked polder prematurely because the frightful desolation made him almost physically ill. But shortly thereafter he got to know the landscape which, far from van Gogh's origins, became the painter's destiny: Heidegger made his first trip to Provence. He went to Provence frequently—less on the trail of van Gogh, of course, than on the way to Cézanne. From then on, our conversations about art and works of art took place entirely in the light of the French painters, who became central for Heidegger. In the exhibitions at the Beyelers' gallery, he saw a series of late masterworks, as well as paintings by Cézanne in the art museum in Basel—where at that time one of the most beautiful versions of *St.*

Victoire Mountains hung on loan. Then there were Rilke's *Letters on Cé-zanne*, which at that time had not yet appeared in a separate German edition. Heidegger took a lively interest in the plans made (together with Clara Rilke) for this edition and in my work on it. But his preoccupation with Paula Becker-Modersohn also brought him back again and again to the French painters as her most important models.

The first conversation that casually touched upon the topic of Cé-zanne took place at Heidegger's home in Zähringen on a November evening in 1947. It was during my first visit to the Heideggers after the war. I had seen a painting by Juan Gris at the exhibition of modern French painting (which was the official reason for my trip); it was a paraphrase of Cézanne's painting of a woman in a red chair. The conversation among the three of us—Dr. Ingeborg Schroth, who was Heidegger's friend and the assistant at the Augustinermuseum in Freiburg, took an active part—soon turned from the modern French painters in the exhibition to Cé-zanne himself and to Rilke's letters on Cézanne's art, which Clara Rilke had only shortly before entrusted to me. At that time Heidegger was working on a memorial address for the twentieth anniversary of Rilke's death, which he gave to a private group. He read to us one of the poet's letters, dated 18 October 1907, in which Rilke speaks of the great turning in Cézanne's painting—"this single thing, on which everything depends"—and repeated with emphasis the sentence about "the work that no longer had any preferences or fastidious overindulgences, the smallest component of which was tested on the scale of a continually moving conscience and which gathered up beings in their color-content so integrally that a new existence without earlier memories sprang up on the other side of color." Heidegger illustrated this thought of such a correspondence from other places in the letters. For example, a letter that refers to the conversation Rilke had with the painter Mathilde Vollmöller says that Cézanne regards color as no one else has ever done, solely in order to make the thing out of it; color then disappears in the "realization" of the thing—with no residue of color. Heidegger referred to another place in the text that was important for him: the reference by Rilke to Baudelaire's poem "Charogne" (Carcass), where one reads that artist's concern with appearance must first have been so well mastered that it sees even in what is horrible and apparently repugnant only what is—the being "that, in the midst of all else, prevails."

Because of the preparation for the edition of Rilke's *Letters on Cé-zanne* in the following years—after my move to Freiburg—our conversations often touched upon this series of letters. And I gradually became

aware of the extraordinarily intimate way in which Heidegger was connected to the appearance and being of the painter. Once in a while one
hears that there were some similarities between Heidegger's and Cézanne's outward appearances—namely, in the look of the piercing eyes;
one needs only to be reminded of that well-known self-portrait by Cézanne that is in Bern. It is possible that something of the inner, essential
relationship was expressed in the outward appearances. Ursula von Kardorff once saw Heidegger sitting opposite her, at the home of Countess
Podewils in Munich. Observing him in conversation with his neighbors
Orff and Guardini, she was reminded of a peasant from southern France,
as she said later—a "Cézanne type" in his quiet serenity. However, it was
not only in their physical appearances that the thinker and the painter
appeared to be related to each other; it was their whole manner of being
that brought the two men close. Both of them dedicated themselves to
their task with the same unconditional devotion, merging totally with
their work. Both of them renounced much for the sake of their work. But
"renouncing does not take away, renouncing gives"—as one reads in
"Der Feldweg" (The Country Path). The work of both men affirms this.

More than once, Heidegger returned from a trip to the land of Cézanne and encouraged me—not without urgency—to bring together in a
book all the paintings of the master that show the mountains and to write
a text for it. Of course, a prerequisite would be that I myself go to Provence and look on the St. Victoire Mountains with my own eyes. For even
the best reproductions of the paintings and watercolors are not capable
of showing what the "holy mountain" has to say and what the painter
then transformed into the language of his paintings. In order to convey
something of this dialogue, one must himself have seen both—the mountains and the paintings.

In his book *Dialogue avec Heidegger,* Jean Beaufret reports that Heidegger made a remark at the beginning of his lecture in Aix (1958) that
was in no way intended just to "break the ice" with the audience; rather,
it gave expression to his experience of thinking. Heidegger began by describing the pathway to the quarry at Bibemus—up to the point where
the St. Victoire Mountains become visible. Then he said that there he had
found Cézanne's pathway, "the pathway to which, from its beginning to
its end, my own pathway of thinking responds, in its own way."

Whoever thinks that this is a matter of an artistic experience is
wrong. What is meant here is found in the lines that Heidegger dedicated
to the poet René Char on his birthday in 1971 ("Pensivement"): "In the
late work of the painter, the tension of emerging and not emerging has

become onefold, transformed into a mysterious identity. Is there shown here a pathway that opens onto a belonging-together of poet and thinker?"

There is a photograph of Heidegger that shows him sitting in front of a view of the mountains. Fédier, who was accompanying Heidegger at that time, wrote that this was one of Cézanne's paths on which one reached the edge of a precipitous rock face; below is the dark green of the trees and the red of the earth, in the depths the water of the Zola Dam—and on the other side the St. Victoire mountain range. There Heidegger sat on a rock and looked. His friends were reminded of a remark by Plato, who once wrote of the amazingly still posture that Socrates sometimes assumed when deep in thought. But Heidegger was not engrossed in his thinking. "He sat very still, over against St. Victoire, looking at the mountains. He sat there like that for a long time. I could not say just how long; this kind of time is nonmeasurable. 'I love the harmonious blending of shapes in my fatherland,' Cézanne said. Heidegger perceived that blending—something that is very difficult to achieve. For within it is hidden the unpretentious unity of the world, its inner character, being itself."

What Fédier describes here was, to use another phrase of Cézanne's, *une minute d'équilibre*—a moment of the equilibrium of the world.

The path or way of Cézanne. The older Heidegger became, the more he perceived this way to be his own way—as if he had the same way to go. It is a task left to the future to illuminate the relationship of their ways and to make that relationship fruitful for thinking. To be sure, it has nothing to do with art history.

Picasso and Braque

In his essay "Heidegger and the Thought of Decline,"[7] Fédier has explained how Cézanne opened the way for Heidegger to the two pinnacles of Picasso and Braque, both of whom had their origin, or found their seed, in Cézanne. This does not mean that the philosopher saw an overcoming of Cézanne in these two painters—as if Heidegger had fallen into the pattern that art history likes to call "development." Quite the opposite! It is the secret of the source that it holds more than what flows out of it; the source hides the sea within it. Fédier writes further that perhaps the contemporary history of painting, seen in terms of its high points, is nothing but a resplendent fall from what Cézanne's painting had been at his time.

For Heidegger, the experience and contemplation of the source remained the decisive event. He saw Picasso with a certain "observer's" distance, although individual paintings by Picasso touched him deeply. Once Martin Nagel sent him a postcard with *Bread Bearer* on it. When they met again later, Heidegger reminded him of it and told him how much the simplicity and austere interiority of the painting had moved him. From this impression, it was clear that the homely content of the painting played a role for Heidegger. In general, this fits with the way that the human being or the thing in each picture had much more to say to him than the artistic form as such—one has only to remember *Peasant Shoes*. Heidegger was touched most deeply when *both* aspects came together in a meaningful statement (as in Picasso's *Bread Bearer*).

Over the years, Heidegger was able to see a whole series of Picasso's masterworks, in exhibitions at Ernst Beyeler's gallery in Basel. Sometimes he was drawn to Basel by Beyeler's beautiful catalogues—sent to him in Freiburg by Frau Hildy Beyeler as an enticement to their philosopher friend. Occasionally, on our hikes in Zähringen or over a glass of wine in the Jägerhäusle or the Falken, we would talk of the phenomenon of Picasso—to which my own enthusiasm often succumbed prematurely, whereas Heidegger sometimes expressed doubt. When his old friend and student Inge Schroth gave an eloquent description of how Heidegger does the same thing as Picasso in the dismantling of the object—when he speaks of the necessary "destruction" in philosophy—Heidegger responded with silence and smiled suggestively.

Once, on our way to Basel, we got into a heated discussion about Picasso's artistic greatness, without reaching any satisfactory conclusion. Shortly thereafter Heidegger wrote me, "Picasso and 'artistic genius'— this is true, without a doubt. But I still do not see whether this artistic genius is capable of making manifest for art even its essential place in the future. Perhaps that is not an issue for art—but then what is the work of such artistic genius? Where does it belong? In my lecture in Munich, this was the question I barely intimated to the 'artists'—but it neatly passed them by or went over their heads. Perhaps one has anxiety—an essential one—in asking this question. But as far as I see it, at least, this is the next step."

In Munich Heidegger had said, "The more questioningly we think the root-unfolding (*Wesen*) of the technical, the more mysterious becomes the root-unfolding of art." Heidegger's way of questioning no longer had anything in common with traditional art criticism. Another letter from the fifties illustrates this point. He writes that he has just returned home after spending several days visiting power plants under the direction of professors from technical colleges. "The root-unfolding of the technical becomes more and more essential for me. But the way toward it is long, and there must first be clarity about the work of art and the power plant." It is a sentence that is hard for artists as well as art historians to understand—an almost inflammatory sentence, but one that points to a decisive connection in a world in which art—to repeat Hegel's sentence again—is no longer the highest way "in which truth provides existence for itself."

Among Georges Braque's aphorisms is one that we could designate as being especially close to Heidegger's thinking: "Science settles things; art unsettles them." Heidegger saw such unsettling not least of all in Picasso. But this was always connected to one's own position. For, as Heidegger once noted, all of today's art—whether surrealistic, abstract, or objective—is essentially metaphysical. In Cézanne, however, a turning in "the work" is being prepared—a turning that then became apparent for the thinker in Paul Klee.

Did Heidegger see Braque, a painter whom he loved, as working toward this turning? We never spoke about that. He liked Braque for the absolute superiority of his human and artistic character. After Heidegger visited him once in Varengeville, he spoke of Braque as his "good friend." And Braque wrote on a lithograph for Heidegger's seventieth birthday, "Echo begets echo / everything reflects back / For Martin Heidegger."

Paul Klee

We have already spoken frequently about Heidegger's lectures entitled "The Origin of the Work of Art" and their well-known, evocative presentation of van Gogh's *Peasant Shoes*. But what is not known is that Heidegger once thought about writing a second part to "The Origin of the Work of Art"—and that what would have given rise to it was the works of Paul Klee.

I can no longer recall exactly when it was in the fifties that the work and figure of Paul Klee entered our conversations on art and artists. Was it from my frequent conversations with Georg Schmidt in Basel, which almost always centered on Klee and which I as often as not reported to Heidegger? Was it the occasion provided by Rilke's letters to Klee, which Felix Klee made available to me for a publication? Or was it with the overwhelming impression I received from Klee's legacy in his apartment in Bern, which his son showed to me, with commentary, during a long visit one evening? At any rate, as soon as Beyeler, by a stroke of luck, succeeded in acquiring the Klee collection of the American industrialist David Thompson and brought it to Basel, the topic of Klee moved rapidly to the center of my conversations with Heidegger. I had hoped that this would lead to an encounter between the philosopher and the work of the artist. This encounter turned out to be of crucial significance for Heidegger.

Thompson's collection is one of the three largest Klee collections in the world. Before Beyeler sold this collection *in toto* to the city of Düsseldorf in the state of North Rhine-Westphalia, he decided to make it available to his wide circle of friends: artists and lovers of art, scholars and writers, from all over Europe. These works by Klee—eighty-eight oil paintings, watercolors, and drawings—exercised their effect in a quite astonishing way within the space of an old, vacant aristocrat's house in St. Alban (a suburb of Basel), in a series of small halls and well-proportioned rooms, some chambers, and a magnificent, wide stairwell. It seemed as if this art had been created specifically for such rooms, with their noble tranquility, intimacy and quiet, old woodwork, and windows that let in light that was sufficient but not too exuberant. And one had a view of the lawns and the clusters of trees in the old gardens. In such an atmosphere, Klee's paintings seemed to feel at home.

A stream of art lovers immediately came to the quiet suburb of St. Alban. Whoever had any connection with Beyeler wanted to visit the provisional Klee museum. Enthusiastic as I was about the event in Basel, where one could see more than two dozen works belonging to the highest ranks of the artist's creation, I first brought Hans Jantzen from my circle of acquaintances to the "Klee House." He was a former professor of art history in Munich and Freiburg and a close friend of Heidegger. It was not too long before Heidegger announced his own visit to the "Klee House." After the Beyelers and Pastor Hassler had greeted him, we left Heidegger alone for hours with Klee's paintings, as he had requested. He came to the pastor's house, which was adjacent to the "Klee House," for lunch and to rest for an hour. But then he could not wait—he called me, and we returned to Klee.

The encounter with Klee's work in the quiet of the old house had apparently affected Heidegger more strongly than I had anticipated. For Heidegger, this was very likely the third or fourth round of viewing the paintings. Although little was said during our tour of the rooms, it remains unforgettable to me. Heidegger would occasionally call me over in order to ask some question or to express his amazement. He was not captivated by the gems that immediately catch one's eye. Rather, the inconspicuously restrained pieces were the ones where Heidegger spent more time and to which he returned again and again, in order to experience them anew. There was, for example, the melancholic tranquillity of *Gedanken bei Schnee* (Thoughts in Snow), the pressing inescapability of *Beladenen* (The Burdened Ones), and the almost painful pathos of *Heroische Rosen* (Heroic Roses), losing their glow in the autumn frost. Heidegger stopped in front of *Patientin* (The Woman Patient)—a painting that reminds one strangely of Grünewald and that seems to reach with its root fibers into the deepest recesses of vegetative pain. He said, "Our friend Nagel should see this painting. For no clinical probing ever reaches as deeply into illness and suffering as this painting does. A physician can learn more here than from medical textbooks."

There was another painting that captivated him for a long time. Having had a remarkable relation to thunder and lightning all his life, Heidegger could hardly tear himself away from Klee's *Bunter Blitz* (Colorful Lightning). It reminded us of the fir tree that lightning had struck down just on the upper side of the hut above Todtnauberg. The little gouache *Ein Tor* (A Gate), painted in 1939, the year of Klee's death, brought a deep silence upon Heidegger. After a while he said in a somber tone, "This is the gate through which we all must at some time pass: death." Later on, Heidegger asked to see this painting again and again, since Beyeler—remembering the effect it had had on the philosopher—did not sell it, but kept it in his possession. Then a series of exquisite, somewhat witty and ironic drawings opened up a wide world of surprises. Among these drawings, those that dealt with the "juggernaut of technology" received Heidegger's special attention.

It was late in the day before we could take leave of the hospitality of Pastor Hassler and return to Freiburg, promising to come again soon. Everyone was inspired by what they saw. The atmosphere seemed to vibrate with Klee's cheerfulness as well as with his deep seriousness.

When I returned to Zähringen to arrange for the second trip to Basel, it turned out that Heidegger had in the meantime discussed the exhibition in detail with Jantzen and had had additional thoughts about it. With regard to the plan for a publication about the collection—as it had been proposed to him—Heidegger smiled and said, "Would I be the one to write a foreword?" He said that for him there was a special difficulty, resulting from the following: It is not yet clear whether Klee's own interpretation of his works ("cosmic," etc.) actually represents the whole of what happens in his creation. Besides, the whole Tachism is probably a consequence—resulting from an (unconscious) misunderstanding—of this erroneous self-interpretation which takes place at one of the most risky points of contact between metaphysics and what is to arrive.[8]

Heidegger went on to say that Klee's "philosophical" struggles with "assertion" do not happen accidentally or incidentally, but out of necessity, and that therein lies the difficulty. And yet Klee does not know what is happening—namely, that art now gets transformed. He, Heidegger, should now write a second part to "The Origin of the Work of Art"!

Following this conversation, Heidegger discussed Hegel's oft-quoted statement that art, when seen from the side of its highest determination, is a thing of the past. While affirming the statement, Heidegger nonetheless added that even that would first have to be shown. For him, it was of utmost importance to learn what became of Klee's relation with the Greeks. Heidegger did not know anything about the close relation of Klee to the artistic world of Goethe, as that has rarely been a subject of research. Klee's relation with Goethe's world would have awakened Heidegger's interest—much as did Klee's numerous relations with the poets of his time, documented in his extensive correspondence (now in possession of his son Felix Klee).

Heidegger considered this man, Paul Klee, to be an enormous phenomenon. He requested that I think over what we had discussed in regard to Tachism, which was much talked about. For Tachism the principle seems to be "letting things run," whereas in Klee there is inevitably a "whole" to be seen.

After that, Klee was the subject of many of our conversations, especially since I myself often worked on his art and enjoyed giving reports of that work to Heidegger—especially when it had to do with exhibitions. I showed Heidegger almost all of the work that originated in this way. In this context, there was an episode that showed in a characteristic way how Heidegger on the one hand participated in my activities and on the other hand took part in the Klee phenomenon. With Georg Schmidt's help, I had made a forty-five-minute program on Paul Klee for television. I was proud to have used some extremely fine material, including lesser-known paintings and drawings. I had no idea that Heidegger had seen this program at the home of an acquaintance. I tried to tell him about it on our next walk in Zähringen, not hiding my satisfaction with the production, hampered as it had been by many difficulties. After my first sentence, I noticed that Heidegger held an entirely opposite view. His opposition had nothing to do with assessing and judging the artist Paul Klee. But I had to swallow the more painful reproach of having done something more or less detrimental to the great master. Heidegger maintained that, for an artist like Klee, the medium of television means nothing short of death for his creations. The random movement of the camera forces the eye to take certain leaps that hinder an intensive, quiet viewing as well as a thoughtful staying-with (*verweilendes Nachdenken*), which each single work and the relations within it deserve.

However well thought out my Klee program for television may have been, it worked destructively precisely in regard to what transpires in this art. It had blocked the way to Klee's art, because from the very beginning the proper access to it had been misplaced. (And all of this is true even only from the standpoint of the graphic, of the line. To provide an impression of Klee's colorfulness through television is impossible anyway, since every shade of color is falsified.) The reasons for Heidegger's detailed "chastisement"—which I can only hint at here—were discussed in detail in our long conversation. Last but not least, Heidegger had missed the tenderness and intimacy that flourish in between Klee's lines—and he missed the failure to bring out what is profoundly ominous. In the end, I had to admit defeat. I took the matter to heart; out of responsibility to art and its language, which in any case are threatened by reproduction, I made no more television programs on art.

Even after the Klee exhibition in Basel was taken down, the artist remained a frequent topic of our conversations through all the years thereafter. In his letter of 21 February 1959, Heidegger wrote, "It was a beautiful evening. Let me add that what you said regarding Klee— namely, what in an essential sense is 'poetic' in every art—this you must bring to light in Klee's work and his person. In this respect what I tried to say at the end of the essay on art is insufficient—*language!* If only you would write *the* Klee book! In Klee something has happened that none of us grasps as yet." His confidence that I would succeed in writing such a book on Klee far exceeded my capabilities. Georg Schmidt once told me, as emphatically as possible, that Heidegger himself was the only one who could write *the* book on Klee. This was after a memorable conversation, on a mild day in April in the garden of Schmidt's house in Binningen. Heidegger had stopped off for a while on his return from a visit to Ronchamp, exuberant from his impressions of the pilgrimage church by Corbusier. A discussion took place on determining the place (*Ort*) of art—a discussion in the literal sense of an *Er-örterung*, culminating in Klee. With his wonderful sense for tracking things, Schmidt noticed the relation of his guest to Klee and to that which has entered the world with Klee's art: "something that none of us grasps as yet."

On his visit to the Klee Foundation in Bern, Heidegger found all the riches that Klee could offer spread out before him. It was here that certain things became clear to Heidegger, such as the relation with Cézanne (*Kleine Felsenstadt* [Little City of Rock] or *Harmonisierter Kampf* [Harmonized Struggle]). When the lecture "Time and Being" was broadcast on radio from the University of Freiburg, Heidegger wrote to Hildy Beyeler that when she heard the titles of the paintings *Heilige aus einem Fenster* (Saints from a Window) and *Tod und Feuer* (Death and Fire) at the beginning of the broadcast, she should take that as a greeting. For Heidegger never forgot those early encounters with Klee in Basel. He said that works such as *Heroische Rosen* (Heroic Roses) are not paintings, but feeling. Klee was capable of making moods "visible" in pictures. *Heilige aus einem Fenster* offers a whole world. The less we think of Klee's paintings as presenting objects, the more they "appear" (in the sense of the Greek φαίνεσται).

Heidegger knew what Novalis meant when he wrote, "The greatest works of art are not kind." Regardless of the superficial "enjoyment" that we fancy we are getting from them, hidden in the paintings of Klee is the thorn of a claim that is not easy to satisfy. All his life, Heidegger was grateful that the way to Klee had been opened up for him in such a unique way through the Beyelers: "Hard to believe that such loyal protectors of Klee's work lived so close by."

The "Posthistorical Picture": A Digression

Nonobjective art was a wave that flooded everything. After the war it burst upon the art scene of Europe, such that it was impossible for previous development simply to continue unbroken. It would have been surprising if Heidegger and I at that time had not discussed this wave of nonobjective art. As for myself, I began to write my first book reviews and critical articles, especially after I made the acquaintance of the painter Gerhard Fietz (who belonged to the circle of Willi Baumeister and Adolf Hölzel); and I met frequently with young artists, as well as the famous art collector Ida Bienert from Dresden and the English art critic John Anthony Thwaites (who exercised a strong influence in Munich and introduced me to William Grohmann, also a famous writer on art).

Because of a particular personal situation, the problem that emerged with the appearance of abstract art was reflected in my correspondence with Heidegger. In view of his association with art and with artists, what he wrote in these letters should not be ignored. A small work of art given to me as a present one day in 1947 by a young friend, the painter Mathias

Goeritz from Berlin, acted as a particular occasion for confronting the novel questions that were being discussed everywhere. This abstract gouache, full of rhythmically moving, powerful lines and tender, colored melodics, occupied me for a long time; and it seemed to me to suggest many hints and answers. I told Heidegger about this gouache and mentioned that I would like to write an essay about it. Two months after my visit to Zähringen, Heidegger wrote, "You are probably busy now with the essay you planned to write. Reflection and statements about art works have something unfortunate and awkward about them; there is no need to discuss the fact that the immediate experience of art works comes first. However, just as the opportunity and the space for the arts are lacking, so is the ability for such experience confused. For this reason an incisive reflection is needed. It seems to me that you belong to the realm of such tasks rather than to the business of history. It is good that everything can be accomplished outside the realm of the university. If you have a small circle of friends who work with you, it guarantees stimulation and inducement. For without the right atmosphere and real encouragement, we cannot build anything. Indeed, such assistance has become rare and insufficient in our befuddled and confused world."

Personal circumstances forced me to postpone work on the essay for a long time. It was finally completed in 1949 and frequently presented as a lecture in private circles. I sent the text to Heidegger, who in the spring of 1950 responded as follows: "For weeks I thought that you must have been brooding. . . . Your lecture is *excellent*. What is difficult and elusive is the method of destruction that is clearly and conclusively carried out by reflections on art as practiced up to now.[9] I would not draw back from the clear disengagement from art historians, but I would tone down the cutting remarks about them, because we are everywhere on the point of a *turning;*[10] And if we hold out in this, we have already done enough. Certainly one must have the picture before oneself, in order to follow each step properly.

"There are many questions with regard to what is prehistorical and posthistorical. Even today, those who hear it and read it are not yet familiar with the distinction made in *Being and Time* between *Historie* and *Geschichte.*[11] I am also not quite clear as to how your painter understands that posthistorically. Here one could sense a rejection of all history, as in Gottfried Benn, who does not come to terms with this question through thinking but perhaps does so artistically.

"Something else: the question raised in the lecture—*what is* the exhibited work of art?—does not yet seem clear in all respects. The question that could be hidden behind all of this is whether there exists an *art work* at all. Or does art become untenable along with metaphysics? Is there perhaps, behind the uneasiness brought about by a nonobjective art, a much deeper shock? Is that the end of art? The arrival of something for which we do not have a name?"

Sculpture: Wimmer and Chillida

After we have shown the connections between the thinking of the philosopher and art by using some examples from our epoch—and the connections are, by no means incidentally significant—it seems logical to ask whether such relations obtain only with respect to painting or whether they also apply to the plastic arts. Admittedly, no sculptor attained the same importance for Heidegger as Cézanne did among the painters. Yet it would be a serious omission to overlook Heidegger's position on the plastic arts—especially since in his later years he formulated one of his most significant statements on art with reference to a modern sculptor.

In examining Heidegger's relation to sculpture, there are two issues that might be easily confused. The first concerns sculpture as such, which in the work of the famous Basque Chillida became for Heidegger the question concerning art as such. The other issue, however, concerns Heidegger's relations to individual sculptors, an issue often closely linked with sculpting problems in their busts of the philosopher.

Although one might suppose that the shape of Heidegger's head would have provoked every painter to reproduce it, none of the great portrait painters of our time tried to do so. Apparently, it more strongly aroused the desire of sculptors to give it a plastic form—in the sense of Hegel's statement that it is above all in sculpture that "what is interior and spiritual becomes manifest in its eternal tranquillity and unity. Only that external thing that still preserves itself in this unity and tranquillity corresponds with this unity and tranquillity itself." In describing her encounters with the philosopher, Ursula von Kardorff above all stresses the tranquillity that emanated from him; this tranquillity is especially characteristic of his head, which brings together in an unforgettable unity his robust peasant origins and the traits of wide-open perception and most delicate sensibility. To find something similar in the art of sculpture, one would have to go far back and let the heads of antiquity file by until one arrived at one giving a similar impression of rank—perhaps Aristotle's bust in the Ny-Karlsberg Glypthothek in Copenhagen, which reminds one immediately of Heidegger. For, as Hegel put it, "The spirit represented by the art of sculpture is the spirit that is pure in itself and not one dispersed in many ways in the play of chance and passion."

The sculptors did not find it easy to represent or to make visible this spirit. Perhaps Gustav Seitz was most successful in his bust of Heidegger, which gives a strong overall impression with apparently simple and well-conceived abstractions, similar to Seitz's small-bust portrayal of Heinrich Mann or Bertolt Brecht. The stone bust made by the North German sculptor Hans Kock is somewhat different, having a heavy, blocklike character; its solid compactness brings into play something of that austere air that belongs to the appearance of what is represented. Particularly famous is the bust of Heidegger by the Bavarian sculptor Hans Wimmer, which exists in different versions. Both being members of the Bavarian Academy of Fine Arts, Heidegger and Wimmer had met in the circle of Count Podewils, who initially suggested the plan for the bust. The work that the artist began was changed again and again over the years during frequent meetings in Munich. Alongside a terra-cotta bust there finally emerged, through continuous reductions, a highly plastic creation: a clay mask that supported the idea that the spirit of the one who was represented should be speaking, as it were, through this mask, as with personae in ancient Greek theater.[12]

Wimmer's mask, which Podewils presented to the Academy of Fine Arts upon his retirement from his post, is often praised. Heidegger hardly spoke about it. Was he himself really convinced by this unique work of art? Whoever sees the mask will initially experience surprise, which soon will be accompanied by shock or even doubt—all of which will be difficult to appease in spite of the insight into what the sculptor wanted to achieve. The longer we look at the mask, the more we have the impression of something half-made and unresolved. It is as though the vacuity of the product is not filled with spiritual life—the open sockets of the eyes, without the gaze and pierced through by light, remain mere holes deprived of the power of looking.

If we examine the sculptor's sketches, which he drew in changing situations and from the most varied angles, in the lecture hall or in conversation, then our dislike increases. If we find that in the frontal view of Wimmer's early bust of Heidegger there is something strangely wry and essentially alien to Heidegger, then we conclude from Wimmer's sketches that, although here the artist perceives some of the traits congenial to his own temperament (the rootedness and closeness to the earth[13] of the Alemannic character peculiar to the "inner Heuberg"),[14] almost to the demoniac, Wimmer nevertheless largely fails to grasp Heidegger's spiritual being. If these sketches appear exaggerated and often theatrical to the point of being grotesque, then it must be said that Heidegger was neither a dandy nor a gnome. And when he occasionally appears on Wimmer's pages as a forest elf, then that is a malicious misunderstanding. The man who unsettled a whole world of thought is not present in these sketches, and thus the "mask" is also problematical.

As for other sketches by sculptors, the highly successful sketch of Heidegger's head that Bernhard Heiliger drew with a few strokes and later published as a lithograph (see page 2) has become famous. It originated in one of the festive gatherings organized by the St. Gallen publishers and by the gallery directors Franz Larese and Jürg Janett in the castle of Amriswil in Switzerland, where artists, painters, and sculptors occasionally came together with writers and poets such as Ezra Pound, Ungaretti, Cioran, and others. Heidegger eagerly took part in these events, to which Larese would issue invitations whenever there was a new exhibition in his gallery. It was there that Heidegger became acquainted with Eugène Ionesco and talked with lyric poets such as Max Hölzer and Jean Dupin. On one such occasion Santomaso made a sketch of Heidegger. Among other things, the festive marches composed by Paul Huber and dedicated to Hans Hartung, Carl Zuckmayer, and Martin Heidegger bear witness to the relaxed cheerfulness of these events.

On one such evening, after a Zadkine premiere in St. Gallen, the philosopher met the sculptor at the dinner table in the old castle. They sat next to each other as honored guests. Yet Ossip Zadkine did not produce a bust of Heidegger. What he drew then, in the autumn of 1965, should be related here as an anecdotal arabesque. While people were busy giving after-dinner speeches—to which Zadkine was only half listening—he started to draw on a piece of paper lying nearby. Heidegger, as he reported later, was at first amazed and then pleased to see how there appeared a fairy plant in blue, spreading as if transparent, full of fantasy— a plant that is associated with the artist's sculptures. When Zadkine finally put his pen in his pocket, his neighbor asked if he might keep the drawing as a souvenir. Yes—if he would like it, Zadkine said with a laugh. He signed the small work of art with the famous "O. Z." and gave it to Heidegger, who in turn added his initials, the date, and the place. A few days later Heidegger showed me this drawing and wanted to know whether I would like to have it. Thus I came to own a Zadkine sketch with two signatures on it, unlike any other of the sculptor's sketches.

In the face of so many only half-successful sculptures and sketches, one might wonder whether the philosopher's head could ever be captured in a work of art. Hans Wimmer, who once said that some people are better heralded "in poetry than in sculpture," undoubtedly worked extremely hard on Heidegger's appearance, without succeeding in producing a convincing representation. To reproduce the philosopher in sculpture, to show his head "as not variously dispersed in the play of chance and passion" (to quote Hegel again) has been an almost unsolvable difficulty. This task could succeed only if the artist fully understood him. Is it too much to say that that is what presumably has been missing? One has the impression that the artistic interest triumphs over the concern with the thinker himself. But who would want finally to blame the sculptor for this?

In only one case does Heidegger seem to have found a real match in his encounters with the plastic arts—or, to put it more precisely, with the work of a contemporary sculptor. However, this case had nothing at all to do with a bust of Heidegger. And it is significant that Eduardo Chillida subsequently stated, in a conversation in Basel on 14 June 1982, that he would like to preserve the memory of Heidegger—the greatest man he had ever met—in a series of etchings. "In remembrance of Heidegger" [15]—thus not a bust, but an artistic inscription in another language!

Juxtaposing the names of the philosopher and the plastic artist who worked with iron and stone—each belonging in his own way among the great figures of our time—may be surprising at first glance and needs explanation. I must confess that I was partly responsible for their meeting each other. I met Chillida for the first time in the spring of 1962, at his grand exhibition in Zurich, and was deeply impressed by his sculptures, which showed a spirit entirely different from what one was accustomed to seeing in the more recent exhibitions both at home and abroad. Later I reported to Heidegger in detail a lengthy conversation I had had with the artist, because it seemed to me that there was a whole series of amazing connections between the thinking and the work of the two men. I was able to tell Heidegger about Chillida's way of working, in which one detected the pride of the skilled craftsman who had learned a great deal from the ironsmiths of his Basque homeland and who nevertheless avoided anything in his works that produced mere effect, anything that was merely "stimulating." Thus there emerge from flat surfaces that are without seam or crack very sharp gestures of form in which nothing is left to chance. I told Heidegger what the sculptor had said: "It is not the form with which I am concerned, but the relation of forms to one another—the relation that arises among them." Thus we touched upon the fundamental problem of this sculptor, namely, the incorporation of "space" in his work.

This aroused Heidegger's interest. Since his lecture in Darmstadt entitled "Building, Dwelling, Thinking," he had been constantly occupied with the issue of space and with the question whether "space" as conceived by Galileo, Newton, and modern natural science is identical with space in art. How, then, would Chillida understand "space"? We spoke in English; and to the question of what in his opinion is meant by *space* and *espace*—concepts that indicate the Latin *spatium*, "extension," and therefore something measurable—Chillida immediately and vehemently objected. He indicated to me that he does not take space as it is understood in physics; what can be calculated would not interest him. This seemed to me to be all the more significant in light of the fact that, with reference to Chillida's works in plastic art, one frequently speaks of forms that "encompass space" or that "firmly establish themselves in space." Finally, I could tell Heidegger that for this artist space must be something other than what we have long been accustomed to understand only as measurable and surveyable. But which space?

In our conversation at that time, Heidegger touched upon those thoughts that he would later intimate (rather than elaborate on) in the short essay "Art and Space" (St. Gallen, 1969). Above all else, he was concerned with the meaning of *place*, the Greek *topos;* in the lecture at Darmstadt, he used the example of a bridge across a river as an instance of an "instituting" that establishes "place" through human work. From then on, it was the "place" as represented in the plastic work of Chillida that concerned him. We spoke of the *Aeolian Harp Made of Iron*, the *Comb of the Wind*, and *The Praise of Ether*—sculptures that are related to the elements. And then we spoke of other works in which the spatial relation is inverted, as it were, so that what is outside becomes the inner space and one is tempted to say that what the observer does *not* perceive with the physical eye becomes important. With reference to such points that are withdrawn from the gaze of the observer, there where one feels the very heart of the sculpture to be, the word *segredo* was frequently used—mystery, precisely in such works as the powerful *Autour de vide,* which seems to struggle to come to terms with the world of technology and which, according to the sculptor's own opinion, betrays a congeniality with the Greeks when it begins to shine in the light. These works, with their terse and reserved lucidity, have at best only an external connection—and fundamentally no connection at all—with contemporary expressions of the *Zeitgeist,* such as "minimal art."

At the end of our conversation in Zurich, Chillida made a statement that provoked Heidegger to listen all the more attentively. The sculptor said that he was interested in space above all as something born of time. Again, what he meant had nothing to do with physics or with measurable time. Instead, he had in mind the time of music, its tempo; he pointed to some of his works, like *Musica callada* and *Musique des constellations*— sculptures in which, in ever-new variations, a nonmeasurable relation to space seems to resonate. I was able to illustrate the account of my conversation with the artist with the help of a few photographs—and mentioned that the most beautiful and birdlike version of the sculpture *Dream Anvil* belonged to Georges Braque. Such a wealth of relations aroused Heidegger's continuous interest; and it pleased him very much when, in 1968, invited by the gallery in Erker, he was able to meet the sculptor in Hagenwil Castle. Unfortunately, I did not witness the meeting. But I noticed later that it led Heidegger—at Larese's request—to write the essay "Art and Space" directly on the lithographic stone in St. Gallen—a labor that was not easy for the philosopher, who had no practice in such exercises in art. A unicum in his entire work!

However, he returned to Freiburg contented and happy. Without too many words, the sculptor and the thinker had understood each other. When at the end of November 1968 Heidegger sent the short essay (which later appeared in standard type) to the artist, he wrote that these observations dealt with the riddle of art, with the riddle that art itself is. He also pointed out that the issue is not to solve the riddle; rather, the task consists in seeing it.

"Occasionally we have the feeling that for a long time now the thing-character of the thing has been violated and that thinking has participated in this violence. That is why one rejects thinking instead of trying to make thinking more thoughtful." And at the end comes the dedication: "For Eduardo Chillida."

Heidegger and the plastic arts: What this relationship amounts to becomes clear from an entry by the philosopher, to be found among many valuable Heideggeriana at the Erker gallery. This inscription gives the result, as it were, of the dialogue between the thinker and the sculptor. In Heidegger's own handwriting, it reads, Δοκεῖ δε μέγα τι εἶναι καὶ χαλεπὸν ληφδῆναι ὁ τόπος (But it seems to be something very powerful and difficult to grasp: the *topos*). These words of Aristotle are still valid today.

7
Greece and Buddha

In a Greek Light

I still possess a small scrap of paper on which Heidegger wrote his own translation of the first verse of Sophocles' *Antigone*. This slip of paper goes back to those days in which an unusual event occurred in Munich: the performance of Sophocles' tragedy in Hölderlin's translation and with music composed by Carl Orff. Heidegger came from Freiburg specifically for this performance. Before I took him to his train for the return trip to Freiburg, we met in the morning in one of those small shanty cafés that are now long gone but that existed then around Munich's main train station in the landscape of destruction from the air war. Over breakfast we had a lively discussion about our impressions of the evening before. We had a long conversation concerning the various translations of Sophocles' works in German. Using various examples, we contrasted Hölderlin's rendition with that of the classical philologist Karl Reinhardt, whose translation had just then come out and whom Heidegger esteemed highly.

Our discussion finally focused entirely on the first line of the tragedy: Ὦ κοινὸν αὐτάδελφον Ἰσμήνης κάρα. Heidegger explained to me that this verse, when translated into German literally, should read "O Haupt, das du gemeinsam mit mir den Bruder hast, Ismene" (Ismene, O leader, you who share the brother in common with me). This cannot be rendered in German; at any rate, it should not be rendered as Hölderlin does, with "gemeinsamschwesterliches" (in common sisterhood), because then we will miss what is crucial, namely, "das Haupt gemeinsam mit dem Bruder" (the leader shared in common with the brother). For these words of the first verse already indicate the relation to the brother—a relation that is crucial for the entire tragedy. When I inquired how *he* would translate the verse, Heidegger deliberated awhile and then wrote on the slip of paper mentioned earlier, "Oh auch mitbrüderliches oh Ismenes Haupt!" (Ismene, O you who share in brotherliness, O leader!). This, he added, is not "German"; however, in terms of meaning and also sound, it is almost exactly what Sophocles says.

159

I do not offer this brief glimpse into Heidegger's "Greek workshop" for the sake of philological subtleties, but only to indicate Heidegger's relation to the Greek language, which was in no way different from his relation to his mother tongue. It was in many ways a relation characterized by hearing, which in the end may have had something to do with Heidegger's musicality. This relation was never a scholarly and philological one. It is well known that he often suspected the legitimacy of the claim and the privilege of the linguists who insist on etymology, and that he was much criticized by the linguists because of the "arbitrary" character of his translations. He dealt with Greek differently than did the philologists, and, as far as I can tell, in an almost intuitive way, as can be seen from the example just mentioned.

In the gymnasium in Konstanz, Heidegger had a Greek teacher whose teaching must have been excellent. Sebastian Hahn "understood Greek better than anyone else, and we really learned from him." Heidegger always spoke with veneration and gratitude of his Greek teacher, who is buried in the cemetery of his native village Rast, near Messkirch, with the beautiful epitaph *Vir pius / Doctus / Vere nobilis.* (A devout man / Learned / Truly noble).

The association with Greece runs through all of Heidegger's lifework. It is a critical debate with Greece, with its language and thinking— not to be confused with "antiquity" in the sense of that word as coined by European humanism. How decisively Heidegger distanced himself from everything Roman—and the Latinness in it—need not be discussed here in detail. It suffices to refer to the statement in his first lecture course on Heraclitus in the summer semester of 1943 ("The Beginning of Western Thinking"), where he says, "The Romans notoriously failed to grasp Greek thought"; and to mention the remark that he repeatedly made in the lecture and discussions about the decisive transformation of the concept of truth from ἀλήθεια as "unconcealing" to *veritas* as "correctness."

If we glance at the titles of Heidegger's lecture courses in Marburg and Freiburg from 1923 to 1944, we will notice how significant the dialogue with the Greeks was for Heidegger; and we will see a profound transformation vis-à-vis traditional views. These lecture courses do not focus on the presumed completion of Greek thinking in the classical philosophies of Plato and Aristotle, but rather on the early call of "pre-Socratic" thinking, which was once judged a mere forerunner to philosophy but which indeed provides the beginning of philosophy. With the names of Anaxagoras, Parmenides, and Heraclitus, this beginning claims a priority that befits originary thinking. For Heidegger, the entire culmination of philosophizing, its unfolding and its decline up to Hegel and Nietzsche, stands in this light.

The performance of Sophocles' *Antigone* in Hölderlin's translation and with music by Carl Orff, as mentioned earlier, was an event that reached far beyond Munich. It had an effect not only primarily on the world of theater; in its uniqueness, and even radicality, this performance also touched upon the issues pertaining to spiritual existence and matters of human insight, at a point in time when the openness of insecure humanity to essential claims had not yet been stifled by the approaching way of thinking that is devoted to prosperity. The audiences of the long series of performances of this tragedy, which had to be given again the following year, were moved and gripped by a process to which they could not close themselves off. Far removed from any superficial "operatizing," Orff the musician succeeded in creating a work which by unifying the sounds—initially strange, harsh, and often aggressive—with the power of the poetic word almost perfectly evoked a bygone world. No one who saw *Antigone* then, who entered the space of the Prinzregent Theater—a revered place originally conceived for the great performances of Wagner—could avoid the message that became audible and visible in this performance. One could almost say that one was exposed to a spiritual venture there.

Special, fortunate circumstances coincided in this performance at Munich as they presumably will never coincide again. The work was first performed two years earlier in Salzburg, but in an atmosphere that was not entirely suitable for it. The cast in Salzburg, which could be called simply an ideal cast, was able to be brought over to Munich: Christel Goltz as Antigone, Hermann Uhde as Creon, and Ernst Häfliger as Tiresias. Under the direction of Georg Solti, the performance fulfilled in a unique way the intentions that had guided the composer in creating the music, namely, his concern with the sound-world of antiquity, both in song and orchestral accompaniment. This represented a significant step beyond the misunderstandings which, although productive, had led to the development of the opera in Italy. Those who experienced all this in Munich at that time will never forget it: the powerful choral scene, the appearance of Creon and Antigone, their shocking path to death, the prophecies of the deranged seer, and finally the collapse of the proud king. Those present were gradually moved by an increasing feeling of the religious significance that the performance of this tragedy had for humans in antiquity—from the first, long-drawn-out lamentation of the king's daughter, to the almost earsplitting fortissimo that the playing of the stones introduces like a hammering, all the way to the somber denouement of the play, after which an audience of over one thousand remained silent for several minutes.

As a storm of applause broke out, Carl Orff saw a man approaching him in the dim light of the stage whom he initially mistook for a stage worker. But then this stranger suddenly grabbed Orff's hands and, touched with emotion, said to him, "Thank you for bringing ancient tragedy back to life. My name is Heidegger." Clemens von Podewils reports this outstanding event in commenting on Orff's musical work. Two human beings belonging to the creative class had recognized at that moment their nearness to each other: one gives a new life to the original unity of the Greek verse and song, the other calls thinking—which is getting lost in science—back to itself out of the original meaning and power of words. What was common to both men was language.

In 1952 Heidegger saw the performance once again. In those days discussions centered again and again on the event of that performance, which, despite the modern stage, exercised an almost magical effect on all who were sensitive. Whoever felt devoted to the Greek spirit—poets, writers, artists, and scholars—all came to the capital city of Bavaria, often attending the performances more than once and speaking openly of ancient themes.

Besides Heidegger's short meeting with Orff and Solti behind the scenes—a meeting brought about by their shared pleasure over the success of *Antigone*—there is one thing I recall from the encounters and conversations of those days that brought Heidegger and the singer of Creon together at my house at Icking. An excellent singer—who embodied the Theban king in an incomparable manner, not only in terms of his vocal capacity as a bass-baritone, but also because of his stately figure, impressive posture, and noble bearings—Uhde came from Bremen. We had gone to the same gymnasium there. Heidegger was so impressed with Uhde that I had to invite the singer to come to Icking on a day when he was not performing, in order to meet Heidegger. This meeting, which took place one afternoon around the tea table and without the presence of curious people, went extremely well. For as soon as the philosopher and the singer began to talk, it became clear that the singer not only had studied Hölderlin's words—which he had to sing—but had also studied and understood the entire original Greek text beforehand. Only in this way was it possible for him to enter so fully and empathetically into the tragic event of the poetic work and to bring Creon to the stage—not to play the role, but to *be* the king, really and truly, in his proud arrogance and his terrible suffering, down to his every gesture and tone of voice. Thus this conversation was concerned not with external matters, but with the content and significance of the tragedy, which one can grasp only if one is entirely versed in the Greek and its living spirit. Heidegger was deeply impressed with Uhde and frequently returned to the conversation he had had with this noble and artistically sensitive man, whom he valued highly—both as a human being and as an interpreter of a world that was so significant for Heidegger. That is why he was so taken aback by the news of Uhde's sudden and early death, which later I had to bring to him. (Uhde died on the stage in Copenhagen during the first performance of a modern opera.) Heidegger spoke of this death as a heavy loss. He did not want to see *Antigone* again with another cast that would perhaps turn Creon into a theater king.

I had another conversation with Heidegger about *Antigone* in the following year when he came to Munich to see the performance again. In the guest book that I kept in Icking, Heidegger wrote on 27 April 1951, Ἀγχιβασίη / going into the nearness / Heraclitus, Fragment 122 / after discussing *Antigone*." It was an attempt, drawing upon a fragment of Heraclitus, to get near to an unfathomable topic, to which Helmken—an energetic participant—held fast two days later, with Creon's words to Tiresias: εὖ γὰρ οἶδότι / θεοὺς μιαίνειν οὔτις ἀνθρώπων σθένει, which in Reinhardt's translation reads "Denn der Mensch ist zu gering, Gott zu entweihen" (For man is too small to desecrate God) (lines 1043–44). This was the topic! And this was an example of why the experience of this tragedy became a serious and holy matter in those days.

Hofmannsthal once wrote, "A trip to Greece is the most spiritual trip that we ever undertake." Dealing with the thinking of the Greeks nurtured in Heidegger the desire to transform the spiritual pilgrimage into a real trip to Greece—a trip that would enable an encounter with those places whose names were so familiar to him and whose light Hofmannsthal admired. However, this desire of many years ran up against external circumstances again and again. Even plans for such a trip that were once worked out far in advance with Kästner came to nothing, as I indicated before. Heidegger had already turned seventy by the time Helmken, my friend from Bremen, finally succeeded, by way of inexhaustible initiative and practical preparations, in bringing about a joint trip with Heidegger in the early spring of 1962. They went by ship from Venice to Olympia and Corinth, and from there over a short stretch of land to Epidaurus (where Heidegger visited the shrine of Zeus in Nemea);

they continued on to Crete, Patmos, Rhodes, Delos, and then Attica, ending with a visit to Delphi and the return to Venice. I am sorry to say that I could not go along on that trip.

It was typical of Heidegger that he refused to use even a well-meaning "introduction" to this trip. Someone had sent him a widely read new book about Greece by the writer Peter Bamm. In response he said that he was not too happy with the book, "which is written as a secondary text and which actually mixes what is Greek with Roman and Hebraic elements. The success of the book obviously rests on this mixture. Preparation for the trip consists in bracketing out all preconceptions and in keeping oneself ready for that which is there—in Greek terms, for that which, unconcealed, emerges (*anwest*) in the light."

Heidegger's trip to Greece was not concerned with what people nowadays see and admire as "sights." In any event, what for him, the questioning one, was worthy of being seen he found in abundance in the course of the trip, and he received it as something more than the answer he had sought. There are no letters referring to this trip, nor any other written accounts—except the one that he wrote for his wife, a participant in the trip, in order to gather up certain memories of the days in Greece. This account was and will remain inaccessible to outsiders.[1] When he later spoke about his experiences in Greece—which happened only infrequently, since he remained largely silent about what impressed him most strongly—it was usually not the details that he discussed, but the all-encompassing physical light peculiar to Greece. Like Hofmannsthal before him, Heidegger experienced the "lesson of the light designed for the thoughtful observer" (see Hugo von Hofmannsthal's *Greece*, published in 1922). However, while Hofmannsthal—the writer in love with words—attempted to describe this light by transforming it almost romantically and perceived in it not only everything he came across but also "the philosophical world of thought peculiar to the Greeks . . . like a chain of mountain summits," Heidegger's experiences were by contrast far removed from any enthusiastic revelry. He sought what is simple and found therein the fullness and richness of what has the character of a beginning. He heard what the rocks and the skies had to say at the exit from the processional way in Delos, flanked by lions, or between the newly re-erected pillars of Hera's temple in Olympia. It was Hölderlin's ode that gave him his lead.

After he returned from this trip, the overwhelming impression he had received from the flood of light in the Cycladic archipelago did not leave

Heidegger in peace. A longing for the "beloved Greece" remained. Thus he later traveled many times to Greece, once staying for a while in Aegina; finally, in those months of the year 1967 that were overshadowed by revolutionary unrest, he was invited by the Athenian Academy to give a lecture and once again went to Athens. Sicily (Greek in a wider sense), where in Taormina he wanted to recuperate from a serious illness, could not replace Greece for Heidegger.

One could almost say that it was rather Provence that renewed Heidegger's contact with Greece—Provence, with its poor interior region, whose monotony, as Hofmannsthal put it, often reminds one of Greece "in a silent solitude" ("it looks like the hills where Antigone visits the corpse of her brother"). Was it only accidental that Heidegger held his lecture "Hegel und die Griechen" (Hegel and the Greeks) for the first time in Aix-en-Provence? Moreover, the seminars he gave in Le Thor in 1966, 1968, and 1969, as the guest of René Char, were open dialogues that above all centered on how to find access to the Greek word. These seminars focused on the poetic aphorisms of the pre-Socratics; Heidegger turned inquiringly to the traditional statements on logos, physis, world, conflict, and fire in the light of the Heraclitean logos—recalling finally Parmenides' poem, according to which "thinking and being are in truth the same."[2] That is how what is Greek came to be articulated on the ground provided by Provence—with its Greek light, if we are to believe Maillol. For the sculptor Maillol, forty years earlier, had pointed out to a guest how much Provence looks like Greece and that he had found "real Greek light" again in Elne, in neighboring Roussillon.

Heidegger's attention to and concern with what was Greek has deep roots. During his entire life, he was basically on the way to Greece and the brightness of the Greek islands. The following poem by Constantine Cavafy could serve as an epigram for the life sojourn of Heidegger:

Keep Ithaka always in your mind.
Arriving there is what you're destined for.
But don't hurry the journey at all.
Better if it lasts for years,
so you're old by the time you reach the island,
wealthy with all you've gained on the way,
not expecting Ithaka to make you rich.
Ithaka gave you the marvelous journey.
Without her you wouldn't have set out.
She has nothing left to give you now.[3]

The Monk from Bangkok

"Count Kuki has a lasting place in my memory." This sentence—which stands at the beginning of the dialogue on language that Heidegger placed between the texts of his lectures on Trakl and George in *On the Way to Language*—says more than it at first seems to. For, in recalling the Japanese count, a pathway opens up for Heidegger. It is the pathway that connects Heidegger's thinking with the world of the Far East.

The work whose title ("Aus einem Gespräch über die Sprache" [A Dialogue on Language])[4] characterizes it as part of a larger piece is one of the lesser known works of the philosopher. But it belongs among those that were significant in his own eyes. For in the coming together of an unnamed Japanese and an inquirer (easily recognizable as Heidegger), the course of the dialogue approaches the root-unfolding (*Wesen*) of language in a way that is peculiar to Heidegger's later work. It should be noted that this happens by way of a thoughtful association with a Japanese.

First, of course, we must ask whether Heidegger had any relationship at all with the world of the Far East and, if so, what that relationship was. Anyone who knows a little about Heidegger's life will have to respond positively to the first question. As early as the 1920s, Heidegger developed personal relationships with Japan. The same Count Kuki—introduced to the French language by the young tutor Jean-Paul Sartre, whom he told about Heidegger—was not the only Japanese student who then or later attended his lectures in Freiburg and contributed to his seminars. These students conveyed Heidegger's thinking back to their native country, where it was energetically taken up and sometimes understood even better than in Europe. Heidegger's writings were soon translated and read in Japanese.

In what is this understanding grounded? Why does the age-old legend "The Ox and Its Shepherd" (later translated by Hartmut Buchner) seem so strangely close to Heidegger? How did it come about that one of the poems composed on the occasion of the philosopher's death was written by a Japanese? Keiji Nishitani, the one who wrote the poem, and Koichi Tsujimura were both his students. Features that are common to Zen Buddhism and Heidegger have often been emphasized. Heidegger himself recognized his own thinking in many of Zen's views and found in Eastern thought much that he considered essential. Precisely because he met with so much misunderstanding and lack of understanding in the

West, Heidegger felt himself drawn more and more toward a world that received him so readily.

But even when he knew that men like Nishitani and Tsujimura understood him, he did not let himself believe that this was generally the case in the Eastern world of thinking and teaching. In a conversation in his last years with a German religious scholar, Heidegger was skeptical about "what his Japanese friends made out of his philosophy" and said that "he has difficulty believing blindly that thoughts in a language so foreign would mean the same." Perhaps the American editor of the writings of the Zen Buddhist Suzuki is right when he says that there is much in Heidegger's thinking that cannot be found in Zen and much more in Zen that cannot be found in Heidegger's thinking, but that the many points of agreement between Zen and Heidegger nevertheless remain exciting. In any case, it would be a mistake to want (as some have) to construct, over-zealously though with good intentions, a kind of thought-harmony that would span the peoples and to attempt a direct equation of Zen with Heidegger's many paths of thinking. The fact that for years Japanese, Vietnamese, Indians, and Siamese listened to his lectures does not prove such an equation. It does, however, indicate that thinking in the Eastern world encountered in Heidegger another congenial thinking, different from the calculative thinking of the modern West. This congeniality does not find the course of "Der Feldweg"[5] strange. (How excited Heidegger was one day when he gave me, as a gift, its Japanese translation, which he himself was not able to read!) What clearly emerges from the dialogue with the Japanese mentioned at the beginning is that caution is necessary in regard to these issues and that too-hasty movement can be damaging. Above all, this dialogue brings out what Heidegger never lost sight of— the dangers that threaten a thinker as soon as he steps on the insecure bridge that connects various languages. How seldom we succeed in finding a word, a sentence, or a concept in the foreign language of a dialogue partner that correctly and completely mirrors the thought. How often we suspect a certain fallacy with the first step we take. What possibilities of being led astray result from each new expression, without anyone's noticing.

A dangerous obstacle in communication is English, which is basically an unphilosophical language. Yet it is through English that Europeans gained access to the philosophical sources of the East. However rich English is in terms of vocabulary, it suffers a significant lack when it comes to words of *thinking*. Let me marginally mention one example.

In the 1950s, Heidegger asked me to pass judgment on a few pages he had received of the English-American translation of *Sein und Zeit* (Being and Time). Returning those pages to him after a few days, I strongly advised him against authorizing that translation. It certainly was the result of a great deal of effort, but almost every sentence either missed an essential point or failed to consider a perhaps-significant nuance of meaning. This was confirmed when we went through the translation sample together. At that time it seemed as though an adequate translation of this work would not be possible at all. Although more-sensitive attempts have since replaced the initial, inadequate translation, the conviction remained that in translating Heidegger there will always be an irresolvable remainder. At the same time, it cannot be denied that Heidegger's thinking is more appropriately brought to another shore in French or Spanish, for example, than in English.

The Japanese scholar Kakuzo Okakura wrote, "A translation is always an act of violence." And as a Chinese writer of the Ming period states, even the best translations can only be like the reverse side of a brocade: "Indeed, the threads are all present, but not the elegance and subtlety of the color and the design."

As far as Heidegger's relationship to the Far East is concerned, I often had to think in those days of the works of the two great artists whose forms and intentions were frequently associated with the Japanese. Heidegger had known Julius Bissier since his school days, and he became associated with Mark Tobey much later, in Basel. In their later creations, both painters, each in his own way, presented forms that recall something of a Buddhistic submersion and that Europeans felt as being inspired by the Far Eastern spirit. This is the case with Bissier's large, sketchlike watercolors and with his delicate and sophisticated miniatures, one of which carries the following lines: "Life's things lose their names, the entrance opens onto the land that has been thought." And many of the later color drawings by Tobey, who himself was in the Far East, speak an Eastern language without imitating that language. Both artists opened for art a window toward that world. Was it the same with Heidegger?

In Heidegger's study hung two sayings of Lao-tzu that Paul Shih-yi Hsiao, at Heidegger's request, had written on parchment rolls in Chinese characters. They are two lines from the fifteenth saying of Book One. In Walter Stroltz's translation they read:

Wer aber ist imstande, ein quirlend Wasser durch die Behutsamkeit der Stille zu klären?
(Who can clear the muddy water through the care of stillness?)

Wer aber ist imstande, die Ruhe durch die Behutsamkeit dauernder
Bewegung zu erzeugen?
(Who can bring about rest through the care of continued motion?)

For a long time a Japanese engraving by Moronobu showing a Zen
monastery, which I had given to Heidegger on his seventy fifth birthday,
hung next to these parchments. The engraving had belonged to my grandfather Wiegand's collection, the largest portion of which had been presented to the art museum in Bremen. During his first visit to Bremen,
Heidegger had carefully viewed what was left of this collection in my
family's possession, after he had unexpectedly read and interpreted a simile of Chuang-tzu (as I reported earlier). Thus he gave witness to his relation to a world that was familiar to the people of Bremen because of their
commercial connections and because of some precious collection items in
their museums. Many years after that "Japanese tea hour" at our house,
where he admired the colored woodcuts of Sharaku and Hokusai and
was deeply impressed by one of Utamaro's works (which showed a tiny
red beetle in the midst of a grayish world of grass), he once again talked
about Chuang-tzu in Bremen. During the seminar that Heidegger held on
the topic "Bild und Wort" (Image and Word), he placed the legend of the
belfry at the center of discussion. Once, when I had to write a report
about an important exhibition of Zen paintings and designs in Zurich,
Heidegger drew my attention to the relevant literature that he considered
significant.

As important as these contacts with the art and intellectual world of
the Far East was Heidegger's encounter with Emil Preetorius. He came
into frequent contact with Preetorius during sessions of the Bavarian
Academy of Fine Arts in Munich, whose president Preetorius had been
since 1953. This unusually versatile and productive illustrator, designer,
book artist, and stage designer possessed one of the largest and most valuable collections of East Asian art in Germany. Despite his age—he was
already seventy years old when he was elected president of the Academy—he was intellectually bright and fresh, was full of ideas, and had
the power of persuasion. He was repeatedly elected president; for fifteen
years he occupied the top position in the Academy, thus molding its character. He died in 1973, almost ninety years old.

He was one of the very few at Bühlerhöhe who was a genuine dialogue partner for Heidegger. The philosopher was amused, rather than
put off, by the often-strange mannerisms of the world traveler and intellectual manager—who stages Die Walküre one day in Paris, discusses the

decor for a performance of *Figaro* in Stockholm two days after that, and a little later assists a Japanese exhibition in London. Preetorius's contribution to a festschrift for Heidegger in 1959—on a word of Novalis—provides glimpses into what took place between them when they were together.

Inevitably, they also talked about Preetorius's collector's passion, which was admired by amateurs and professionals alike. On one of his visits to Munich, Heidegger was invited to see Preetorius's collection from the Far East, which was kept in his apartment in a high rise near Prinzregent Theater. Remembering the Japanese colored wood engravings that he had seen at my parents' house and considering my interest in the matter, Heidegger suggested that I accompany him. Preetorius readily accepted this suggestion. This turned out to be an unforgettable day; visibly excited by the interest of his guests, Preetorius spread out his treasure piece by piece, without being able to show them everything. The collection contained more than a thousand pictures, among which were many Japanese paintings; in addition, there were draperies, beautiful carpets, sculptures, and magnificent pieces of porcelain. Most of these pieces came from China and Japan; there were some riches from Korea as well. Heidegger was profoundly impressed by what he saw and asked many questions, to which Preetorius responded out of his immense knowledge. When we left around noon, it was not easy to go back to daily life in Munich.

However peripheral these remarks about Heidegger's relation to the East may be, I once witnessed directly his contact with the nature of the East, an event I will never forget. It happened when a Buddhist monk from Thailand visited Heidegger in Freiburg. The visit, arranged by the Southwest Radio Network, led to a conversation between the philosopher and the monk, as the latter had requested. This was one of those rare occasions on which Heidegger—against his inner conviction—reluctantly put himself within reach of the public. The visit became public knowledge through the broadcast of the Baden-Baden television studio. What was not known publicly was the more significant meeting that took place in Freiburg.

Thus the encounter with the monk had two parts: the television broadcast in Baden-Baden, and the discussion that took place at Heidegger's house in Zähringen—in strict privacy—for several hours, before the broadcast. It was only because this discussion went so well that Heidegger finally complied with the monk's request to speak once again in front of the television camera, to prepare a program specifically for Siamese

Buddhists. However, as is almost always the case on such occasions, the repetition of the meeting, with specifically prepared questions and responses, was a pale reflection of the first and spontaneous meeting, which took its course without prior arrangements. It was Heidegger's wish that I be present on both occasions. Thus, in a hotel in Baden-Baden during a brief tea hour prior to the television broadcast, I heard the monk speaking with amazement about his many impressions of the West—especially his impressions of things he was shown proudly as "achievements." I remember specifically his bitterness about "warehouses" for the elderly and children created in Germany in order "to get rid of them." Just as children belong in the circle of the family, and not in nursery schools, so also do the old people. Their experience demands respect and should be utilized by the youth. In Bangkok there is also a nursing home; but it is not occupied, because no one wants to push old people aside without, in doing so, being hated by everyone. What a contrast!

Almost thirty years old, Bhikku Maha Mani was the son of a peasant from Thailand, and as a monk belonged to the oldest of the four hundred temples in Bangkok. There he taught philosophy and psychology at the Buddhist university, was the shining star in his monastery school, and was highly prominent among the spiritual leaders of the East. The national radio entrusted him with broadcasting programs in the subjects he taught, and one of the most popular of these programs was "Buddha's Light Hour." Maha Mani was sent on a trip to Europe so that he could get better acquainted with modern Western reality. Without the slightest prejudice, he approached the phenomena of the technological epoch and the problems they posed and was convinced that technology would lead to a better life if one was not enslaved by it and used it moderately. He took television to be a challenge to the elite of every country to turn to as many people as possible. It was not until he was in Europe that he seemed to realize that there is a danger in the magic this medium produces.

The monk's statements during his trip, his brief conversations with workers, his fellow countrymen, scholars, clergymen, and functionaries were marketed at that time as one of television's usual cultural programs. But despite all the interest he took in the factories and institutions that he was shown, he was interested basically in one single encounter, for whose sake he had traveled to Germany. He wanted to meet *the* philosopher, who among all those alive thought and spoke, in his opinion, the most profoundly about technology. And that philosopher was Martin Heidegger.

I do not remember the details of the arrangement that Heidegger
made with television after overcoming many difficulties in regard to the
television interview. It was certainly only his long-standing sympathy for
the spiritual world of the East that prompted him to make himself available at all for such an interview. I was a little surprised when I heard
about the arrangement made with the television studio in Baden-Baden.
Heidegger still wanted to meet the monk first and to discuss with him
what was to be said in front of the camera. This Freiburg discussion took
place one afternoon in Zähringen. With a respectful bow, Heidegger received his guest at the door of his study. I am sure that Frau Heidegger
placed some refreshments there and offered a cup of tea, but I cannot
recall whether the monk drank anything. He only looked into the eyes of
the man in front of him—to whom he had been carried halfway across
the world by an airplane. I soon realized that this visit was the culmination of his trip and was the ultimate motive for undertaking it. The following is a report of this meeting, which I wrote down immediately, on
the evening of the same day.

"The monk wears a simple linen toga, of rose color (which, he says,
indicates the highest rank in the order). It reminds one of the toga used in
antiquity, which likewise was placed with a sweeping throw toward the
back over the right shoulder. He walks in very light, open sandals that
leave the foot and ankle free. His feet are as delicately built as his hands,
with their fine fingers. As soon as he raises his hands, which have been
resting one on top of the other, they make very meaningful gestures, but
without any passion. Nothing gives the impression of being rehearsed.
Occasionally there are gestures that build toward a magnificent power of
expression; but this happens only two or three times during the entire
meeting. One small gesture is unforgettable; it consists of the right fore-
finger moving horizontally outward from the corner of the right eye.
With a very small frown, the monk sometimes indicates that the translator did not make himself entirely intelligible. Even at its most intense,
when Heidegger almost gets excited, the conversation is never loud. The
monk's voice remains evenly restrained, light and permeated with friendliness. His voice does not betray how deeply he is moved—which he
shows only at the end, in a few words. He had anticipated this meeting as
the culmination of his trip.
"Conversation begins very differently than it would with a European
or American visitor. Such a visitor would put the question directly to Heidegger, asking something like 'What do you think about the relation be-

tween religion and humanism?' (This was the way the topic was initially formulated by the Southwest Radio Network for the program, which Heidegger then rejected.) But the monk is silent. Upon entering Heidegger's study, he surveys the room with astonishment and curiosity. Even the Japanese scroll on the wall behind the leather armchair where he sits fails to tempt him to say a word. Considering our European ways, what an opportunity for starting the conversation the saying of Lao-tzu written on that picture would be! But the monk is silent—because the first word belongs to the teacher of wisdom.

"Heidegger and the monk's companion exchange a few words about the details and the length of the monk's visit. Because the monk does not understand German and looks at me with expectation, I take advantage of a pause in the conversation and tell him that the professor has just learned that the monk has been traveling for a while in our country and that this visit is his last undertaking.

"Since Heidegger notices that the monk is expecting him to say something, he says that certainly his visitor has some questions in mind. The monk's companion responds by saying that there are indeed twelve questions. I translate this for the monk, who smiles at me, looks over to Heidegger, and says, 'No—fifteen!'[6] We laugh.

"Now Heidegger takes up the thread and poses a question that immediately determines the level of the conversation. He inquires about the attitude of the monk and his fellow countrymen in Siam toward modern European technology. What seems to them to be the distinctive mark and essential character of this phenomenon? The monk responds that he does not entirely understand this question, since he is only concerned with whether or not this thing (technology) is 'good' for humans. Then he adds, 'We never say no to a thing in advance.' Heidegger then wishes to know what the monk means by 'good.' Comprehension is already becoming difficult. Sentence by sentence, the vehicle of the English language makes it clear how little this vehicle can do beyond attending to the very basics. On the other hand, the monk realizes quite well that there is no room here for commonplaces. Frequently, he shakes his head in regret and mumbles that he cannot find adequate words in English for what he wants to ask or to say.

"After setting aside his initial question for a moment—a question that later enters the discussion in a different way—Heidegger continues with another question. How do Eastern and Western thinking relate to each other? The monk perceives an obvious contrast between the two. In what does this contrast consist?

"Heidegger is of the opinion that the issue has to do with the role of the mediator. He himself holds to Lao-tzu, but he knows Lao-tzu only through the German mediators—for example, Richard Wilhelm. However, as far as Eastern thought is concerned, it also comes to us in another form. But how does the knowledge of Western thought reach the East? The monk responds that this happens through English books. Even what he himself knows about Heidegger he knows, besides through many oral communications, through English publications. Heidegger, looking concerned, doubts whether the crucial issues could be transmitted at all in that way, since the English language is completely unphilosophical—as the monk himself pointed out earlier. English is much less philosophical than, for instance, French, in which a new word had to be constructed for what Heidegger means by *Sein* (being).

"The monk agrees. He then asks what the crucial issue in Heidegger's thinking is. Is it this *Sein* that so much distinguishes Heidegger's philosophy from the rest of European thinking? Heidegger affirms this; he is concerned with the question of being, which for almost two and a half millennia has been forgotten in the West. (The philosopher explains this once again in the Baden-Baden television interview by saying that meditation on the history of Western thinking has shown him that thus far thinking has never posed this question. But the question is significant because Western thinking determines the being of humans insofar as they relate to being and exist in terms of this relationship and insofar as they correspond to being. This means that, as such corresponding beings, humans have language. He is of the opinion that, in contrast to Buddhist doctrine, Western thinking draws an essential distinction between humans and other living beings, such as plants and animals. 'Humans are distinguished by their knowing relation to being.' The question of being that has been hidden from us in history so far must be posed now in order to find an answer to the question as to what and who humans are.) The monk listens very attentively, but he is still unclear as to what Heidegger actually means by the expression 'being.'

"A long and mutually shared attempt is then made to explain this word—an attempt that demonstrates the inadequacies of the English expression 'The Being.'⁷ I try to show how we take a teacup or a bowl as a being without ever perceiving that which allows a being to be a being and lets a being appear *as* something. Heidegger adds that, for a Westerner, *Sein* (being) equals *Anwesenheit*. It turns out, however, that the English word 'presence' is by no means enough to state entirely what *Anwesenheit* means.

"The monk receives all of this quite attentively, interposing a couple of small questions. It is clear, however, that he is waiting for something else. I take advantage of a brief pause and turn to the monk to ask whether it is not more appropriate to begin his various questions if we are to avoid speaking only about Western thinking and possibly getting stuck there. The monk looks at me with a smile, then looks at Heidegger and states that he has already posed a whole series of his questions and received responses to them. Later on Heidegger says to me, 'You were quite right with your question. But because these people never *count*, we did not notice at all that he put his questions. A European would use words like "first," "then," "thirdly," and so forth. But here there is no such thing as a logical sequence. Rather, everything emerges from the *one and only* midpoint.'

"The monk takes up the conversation and asks in what way technology, which Heidegger understands to mean something different from and by far older than machines, has become a danger for the thinking of Europeans. Heidegger responds by discussing the essential character of European, or Western, science, which in each of its separate realms is already technology. Putting itself *between* human beings and what they inquire about, this science deprives the actual questions of thinking of any foundation. This is so because science is increasingly concerned with what is calculable, while thinking occurs far from any calculation. The responses of thinking do not bring 'results' in the sense that this word has in the sciences. . . .

"The monk inquires whether there is a connection between modern technology (science and industrialization as well)[8] and philosophy. Heidegger answers the question affirmatively, saying that there is a very essential connection between them. Modern technology has emerged from out of philosophy, that is, from modern philosophy, which for the first time set up the proposition that the real is only what we can know clearly, with mathematical certainty. There is the famous statement of the German physicist Max Planck—'Only what is measurable is real.' The thought that reality is accessible to humans to the extent that it is measurable in accordance with mathematical physics determines the whole of physics and technology. And insofar as this idea is thought for the first time by Descartes, the founder of modern philosophy, the connection between modern technology and philosophical thinking is quite clear.

"As the discussion in Freiburg continues, it becomes clear that the separation of subject from object, which occurs once and for all in science and seems to be irrevocable, prevents thinking from actually unfolding.

Even one who is once touched by essential thinking falls necessarily into this separation, which makes Western humanity appear dichotomized. As Heidegger repeatedly points out, we are not really free, but are in a prison that we carry around with us our entire life. His whole life's work, he says, has been devoted to a freeing from this prison. However, this involves fighting the superior power of two millennia—since Plato. The burden of history is present in every process of thinking. But vis-à-vis Eastern thinking, it is this history that actually separates East and West.

"Heidegger is silent, and the monk finally states very calmly, 'We do not recognize history. There are only passages through the world.' Heidegger emphasizes again that this point of difference in attitudes toward the world is what makes impossible a simple comparison of the theses of philosophy in West and East, here and there. Whoever attempts such a comparison is responsible for a falsification, because the presuppositions are different.

"The monk listens as discussion turns to the question of how various formations of religion and its dogma have contributed to enhancing these oppositions. The gap becomes increasingly visible as it becomes clearer that the East does not have anything approximately comparable to 'faith' in the West. At this point the monk raises a very explicit question, which I repeat because of its crucial significance: *Does Heidegger consider it more important to set up a new system of thinking, or would he put emphasis on the necessity of religion?*

"After I translate this into German, I suggest to Heidegger that he should first eliminate everything that is understood to be a system. Thus Heidegger states that he has no system. What matters is whether one can co-enact Heidegger's path of thinking. The only significant thing is 'to be on the way.'

"The monk indicates complete agreement. Then he repeats the second part of his question. With an almost passionate determination, Heidegger then wants to know what the monk takes religion to be. Dogmas and doctrines? Or that which constitutes their origin? Then he turns to me and says, 'Now you must really try to make clear the difference between Christianity and being Christian (*Christlichkeit*)'—which turns out to be a difficult matter. But a further explanation is not necessary because the monk says quite simply that by religion he understands the teachings of the founders ("sayings of the founders")[9].

"Excited and very determined, Heidegger responds by turning to me and saying, 'Tell him that I consider one thing alone to be crucial—

namely, to follow the words of the founder. This alone—neither systems nor doctrines and dogmas are important. *Religion means following.*

"The philosopher and the monk silently look at each other for a long time. Do we all now think on the same thing—Buddha and Christ? This is the first high point of the discussion.

"After a while Heidegger calms down and asks me to tell the monk once again that the oblivion of being discussed earlier—along with the ensuing dichotomy and prison—is responsible for the fact that we Westerners are closed off to the sphere of the holy. (Since the English word 'holy' is easily misunderstood, I try in translation to work with the word 'das Heile' [the whole], which I make intelligible after several definitions and after drawing upon the notion of harmony.) Heidegger then adds, 'Without the holy, we do not come into contact with the divine; and without being touched by the divine, we have no experience of God.' He says that no one understands this.

"The monk, who understands the last sentence without translation and who throughout watched Heidegger with close attention, turns to him and says warmly, 'Come to our country. Everyone will understand you.' For a long time there is silence in the room.

"Once again Heidegger takes up the question of whether it is necessary to describe a new path of thinking or whether it is important to stress more strongly what religion has proclaimed so far. He believes he has already made clear to what extent a new way of thinking is necessary. This new thinking is necessary because we cannot raise the question concerning humans from within religion and also because the Western relation to the wholeness of the world is today no longer transparent, but confused. This confusion stems in part from the various orientations of the faith of the church and in part from philosophy and science and from the remarkable circumstance that in the modern world science itself is considered to be a kind of religion. The task of thinking today, according to Heidegger, is new in that it requires a whole new method of thinking.

"As Heidegger explained later in Baden-Baden, this method can be attained in the immediacy of a dialogue between human beings and to some extent by practicing 'seeing in thinking.' This kind of thinking can initially be enacted by a few people, but it can then be passed along through various realms of education to other people. Then Heidegger adds, 'Let me give you an example. Nowadays everyone in Germany can handle a radio or television set without knowing what physical principles underlie their operation—without knowing what methods were required for investigating these principles. There are methods whose actual character is basically understood by perhaps four or five physicists. The case of thinking is similar. This thinking is perhaps so difficult that only a few people could be educated in it. . . .'

"When Heidegger leaves the room briefly to get a book—despite the monk's statement that he would rather read it later, that right now he does not wish to look at a book because it is so refreshing to speak with Heidegger ('because it is so fresh speaking with the Professor')[10]—the monk turns to me and says that this is a good discussion. He wonders why the professor does not want this discussion to reach all human beings. Would I be able to tell him he should present it once again in front of the television?[11] He, Maha Mani, would then like to show Heidegger to his people; he adds, 'In my country people revere him very much. In Germany, however, when I asked many people on the street whether they knew who Heidegger was, no one knew the name. Why not? In our country people know and respect the names of the wise ones. I also asked intellectuals; they were informed, but that is not interesting.'

"At this moment Heidegger returns. The monk politely takes the book that Heidegger hands him and reads carefully the English sentence that is supposed to explain something to him. Then once again he turns directly to Heidegger and says that Heidegger has undoubtedly thought much about technology—adding, with a look toward the writing desk, 'I am even certain about this.' But why does Heidegger refrain from using the available means in order to address simple people? He and his brothers do that frequently in Thailand. Heidegger should certainly agree that each person has the potential to develop humanity's ability for thinking.

"In his response (to which I add what he said on the television program in Baden-Baden), Heidegger goes back to what he stated earlier. By saying that initially only a few people can learn this new thinking, he could easily have given rise to a misunderstanding—that these people are superior people. 'In truth, every human being as a thinking being is capable of enacting this thinking. But in our system of education and in keeping with our history, only a few people are capable of appropriating the presuppositions of this thinking.' In our Western world, the ability to think, about which Maha Mani talks, is blocked. This ability is covered up by doctrines of philosophy as well as religion. 'We have too much culture.' We are stuck in that prison, so that it is very difficult for the individual to get through.

"But doesn't Heidegger go into his small city ('village'),[12] in order to talk to his people, as one hears? Heidegger responds that yes, he much prefers to speak with his people. This is true. Then the monk asks whether people elsewhere in Germany are also Heidegger's countrymen. If so, why do we always hear people say that Heidegger is too difficult and no one can understand him? Basically, in fact, it is quite simple to understand him; one must only listen properly. Why does Heidegger never go to the people?

"Heidegger is noticeably affected. He tries to explain that it has primarily to do with the development of thinking, which was addressed earlier in various ways—namely, with how the predisposition of thinking he described makes people lose their openness to simple hearing (and listening). For instance, if he spoke to Catholics, Catholicism as such would stand in the way (though there are always individuals who, exceptionally, could suddenly be affected). Even the best theologians, Catholic as well as Protestant, take from what he says only what fits their own views. Even they refuse to see the whole of his thinking, of what he says.

"The monk suggests that perhaps it depends on precisely these individuals—and that they are everywhere. Heidegger responds that he can reach them only through dialogue and not through the technological means. Here I make an interjection and suggest that, through his lectures and speeches, it has frequently happened in his life that Heidegger reaches individuals—and I mention myself as an example. And he *writes*, too, I add.

"Heidegger smiles and, in agreement with what I just said, adds that he has often been told that those who have heard him speak also *read* his text as if they *hear* it—he is thus present even in reading. . . . At this point the monk interjects that so far he has read little by Heidegger and has only heard other things about him. But throughout the monk's trip across Europe, Heidegger has nonetheless been his companion!

"Still, Heidegger insists that television is not a genuine means, because what is said through television is not binding and is subject to distortion. . . .

"The monk abandons this topic and raises a final and crucial question. What, in Heidegger's opinion, should be done to overcome the pre-disposition and the prejudice so that unity is restored beyond the dichotomy? Heidegger answers that the way can be opened only through releasement toward things and openness to the mystery.

"The reservations about religion and its failure in the present state of the world, merely touched upon earlier, are discussed. Maha Mani asks whether religion, as well as philosophy, should be 'abolished'[13] because—despite their existence for millennia—neither succeeds in bringing about peaceful coexistence among humans. Heidegger emphatically disagrees. He says that we cannot and should not abolish thinking and faith because they do not achieve what they have striven for throughout a long history. And we cannot abolish this thinking and faith, because humanity's root-unfolding, its *Wesen,* is finite: In accord with this root-unfolding, humanity is always required to engage in new attempts. With respect to the present time, Heidegger would suggest that a meditation on what humanity is and who humanity is is necessary—today, when there is the danger that humanity will one day be entirely delivered over to technology and that it will become a regulated machine.

"The monk, who is obviously concerned with a practical attitude in life and with harmony among people, once again raises a question in this direction. Heidegger finds no common ground on which people could come together in psychological and human terms, given our entire historical situation and humanity's dispersion in various religions, in various philosophies, and in various relationships to science—no common ground on which there would immediately and simply be a mutual understanding.

"Heidegger says, 'We must consider the large difference between a European country, with its history, and a country like the one in which you are at home.' Self-determination of people, which is necessary in every respect, becomes difficult, because today—not only in Germany, but also in Europe as a whole—there is no unambiguous, common, and simple relationship to reality and to ourselves. That is the great deficiency of the Western world, and this deficiency contributes to the confusion of opinions in various realms.

"Heidegger had spoken of releasement and openness to mystery, so the nature of meditation is finally discussed. What does meditation mean for Eastern humanity? The monk's response is quite simple: Meditation means 'to gather oneself.' The more humanity succeeds in gathering itself and concentrating, without exertion of the will, the more it lets go of itself. The 'I' dissolves, until in the end only one thing remains: the Nothing. But this Nothing is not nothing; it is just the opposite—fullness. No one can name this. But it is nothing and everything—fullness. Heidegger understands this and says, 'This is what I have been saying throughout my whole life.'

"Once again the monk says, 'Come to my country; we understand you.'

"Heidegger is quite moved. He closes the discussion by turning to me and saying, 'Please tell him that all my fame in the world does not mean anything to me if I am not understood and find no understanding. Therefore, I not only am grateful for this discussion, but consider it to be a confirmation of a kind that I have seldom been granted.'

"The two stand up and face each other for a while. Then the monk bows deeply and leaves. The dialogue took more than two hours, and now it is night.

"The tension eases only gradually. The Heideggers invite me to stay for the evening meal. But first I must show where Bangkok is in Frau Heidegger's old school atlas. Then we discuss a whole set of individual observations. Heidegger and I are in agreement that the monk's face shows something purely childlike—something between what is animallike and what is spiritual, but without childishness, because of the presence of the highest level of consciousness. His face shows how wholesome his whole being as a man is. His deep-seated eyes are wonderful, and—in contrast to Japanese eyes—look at you fully and openly. In him there is no duality between the mind and the senses. His seriousness and his relaxed cheerfulness are unforgettable.

"Heidegger nevertheless felt strongly that people such as this monk do not have the slightest idea what the technological setting, with which we deal, actually means. They take technology and use it as they would a hammer or a pin. They are somehow little impressed by Western technology—and just as little do they know what occurs as *Ge-Stell*.[14]

"Heidegger was right. A year (or perhaps more) after this meeting with the monk, he phoned to tell me something sad: The monk with whom that good discussion had taken place had left his order and taken a position with an American television company."

I knew how highly Heidegger esteemed Lao-tzu. But only after he died did I learn that at one point he began translating the *Tao Te Ching*. When Ernst Jünger was about to start his trip to East Asia in 1966, Heidegger included a saying of the old sage in his letter to Jünger. I am grateful to Jünger for being able to quote that saying at the end of this chapter devoted to Heidegger's relationship to the Far East—a relationship embodied in the meeting with a Buddhist monk. It is the forty-seventh chapter of the *Tao Te Ching* and reads, in the translation by Jan Ulenbrook, as follows:

Nicht zum Tor hinausgehen
   und die Welt kennen,
Nicht zum Fenster hinausspähen
   und den Himmel ganz sehen:
Geht man sehr weit hinaus,
   weiss man sehr wenig.
Darum der Weise:
   nicht reist er,
      doch er kennt,
   nicht guckt er,
      doch er rühmt,
   nicht handelt er,
      doch er vollendet.

(Without stirring abroad
One can know the whole world,
Without looking out the window
One can see the whole heavens:
The further one goes
The less one knows
Therefore the sage knows without having to stir
Identifies without having to see
Accomplishes without having to act.)[15]

Heidegger could have set a stanza by a late European poet, which mirrors the West, alongside this saying from the East. I am referring to Gottfried Benn's "Statische Gedichte," which reads:

. . . .
Richtungen vertreten,
Handeln,
Zu- und Abreisen
ist das Zeichen einer Welt,
die nicht klar sieht.
Vor meinem Fenster
—sagt der Weise—
ist ein Tal,
darin sammeln sich die Schatten,
zwei Pappeln säumen einen Weg,
du weisst—wohin.

(To advocate positions,
To act,
To travel to and to travel from

are markings of a world
that does not see clearly.
Before my window
—says the sage—
is a valley
where shadows gather,
where two poplars mark the edge of a path—
and you know where it leads.)

8

The Autumn Years

Living in Freiburg

Autumn years are harvest years. What kind of harvest could the philosopher in his old age—he had already passed sixty—gather, in the old place, and after everything that had happened to him? Without ever becoming a philosophical disciple in the strict sense of the term, I, Heidegger's onetime student, enjoyed at that time his growing confidence and soon his cordial friendship. Although giving up the residence in Icking intended for my parents' old age had been done for other reasons and was not directly related to my move to Freiburg, Heidegger's presence in this city constituted something like a secret point of reference for my future life. In the next two decades, his presence meant guidance and companionship to me and in retrospect obliges me to confess my honest and sincere gratitude.

It seemed at first almost unreal to be able to return safely to the place of bygone times, after so many upheavals in the world. It seemed unreal to find, in the midst of the heavily damaged city, the rooms of the beautiful Billing University left almost intact—where janitor Thoma was still working, just as twenty-two years ago! And once again to listen to Heidegger's lectures. The old fascination with those sessions took over again—and yet everything was different. My own life, into which war and war's end had cut deeply and irrevocably, had found its own shape. The old friends were no longer around with whom I used to discuss Heidegger's words far into the night, with a glass of wine in Kopf or in Oberkirch.[1] A true and resounding echo did not seem to emerge from being with strangers with whom I could not easily communicate, as I once did with my fellow students—despite the intensity with which those who attended Heidegger's lectures followed "Der Weg zur Sprache" (The Way to Language). Soon, however, I found new friends. Above all, my relationship with Heidegger himself had changed over these twenty-five years. The attentive attitude of one who listens to a lecture course turned into a friendship, which was no less attentive and which led me to ask myself whether this could be true.

In my copy of the first volume of Heidegger's Nietzsche lectures (which is arranged according to content, not according to the sequence of lecture sessions, and which characteristically carries the remark "the written and printed text lacks the advantages of oral presentation"), Heidegger wrote, "With cordial thanks for your assistance. Freiburg, May 1961." This expression of gratitude refers to the assistance that I provided in correcting the galley proofs, which had taken much time. These proofs were not the only ones that I read. On another occasion Heidegger requested, "I would like to use your skillful eyes again." To participate in this way in Heidegger's work was felt to be a distinction. It required the highest precision and also provided one with opportunities for detailed discussion. It was the galley proofs of his publications that took me frequently to Heidegger's house in Zähringen.

Our work together on the proofs and the discussion of the corrections was usually followed by a long walk, which often led us to the Jägerhäusle—a friendly and somewhat "grandfatherly" place that reflected its comfortable Alemannic name; it had a beautiful chestnut garden and lay on the mountain slope overlooking the city. The Panorama Hotel, which today stands in its place, has failed to preserve anything of the old magic of the place where students and Freiburgers drank their glasses of wine. Heidegger liked this tavern; he often took the table in the corner so that we might talk together undisturbed. I still possess numerous postcards of his, lying between his letters, in which he requests that we work together in the afternoon and then "go to the Jägerhäusle." Our walks in the high streets leading to the Jägerhäusle belong to the most beautiful memories of that period—walks taken up by words that have long since scattered but that have left behind an unforgettable radiance.

After a telephone was installed in Heidegger's house and in mine, the telephone replaced the postcard. We had frequent appointments in the city, where Heidegger liked the old Zum Falken tavern. This tavern, too, fell victim to modernization; and its setting, transformed into that of a first-class hotel, lives only a borrowed existence as a wine restaurant and has retained little of its original charm. Heidegger and I often sat in the Thoma-Stüble of the Falken or in one of its deep window corners and had a glass of wine whose "label" we tested like experts. Once on a winter evening something surprising happened. We were about to leave and were already standing at the exit of the restaurant when a young woman, obviously a student, approached Heidegger, mumbled a couple of words in embarrassment, and handed him a piece of paper. Heidegger was no less embarrassed and looked at me helplessly. I had to laugh; I gave him my pen and told him he should give the young lady his autograph. While he stood there writing his name, I added, "Please do not forget the date. That is important." Radiating delight, the beautiful autograph-seeker bowed to the great man who had fulfilled her wish. Outside in the snow, Heidegger stood shaking his head and said, "Such a thing!" This was indeed his first autograph in Freiburg. I commented, "Yes, Herr Professor, when one is famous, such things happen." Then he laughed.

In a short piece of prose, Frau Heidegger once described the visit of a fictitious student to the Heideggers' house at Rötebuck, which was designed largely according to her ideas and was built by the Heideggers in the still mostly undeveloped suburb of Zähringen after their return from Marburg in 1928. Whoever took the road that led to that house went through something like the experience of the young man she described. The road led from the last trolley stop across the hill in a little more than a quarter of an hour to Rötebuckweg, passing by a couple of constructions that looked half like city dwellings and half like farmhouses; beyond them, in those days, the open land extended up to a forested flank of the mountain. On the left side, almost hidden behind a high, living hedge, was Number 47—a simple house with a shingled exterior and a wide, protective roof. The famous professor was supposed to live here? "The young man walks across the straight garden path between the flower beds toward the door of the house and climbs a couple of steps under a small roof designed for protection from the rain. However, before he rings the bell—beside which he reads on a little card 'Visits after 5 P.M.'—he is surprised. For above the wooden beam of the door, a proverb from the Bible is engraved, something he did not expect to find here. Thus unexpectedly attuned to reflectiveness, he is confronted with yet another surprise upon entering the house. The foyer is wide, separated by a floor-to-ceiling glass wall, and opens into a single, bright room in which there is a piano and an old armchair. Behind these there is another large window, which reaches to the floor and opens onto a terrace half-covered by a protruding higher floor. The terrace provides a place for sitting and in summertime is the center of life for the family. Wide steps lead from the terrace to a garden full of flowers. Thus upon entering the house, the visitor is enveloped by the whole radiating expanse of the meadows and the dark edge of the forest beyond. This is a house that 'seems to absorb the whole of nature.' Adalbert Stifter would have loved this house.

"A door is open on the side toward a living room with a few beautiful pieces of furniture from the Biedermeier period. The waiting student, however, has no more time to look around, because he must now climb a well turned stairway—a craftsmen's masterwork—to the next floor, where beside a huge family closet a clock, made in Hellerau, hangs on the wall—the pride of the family. Now things become serious: The professor is waiting."

How many visitors will remember most clearly Heidegger's study, whether they entered it once or more often? This study seems dark, as the walls are covered with wooden bookshelves and the light streams into it through an ivy-clad window in the northeast corner of the room. The large writing desk in front of the window has often been described, with a simple chair from which the writer, when looking up, could see all the way to the tower of Zähringen's ruins. Beside this desk there was the leather armchair in which generations of visitors sat, from Bultmann and Sartre to the nameless student who would not forget this visit. Nor would he forget the confusing look of the writing desk—covered with numerous slips of paper (spread out according to an unfathomable system, many with only a single word in German, Greek, or Latin), along with the earliest drafts covered with yellow, green, and blue arrows: the "switching yard" of a railroad station, as Heidegger's brother Fritz called the manuscripts. But there were also days when there were only a few pages on the desk, in strict order—when the main task of the day had been accomplished and the next step of the project visibly laid out. Otherwise one could assume one had interrupted the work process and would want to reproach oneself for having done so. A small picture frame with a photograph of Heidegger's mother always claimed its place on this desk. Besides a heavily loaded table of books and a couch, this room contained nothing else.

Because it was tailored entirely to the needs of its inhabitants, especially to those of its master, the house in Zähringen was one of the most unforgettably livable houses I ever walked into. When Heidegger left this house after his eightieth birthday and moved to a residence built for his old age on ground level at the lower edge of the garden, some of the Biedermeier pieces accompanied him; but his old study remained almost intact. A younger generation took possession of the big house. The new one was basically like a tent; it was a last station in which the thinker was allotted five more happy years to live. Practical considerations led to this decision, whose planning was clearly in Frau Heidegger's capable hands. Besides, this new residence had a spacious attic for housing the visiting friends and students from France. For, even under the changed external conditions, Beaufret, Vezin, and Fédier did not want to give up their yearly visits, which Heidegger reciprocated in Provence. These French "invasions" occurred regularly in very highly intellectual moods. But the walls of the small study in the comfortable and simple little house at Fillibachstrasse 25 heard other significant conversations. It was in this house that Heidegger discussed the plan for the *Gesamtausgabe*[2] for hours every week with his loyal assistant Friedrich-Wilhelm von Herrmann. And it was also in this house that in January 1976 a conversation took place with his friend from Messkirch, the clergyman Bernhard Welte, in which Heidegger deliberately prepared for the last stage of his way.

Frau Heidegger's interest in building—which was practically confirmed not only in designing the residence for their old age but also in designing the house at Rötebuck in the 1920s—saw architecture as art. This interest was transferred to her husband, noticeable above and beyond Heidegger's lecture "Building, Dwelling, Thinking." This lecture, to an unusual degree, caught the attention of one of the greatest architects of our time, Alvar Aalto. On Aalto's writing desk, friends noticed the volume that contained the text of this lecture and reported this to Freiburg. When I was coming back from Finland, I ran into some young Finnish architects who were likewise talking about that lecture. When soon thereafter I reported all of this to Heidegger, he was very pleased; and he gave me the assignment of taking his greetings to Aalto when I repeated the trip as planned the following year. But the death of the great architect kept me from making a connection between the two men, which I would have only too happily done.

The growing fame and the ever-increasing number of visitors from around the world were sometimes annoying to Heidegger, although a strict family routine kept him enclosed and protected his working hours. I remember the rather amusing incident one Sunday afternoon when a South American family of many members requested permission to enter the house with the desire expressed stammeringly as "Seulement voir Monsieur Heidegger" (Only to see Mr. Heidegger). After receiving permission and inspecting the prodigy while bowing to him, they left without uttering a word. Such worldwide fame had no influence on family life at Rötebuck. It was a simple life, without even the smallest luxury that would have transgressed the set limit. Thus I felt entirely at home when I was occasionally invited to dinner. In the afternoon, following a good custom from Baden, a glass of wine was served instead of tea up in the study; and the glasses that came from Bremen were always employed. Outside of Zähringen, we saw each other less frequently in the city—

except for appointments to meet in Eberhard Albert's bookstore, where Frau Kiehne and Herr Werner would show Heidegger the recent publications. On these occasions he often gave important hints, when we discussed these books.

It was an intellectual banquet when Heidegger came as a guest to my apartment, as he did once in a while. He seemed to feel comfortable there; and he enjoyed the familiar things he knew from Bremen, or the desk at which he had worked in Icking and at which he had written a poem. This was an atmosphere of intimate familiarity. The occasion for such visits was often my request that he recite to a small circle of friends, including guests from the North, and give us an opportunity for a discussion. Then six or eight of us would sit together and have a cup of tea, according to the Bremen custom, until Heidegger would get up, go to the window, and say, "According to my old habit, I would like to recite standing up." This was always his response to such afternoon gatherings. That was how my apartment in Littenweiler was "dedicated" in 1959 ("to a happy dwelling"). This was also how I heard his Nietzsche lecture in November 1960, after I had missed it in Bremen. Later he spoke about Goethe, Schiller, and Hölderlin, and in August 1962 he came with his brother Fritz to show him my "dwelling." On that occasion he wrote Max Kommerell's words in my guest book: "For we depend on being replenished." Heidegger, who was then almost eighty years old, came to my apartment for the last time on that cheerful winter evening of 1967 when he once again met Alberto Wagner.

There are still other memories from Freiburg that well up. Our trip together to see the Japanese film *Rashomon*, which in those days was causing a great sensation, was unforgettable. It was on this occasion that Heidegger's strong interest in the spirit and phenomenon of the Far East first became obvious to me. The "Dialogue with a Japanese" [3] reflects this afternoon at the movie. He attended the chamber music concerts of the Albert Zyklus, which attained a high international status that winter. By contrast, he avoided the theater; like George, he rather disliked the stage. Once I succeeded in taking him to the Wallgraben Theater, where a number of students skillfully and thoughtfully staged some plays of Beckett. This happened after I told him about the conversation pertaining to Heidegger that I had had in Bern with the Irish playwright. Another time I persuaded him to go to an unusually successful performance in Freiburg of *The Marriage of Figaro*, staged by Jean-Pierre Ponelle and directed by Leopold Hager. This full-length performance, which utilized superb acting and singing powers, pleased him extraordinarily. For here Mozart could be seen and heard in near perfection, and it agreed most nicely with Heidegger's as well as my own love for Mozart.

Finally, I recall another evening at the theater—not in Freiburg, but in Bremen, while Heidegger was visiting. For some reason or other, his host and other friends were busy with other things, and plans we had for that evening had to be canceled. So what to do? I looked at the entertainment column of the newspaper and discovered that *Doña Rosita* by Lorca was playing at the theater. Since I had seen the unforgettable performance of this piece by Jürgen Fehling in Munich, it had become my favorite work of the Spanish playwright; and I thought I could propose to Heidegger that we go to the theater that evening. What I did not know was that he, too, liked Lorca very much. That evening something unusual happened. The three of us—Heidegger, a former student of his, and I—sat together watching a good performance of this piece, staged by Hannes Razum; the acting was also satisfying. In the third act, while Aunt Rositas—forced as she is to give up her present way of life—bids farewell to her old high school professor Don Martin, who is ridiculed and harassed by his insolent students, I sensed that something was happening to Heidegger—as if he were peculiarly touched by what was happening on stage. And while the courageous old housemaid was narrating that, when she hears from the coal merchant's shop the professor discussing "What is an idea?" and does not understand it, then she must laugh—saying that "even when I do not know, I still realize that Don Martin is important"— during this scene and finally, as the cruelty of the noisy students returned the professor from his dreams of Parnassus to the world marked by incomprehension, I heard Heidegger quietly whispering, "Yes, that is me." Heidegger seemed to be pointing to himself "with a countenance sealed with sadness," as Lorca indicated in his instructions for directing the play. This was one of those rare coincidences for which one can find no words.

Hikes around Todtnauberg

On the way from Notschrei-Pass to Feldberg, which takes several hours to walk, an excursion in the Black Forest brings one to a lonely-looking inn at the foot of the Stübenwasen mountain ridge. The wooden structure, darkened by weathering, lies at the edge of the forest, which grows up to this high point from all sides only to make room for individual clusters of trees, berry bushes, and wide-ranging meadows of moss. Only a short distance from the inn there are magnificent panoramas: north and northwest to Kandel and, beyond the Rhine Valley, to the mountain range of the Vosges. A little further up, the view opens out toward the south and southwest onto the summit of the Belchen and the sky. On clear days in late fall, the snow-covered summits and ice fields of the Alps glitter across the entire southern horizon—an overwhelming panorama from Säntis to Mont Blanc. If one climbs up a bit higher on the gently sloping side of the Stübenwasen, one sees way down below the farmhouses of Todtnauberg, nestled in the hollow of the valley and scattered over the hillsides. Climbing up still further, one sees to the left the steep Waldkessel of the St. Wilhelm Valley and, with luck, chamois climbing the rocks.

Whenever I arrived at this mountain guesthouse—and this happened each autumn for ten years—I assured the owner that he had set his house on the most beautiful spot of the High Black Forest. The Kirner couple had come from Wiesental and chosen this spot deliberately, carefully considering business interests, but heeding equally the love they had inherited for their native mountains. This was a truly comfortable shelter, which I initially chose upon Heidegger's recommendation and never wanted to abandon. Only after the Kirners—with whom I developed a friendly relationship in the course of time—had moved into the valley because of their age (the elderly Kirner, a genuine Black Forester died shortly thereafter) and the house was leased did I give up living there in the fall. For its time was over for me, too.

But what was the reason it was difficult for me to break away from the Stübenwasen each time? What made it difficult for me to leave this October happiness up there, this most beautiful time of the year when only a few vacationers returned from their excursions and when I was not infrequently the last guest, once even staying until All Saints' Day? What made it difficult to abandon the days when I would leave the inn in the early morning hours in order to greet the distant Alps, when the sun and the blue sky tempted me to wander far away, to be alone in the forest among beeches and to be with the rustling of the brooks—until evening, when I would return to the simple, cozy comfort of the inn? Or the foggy days when the mail carrier from Todtnauberg would ride the whole way up just to bring "Herr Doktor" a single letter—upon which I would invite him to have a glass of kirsch and talk with me a little, until he and his bicycle disappeared down the hill and into the woods? These were days of stillness, like islands in the midst of the pressures of time—stillness for working, reading, and meditating.

The real reason for returning each year to the Stübenwasen had to do with the latter—it was the proximity to the "hut." Among friends and students of Heidegger, this word has a special meaning. For the mountain hut that Heidegger built in the innermost recess of the valley on the slope above the place called the "Rütte," with its few old farmhouses—this hut can as little be separated from his life as the course of his thinking. Was it the slopes, which in winter were covered with deep snow, that initially attracted Heidegger, the avid skier? Or was it the magnificent solitude, pregnant with thought, that drew him there? *Being and Time* was written in one of the farmhouses of the Rütte. Higher up on the mountain slope, Heidegger built the hut, thus creating for himself that simple, ascetic dwelling place for thinking—a place that provided him with the breathing space he needed, away from everything that belongs to the city.

The hut in Todtnauberg became a fixed concept and has often been described. This hut provoked the curiosity of those who had never been there. There were good reasons for not inviting everyone to go there. And to find the hut required perseverance. Heidegger has been accused of wanting to be different because he frequently withdrew to Todtnauberg, when he could have found an even more stringent peace and quiet for work in his brother's house in Messkirch. At times it was also said he was unable to adjust to social convention (which did not mean anything to him). What *was* this oft-mentioned "hut"?

An informed and philosophically educated writer once said that we cannot know who Heidegger the thinker and the man is unless we see the "hut." What did this writer find there? Just the simple wooden structure, without any exterior or interior decoration; and the monklike furnishings of the study, where, as he put it, nothing that would delight the eye was to be found in the thinker's proximity: "Its meagerness works like ice." And then he added, "Near the hut, through a pipe covered with wood, springwater splashes into a wooden trough. This is picturesque, but nothing more." One cannot carry sobriety and studied matter-of-factness in reporting any further than that. This writer grasps and reports what is characteristic and obvious to the eye, but basically he fails to see the significance that these things have *in* the philosopher's ambience and *for* this ambience. Shortly before this writer visited the hut, he had heard the philosopher say that what is creative grows only out of native soil. Here in these surroundings, reduced to the ultimate, inexpressible simplicity and corresponding to the thinker's way of thinking, counter as they were to whatever is merely pleasing, compliant, and flatteringly decorative—in such an environment this writer could have felt the external conditions for that growth. That he characterized the gushing water of the spring out there as "picturesque, but nothing more" shows that during his visit he did not succeed in getting closer to the thinking nature of the man who lived in the hut. Does not this also show how he could arrive at the daring but mistaken claim with which he sums up his report—namely, that the hut proves Heidegger's homelessness?

This was perhaps the worst misunderstanding. Yet there were other kinds of misunderstandings that were no less mistaken—such as the marveling enthusiasm that came in many forms and that culminated in the exclamation of a lady from the city, who said, "How delightful it must be to live here close to nature and to enjoy the passing of the seasons." Upon hearing this, Heidegger became reserved. Was this reserve his way of expressing anger about so much stupidity? "Yes, but only if you think it is fun to live up here and to sit alone behind this desk in winter, when the timber creaks in the storm and the stove fails to warm up the room and loneliness creeps through every hole!" The lady then became silent. One could have quoted to her the following lines by Ernst Stadler:

The green pines of the Black Forest murmur in front of my window as if they wanted to talk about new voyages.
The wooden planks of my hut crack in November storms
and threaten to break into pieces. . . .

Let me merely intimate how things appeared to the lonely inhabitant of the hut, both outside and inside. The thinker who battled against himself up there and struggled with what was to be thought never liked being there unless he could come to his task fully prepared. One is reminded of another small house, not unlike Heidegger's hut. It is in Sils Maria— Nietzsche's loneliness.

There is one description of the hut that is perhaps the best that has been written about it and its inhabitant. It is likely that this description is not known to a larger audience. Because a good or even excellent formulation loses its excellence if paraphrased, I shall reproduce that account here, abbreviating it only slightly. I am referring to the description that Max Kommerell offered Erika Kommerell, after he and Gadamer had visited Heidegger's hut in the late summer of 1941:

"We climb up the large and gently winding meadows, passing by the edge of the forest . . . until suddenly a shack with a shining roof rises up from the ground. Going up a couple of wooden steps, one sees a kitchen, in which a sturdy camp bed is installed. In front of the kitchen there is a room with a table, a couple of chairs, and a very small window. Heidegger emerges from a second room and greets me with a prolonged and peculiar smile. He invites us to sit, pours us a glass of healthy but sour wine from a bottle of Markgräfler, and without much ado begins to recite simply and impressively in a poetic and quiet voice. I am free to fathom the face, which is taut and brown and not at all peasantlike, as it is often described. It is small, elegant, and astute, a little sad, with a certain lostness in the eyes; it is a lostness peculiar to one who, after the most rigorous tests of reason's doubting, reaches the other side of doubt and lives by certainties that he shares with no one—certainties that protect him from others but threaten him through himself. . . .

"Through the small window the sun shines into the dark [ante chamber], and with its sharp and tiny beams seems to remind us that it can still make halos, martyrs' crowns, tongues of fire, and similar signs of prophecy. . . . Sometimes he [Heidegger] has a delicate smile that is just a tiny, tiny bit crazy. How much I liked him because of that. . . . I thought, 'You, with your delicate knuckles, brown skin, and small frame, with your nods, hints, and way of whisking around until the wife appears and forces you back into your usual motions—you have your own way of living, to which not only the hut but also the landscape belongs, a landscape in which you know every tree and every farmer knows you. In the midst of a famous, active, and very public life, you have acquired a measure of solitude, which is necessary for you. Half of the year you surrender yourself here entirely to yourself, and in your work you have the inner passion of consuming yourself, the more noble as it serves no purpose. Regardless of whether I grasp your thinking of being or whether that thinking grasps me, I greet you as one who also takes things seriously and who, despite the reproach of wanting to topple everything, is pleased to look me in the face and to show me the native landscape, since my name sounds likable to him because of a couple of works—and after that as if nothing happened. . . .'

"Another day he invited me to come alone for a while. . . . It was the most perfect and the most immaculate Sunday . . . with the austere solitude of these summits and forest gorges around Feldberg and the long, deeply cut and clearly visible valleys that lie there like the history of a life, especially when the entire chain of the Alps is radiant. . . . Early in the morning I found him sitting behind a small desk in front of the hut and writing, presumably continuing one of those manuscripts—which inside the hut are placed in neat compartments above the writing desk, none of them yet published. . . . He finds his personal dimensions uninteresting and uses himself as a vehicle for problems. Up here his life is a perfect monologue, whereas his reading, as well as his going down to the university and teaching, are increasingly something transitory. . . .

"He invited me to go with him for a hike. . . . With a voice that is a little thin, not deep, but soft and resonant (and when it conceals itself in mumbling has something especially captivating about it), he spoke with me about everything. It became evident that in his loneliness he takes good note of people and things and, in something like a strategy, organizes a thousand things in his memory. For, in spite of the vehemence with which he rejects and despises the possibility of directly having an effect, time is to him a transition through catastrophes; and with his voice and even his eyes he would like to reach out to those in whom he notices something originary. . . . We parted very cordially."

Kommerell's letter contains an entire compendium of key Heidegger words. For anyone who was in the hut often and knew its daily routine, these key words mirror aspects of some of the occurrences one would experience up there. The hut of the thinker sheltered more than the "shack" that it was sometimes taken to be at first glance.

If I wanted to count how many times I took the road from the Stüben-wasen to the hut in the fifties and sixties, I could only guess, because I was invited so frequently to tea in the afternoon. The usual path, which led from the youth hostel of Todtnauberg to the hut and which was preferable in bad weather, took almost an hour. But soon I discovered a shortcut, which left the small street a little earlier, passed over the slopes, crossed a brook, and went through the most beautiful woods. I could make it in forty minutes, with frequent stops in order to pick the last bluebell, daisy, and clover for Frau Heidegger as a decoration for her table. As time passed, I noticed many signposts on this path and was always glad to arrive at the spot where that very old pine tree stood and below which the roof of the hut became visible.

Tea hours were not to take too long; autumn days were becoming too short and Heidegger was anxious to get going. For these walks—"his" walks—which often lasted far into the twilight, were from Heidegger's point of view obviously the real reason for my visiting the hut. The paths we took together often went far—across the mountain at the edge of the forest, toward the summit of the Stübenwasen or toward the Feld-bergsträssle. Another path led us toward the west, past the youth hostel and around the "Horn," along a wooded slope of the mountain that emerged ahead of us. The latter path offered the possibility of walking side by side and was more appropriate for conversing. After first addressing personal matters—Heidegger, in a most delicate fashion, used to inquire with interest about the events and experiences pertaining to the life of his guest—conversation would soon turn to his guest's work plans. In those days I was often traveling during early spring and summer and thus was able to tell him either about important art exhibitions I had visited in Baden-Baden, Karlsruhe, or Basel, or about my trips abroad. I told Heidegger about the exhibition of the *Europa Rat* in Aachen, London, and Stockholm; Charlemagne and Christina of Sweden were occasions for detailed historical discussions. More than once we spoke about experiences with modern art in Munich or in Bern, while personal encounters with Chagall and his daughter or conversation with Beckett, as mentioned before, played some roles in our conversations. It was on one of these walks that I told Heidegger about the unusual impression I received from the art of Mark Tobey—the wise old man whom Heidegger himself got to know later in Basel.

On these walks we spoke not only of artists and art works that interested me—professionally or personally—but frequently also of the poetic forces of our time. We spoke about Rilke and the constantly increasing inflation of the Rilke literature; I frequently brought Heidegger new publications from my large Rilke library and recommended one or another to him. The noises that some writers made about Rilke, which turned into journalism, annoyed him.

Another topic we often discussed was Gottfried Benn. I have already mentioned a conversation I had with Heidegger in Freiburg in which he expressed his displeasure with new works by Benn, which Limes-Verlag released in an almost hasty succession. He was of the opinion that none of the poems contained in these new releases reached the level of those poems that had been offered to the German public a short while ago in the volume *Statische Gedichte*. Then Benn had poems that even Heidegger considered his own, most protected inner possession. And he surprised some people by mentioning Benn's name in response to an inquiry about the most esteemed poem in the German language. By contrast, Heidegger's attitude toward lectures and prose pieces that Benn published at that time was entirely negative. I had to hear him criticize severely Benn's *Probleme der Lyrik*, which Heidegger considered to be a total failure.

The third master of writing who "accompanied" us on some of our evenings and who was at first largely unknown to me was Joseph Conrad. Heidegger thought highly of Conrad and considered him to be a genuine *Dichter*.[4] Once he told me that I would be amazed at Conrad's *The Shadow Line* when I read it. He was right. And I understood why Hofmannsthal considered the little volume *Youth* to be one of the most extraordinary stories in world literature. From Conrad our conversation frequently turned to Knut Hamsun, whose *Last Chapter* was initially the only thing I knew by him. Heidegger considered this to be Hamsun's weakest novel and recommended to me his *Victoria, Hunger,* and particularly the trilogy of *August Weltumsegler,* which was one of Heidegger's favorite books.

As a historian, I was interested in talking about some historical presentations that I valued. I especially liked Ricarda Huch, in view of my innate big-city sensibility. But I had no success with her with Heidegger. He returned her book *Alte und neue Götter* to me half-read. I could have anticipated his reaction. For this book treats "history" most expertly, but from Heidegger's perspective it fails in regard to the event of "Geschichte." [5] Perhaps he found the noticeable "poetic element" of this book less attractive than disturbing. By contrast, he admired very much another woman writer, Marie Luise Kaschnitz. As a North German who was at that time still unfamiliar with Rome, I did not know anything about her until Heidegger mentioned her to me on one of our walks in the forest. Her *Beschreibung eines Dorfes*—a poem in prose that begins close to the earth and culminates by becoming visionary—made Heidegger so happy and enthusiastic that in the winter when this little blue Suhrkamp volume appeared (not yet disfigured by illustrations), he kept sending it out as a Christmas present.

The walks in the course of which we spoke about artists, poets, and often also philosophers always came to an end much too early. Fading light was a warning to return home, and I had still a further way to go. As soon as we arrived at the "entrance gate" where the pathway above the hut branched out, Heidegger would say, "Now, do take the longer way, not the one through the forest, so that you find your way back home. The Kirners will wait for you with the evening meal." That was indeed the case. The Kirners knew where I went and that I did not come back too quickly. Thus I would walk uphill for an hour, guided in the end only by the luminous thread of the road, with the stars of the night shining through the branches above me.

There were also nasty, cloudy, wet, and foggy days up there, on which the appointment for a walk still had to be kept. In an emergency there was the possibility of a phone call through the hut-keeper at the youth hostel. Once on a rainy afternoon I found Heidegger ready to go. He said, "We want to go right away." There was no tea, and Frau Heidegger did not say anything. The philosopher was emphatically silent and did not want to be talked to, so I followed him without a word. Only after a long while and when we were high up in the forest did he say, "Today you must help me break the forest laws." Seeing my amazement and disbelief, he pointed to a small pine tree that had fallen and dried out long ago, now lying there without any of its needles. He pulled out a small handsaw and began to cut the tree skillfully. He noticed my mild surprise and said laconically, "My wife needs wood for the stove." The thought that he was now going to break the forest laws made me a bit uncomfortable, for what he was doing was indeed such an offense. I thought, if we are caught in the act and hanged for it, so be it; this is a situation that does not happen every day. We carried the little tree down through the woods, Heidegger in front and I at the back; and as we were crossing the Feldbergsträssle, we ran into none other than the forester! I was amazed at Heidegger's composure as he struck up a conversation with the forester and continued it all the way to the point where we had to turn toward the hut. When we arrived at the hut, he smiled and said that he had wanted to scare me a little with "breaking the forest laws." Many years ago, he said, he had done the same thing with Gadamer— which I later found confirmed by a photograph in Gadamer's book *Philosophische Lehrjahre*. But this offense is one that the community authorizes, as it permits the inhabitants to fetch firewood from the forest. The forester knew that, too. Today I wonder whether the small handsaw was not just an additional trick. Back at the hut, the tea was waiting and a powerful schnapps helped raise our spirits. We were quite cheerful on this late afternoon.

The peace of mind guaranteed by the consistency of work was something that Heidegger did not want disturbed in the hut. For this reason I valued highly the fact that I was not considered a disagreeable interruption. Afternoons in the hut became a tradition for all the years to come; and when one year I failed to stay in the Stübenwasen, he wrote me from up there to say that he missed me. Besides Beda Allemann and Ernst Tugendhat, both of whom Heidegger esteemed highly, I met only Carl Friedrich von Weizsäcker up there. The latter recalls in his memoirs that Heidegger guided him down through the forest along a path that suddenly vanished where water sprang from under the moss. Since I was present on that occasion, I was able to yell, "Watch out, Professor, it's getting wet there!" Heidegger laughed and said, "Yes, this is the forest path (*Holzweg*)[6] that leads to the sources" (which he did not say in his book). Our walk ended high above Todtnauberg in the dusk as the full moon appeared in the sky and the dome of Belchen rose sharply against the western sky. As the first stars began to shine and the windows of the farmhouses down in the valley lit up warmly, appearing to answer the stars, I felt delighted and expressed my pleasure over this play of light. Von Weizsäcker did not seem to like this poetic talk and started to speak about the physical reasons that the light of the stars and the light of the lamps appear differently to the eye. . . . Heidegger must have noticed my embarrassed disappointment; he laughed and dismissed the lecture, saying, "Petzet, you forget that Herr von Weizsäcker is a physicist and that you cannot talk with him as a poet."

The hut and the poets—this topic needs a chapter of its own. Above all, Hebel's name should be mentioned. A faded color picture of him hung in the corner of the room where Heidegger occasionally recited Alemannic poems to his guests. This was a fixed custom on every 26 September,[7] when the peasant women from the Rütte came up to congratulate Heidegger and were served coffee and birthday cake. No one else was invited to this ritual.

Once, after the war, the important poet Paul Celan visited Heidegger at the hut. I did not meet him myself, but saw the very strong impression he left on Heidegger, who was later deeply moved by Celan's poem "Todtnauberg." It is regrettable that this poem, whose published versions differ from each other in one crucial word, has become a bone of contention. There is a dispute over the meaning of that word because a political shadow looms over Celan's mysterious reference to "eines Denkenden kommendes [or "ungesäumt kommendes"?] Wort."[8] Celan's inscription in the guest book at the hut, which lies at the root of the poem, contains nothing but a hope for the word that is to come—indicating, according to Beda Allemann, the German editor of Celan, an expectation of a coming poet and not of a political admission of regret. This is so because, as Allemann puts it, "When understood sufficiently radically, Heidegger's dialogue with poets, including Celan, points to nothing but a future poet and his work—'future' meant here of course not in a simple way."

Celan's visit made the thinker happy. For the poet understood the spring as the giver of vitality:

Arnika, Augentrost/
Trunk aus dem Brunnen mit dem
Sternwürfel drauf . . .

(Arnica, eye-bright,
the draft from the well with the starred die above it . . .)[9]

From early on, the hut enabled the poetic in Heidegger to come to language, as is quite clear in the short work *Aus der Erfahrung des Denkens*.[10] This work unfolds *Denk-Sätze* (sentences of thinking) from out of a highly poetic attunement and gaze into nature, each of which remains closely connected to nature. The first edition—which was printed privately in Switzerland, a small and loosely bound booklet with handwritten corrections—makes clear that this work was published in commemoration of the twenty-fifth anniversary of the existence of the hut and was intended to celebrate that occasion. The later editions, which juxtapose the words of both spheres [thinking and poetizing], conceal this.

To own a copy of the first edition was like a distinction. Whenever I pick up the small booklet and remember the hut, I recall three lines from Hölderlin:

> Im heiligen Schatten aber
> Am grünen Abhang wohnet
> Der Hirt und schauet die Gipfel . . .

> (But in the holy shadow
> On the green slope dwells
> The shepherd who looks to the summit . . .)

A Hebel Day

Part of the seeming provincialism of which Heidegger has often been accused consists in his loving intercession for Johann Peter Hebel and his poetry. These accusations occasionally become grotesque—lampoons that abandon not only scholarly reliability, but also human decency. Today, in the technological world, we frequently come upon a state of mind that is capable of perceiving the much-discussed phenomenon of humanness (*Humanum*) only in the forms of highly educated, intellectual urbanity and that has either lost or deliberately given up any deep relation to the roots of human origins. In such a perspective, notions like "homeland" (*Heimat*) or "rootedness" (*Bodenständigkeit*) quickly become dangerous and irritating words and are deplored as backward by enlightened knowledge or ridiculed by sociological progress. It would seem that one small step separates "provincial" from political "reactionary."

I mention this in order to indicate the clichés frequently used about Heidegger and to explain the attempts that have been made to discredit him. However, nothing among all this reaches the truth of the matter— what is in jeopardy here is a human being, and this has hardly yet been felt. This is not the place for polemics. But it shows how much more necessary it is to renounce the slogans and to learn how to listen again. And such listening involves above all listening to the poets—in this particular case, listening to the poet Hebel, who is labeled "provincial."

In his laudatory remarks about the recipient of the Hebel Prize of 1960, the former minister of culture of Baden-Württemberg, Gerhard Storz, characterized this recipient as one who "showed Hebel as a poet who belonged to the whole world," who "acquired the right of citizenship" not only in his Alemannic homeland, but also "in the much larger intellectual world of Germany, and indeed of Europe." The recipient, he continued, liberated Hebel from the narrowness of being a local poet and a lovable but minor master and gave back to Hebel his true rank. The recipient of the Hebel Prize of whom the minister spoke was Martin Heidegger. Storz suggested that, by putting his dialogues with Hebel side by side with his interpretations of Hölderlin, Trakl, and Rilke, Heidegger protects Hebel from being mistakenly included as a poet of the people in the notion of "native art" that national socialism advocated.

Another German poet, with whom Heidegger allegedly does not have a good relationship—Goethe—also saw that Hebel "would take his place in the German Parnassus." One of the provocative aspects of the relationship between Germans and their literature is the fact that Goethe understood the Alemannic poems of Hebel without philological assistance. He expressed the hope that the entire treasure of the German language would be made available through a general dictionary; but, he added, "practical communication through poems and writing occurs faster and grips one more vigorously." What was still possible for Goethe is no longer possible for today's readers and audiences. While Goethe understood the elements of "naive language . . . as instilled in a style by fortunate constructions and lively forms"—a style superior to our literary language—Heidegger had to accept his wife's objection that "the gentlemen from Der Spiegel do not understand" Hebel's language, as he was about to recite from Hebel's poems at the hut. To deny Frau Heidegger's objection was presumably just politeness. But, as early as 1804, Goethe indicated that "recitation" is one of the various means for allowing the entire nation to happily enjoy these poems. Thus Heidegger acted entirely in accord with Goethe when he recited the Alemannischen Gedichte in the hut. The audience's willingness was Heidegger's best reward; and his recitations of "Die Wiese," "Der Sommerabend," and "Das Habermus," as well as the magnificent poem "Vergänglichkeit," will never be forgotten by those who heard them.

Although he was born in faraway Heuberg, Heidegger was intimately bound to the highlands his whole life—as was Hebel, though he was driven to the lower regions, toward Karlsruhe. Heidegger could carry on small talk with peasants in their own language. And while he was writing *Being and Time* in the "Lord's corner" [11] of the sooty living room of a farmhouse in the Rütte, he heard the great-grandmother speaking words that were no longer intelligible to the younger members of the family. (He mentioned this in one of his lectures.) It was an expression of a most profound connectedness with the language of that region that in 1960 Heidegger received the Hebel Prize, which Albert Schweitzer and Carl Jacob Burckhardt had received before him.

In his speech on the occasion of receiving the Hebel Prize before a varied audience in Hausen—there were people from the city and the countryside, including a considerable number from Todtnauberg—Heidegger took up those ambiguous and mysterious words of the poem that concludes the *Alemannischen Gedichte*. There Hebel speaks of the grave in "chüle Grund," of the place with a mysterious door "und sin no Sachen ehne dra," which philosophers, in their way of speaking, characterize as "the transcendent." In masterful language, concentrated and simple in comparison with the weighty language of the earlier part of his speech, Heidegger led the audience to that mysterious door "out of which emerges all poetizing and thinking." He quoted lines from a poem by Hebel entitled "Ekstase," discovered by Wilhelm Altwegg only ten years earlier. These lines say that language, even the language of poets, cannot express what is unthinkable:

> Kein Wort der Sprache sagts—
> kein Bild des Lebens malts
>
> (No word of the language can say it—
> no image of life can paint it)

Nonetheless, the unthinkable becomes present through the poetizing word; and what cannot be heard or seen by the senses—the stillness of things, as they light up and abide—comes closer to humans.

When a few days later I sent Heidegger the report I had published on the Hebel Day in Hausen, he thanked me and sent along a transcript of his short speech, adding, "Incidentally, the gentleman from Basel [i.e., from the Hebel Foundation] clearly did not like it that a wholly different aspect of Hebel's nature became visible. They would have liked to keep the 'Boppeles-Hebel'." [12] He then went on to say that as far as the poem

"Ekstase" is concerned, we need a higher level of thinking in order to address this issue properly. He added that he had deliberately left out the last line from the stanza beginning "Die Sprache, die in Tönen schallt." The last line reads, "Wie selig sich's im Nichts zerwallt." This *Nichts* (Nothing), however, is the basis and core of the whole poem and remained so in the subsequent decades of Hebel's life. In this connection Heidegger referred me to a letter from Hebel to his friend Hitzig (of February 1797), in which the poet talks about his studies in Kantian philosophy and arrives at this conclusion: "There is only one system, only one philosophy—ours. This philosophy is essentially different from all the rest in that it resides on a ground which in Kant's case is 'nothing' and in our case is at least *the* Nothing."

If Heidegger had quoted the conclusion of the poem, would his audience have followed him without reservation? Would they not have said, here comes Heidegger again with his *Nichts* (No-thing)? Still the old existentialist! Presumably, no one would have inquired what this No-thing means. Thus the joy of the Hebel Day remained undisturbed, a joy that in the opinion of the poet truly belongs to the seriousness of that day. This could not have been better confirmed than with the cheerfulness and naturalness with which people of the Markgraf region (famous for its wine) held the traditional Hebel Festival, their spring celebration. There could have been no May day more beautiful. This day lighted up the house in which the young Johann Peter grew up and put that *Hebelmähli*[13] in the proper light, as twelve old villagers came together there with the earlier Hebel Prize winners. Lina Kromer recited her Alemannic poems, and Heidegger listened with a satisfied countenance.

This was a day in the spirit of Hebel, which could mislead one who viewed it from the outside into believing that this day had to do only with the Biedermeier flavor, which is alien to our time. But those who are familiar with the letters that the ecclesiastical councillor and prelate from Karlsruhe wrote in his beloved highlands will know better. When conversation with Heidegger turned to Hebel, these letters were never forgotten; and references along these lines continued to have an effect long after— as with *Merk's Wien* of Abraham a Sancta Clara. There is, for instance, Hebel's letter of August 1804 to his friend Hitzig, in which Hebel describes his meeting with Heinrich Stilling and suggests that being with such a man for just one minute transforms him into a believing child: "With such a disposition as my own, I am pleased to know that you consider such a mysticism necessary for religious faith. Only we should never say it because we are supposed not to know it, we are supposed to have mysticism without knowing that we have it and we should have no name for it." There should be no name for such a "quiet little domestic ghost" that is readily bewitched when it is named—and thus more easily goes out of the heart, where it works quietly and calmly, to the head, where it makes much mischief.

Strange thoughts, coming from an ecclesiastical councillor! Stranger still were the thoughts expressed in a later letter to his friend, where Hebel seems to advocate polytheism. Heidegger considered that letter a significant document. Hebel fears that the previous God of philosophy, baptized and preached to, stands on shaky ground. His worshipers are praying to a definition: "Their God remains forever an abstract thing and never becomes concrete." When the poet goes on to say that it is only the faith in which he has been raised that prevents him from "building little churches for the blessed gods" and that he would find satisfaction with one or more gods of this earth who encompass us, who "open up our blossoming buds and help ripen our grapes, on whom we can rely, and who need to be concerned as little as we do with who takes care of other stars," then behind the world of these native poems something else becomes visible that is perhaps discernible in the stanzas of the poem called "Vergänglichkeit." When, in the letter to Hitzig, Hebel suggests further that those gods need not be all-powerful and all-knowing but only powerful and wise enough for us, need not be sovereign but subordinate to gods more powerful and wise "with whom they are to be concerned, not we," then one remembers Goethe's words in his review of *Alemannischen Gedichte*, when he writes that in these poems the higher godhead remains in the background.

Is this the "Boppeles-Hebel"? The "Boppeles-Hebel" was an easy Hebel destined for easy use. Heidegger saw Hebel, the genuine *Hausfreund*[14] (friend of the family), entirely differently. He saw a poet who took his place in the German Parnassus and still holds that place. As Goethe affectionately called him in his memoirs *Sonntagsfrühe von Sesenheim*, he was the "inestimable Hebel."

The Brothers from Messkirch

"And what are you working on now?" This was a question one had to anticipate whenever Heidegger invited one for a conversation, a walk in the woods, or a glass of wine in the afternoon. Himself being an inexhaustible worker, Heidegger could hardly imagine someone who would let a day go by without the toil of work. But he did not consider work as either slavery or a hectic process. Work was for him the steady and un-ceasing responsibility for traversing one's own way and building on it. To him, work was a holy burden, which he carried without forcing or rush-ing himself to do so. Like all the great workers—Kant, for example—Heidegger allowed himself a break from the toil of work. Whoever heard him laugh knew how joyful Heidegger could feel. Heidegger as the always-gloomy "existentialist" is a fairy tale—and an ugly one, at that—which has been propagated intentionally by persons of ill will. In his youth Goethe wrote in a letter, "The pressure of jobs is good for the soul. Once this pressure is relieved, the soul plays more freely." If we replace the word "jobs" with "the task of a great work," then Goethe's remark applies fully to Heidegger, the only difference being that Heidegger was never relieved from the assignment. On the contrary, the assignment be-came more difficult as he grew older. Occasionally he enjoyed saying that he could not do anything better than to think nothing. He said this espe-cially when he felt that someone was pitying him for the difficult work of thinking that he had to carry on. But heard properly, this statement of his had the kind of ambiguity that pleased him.

He took a sincere interest in the work of his friends. However, he could also catch one who was not self-disciplined enough: "Because last time you came unprepared and because Klee is nevertheless quite an im-portant issue for you, I would like to ask you to meet with me on Good Friday at 3 P.M., for a walk in the woods" (22 March 1959). Another time Heidegger added the following sentence to an invitation for a meal: "Then we can at least address your questions, without resolving them." A mere look at the philosopher's writing desk in Zähringen would im-mediately bring me into an atmosphere filled entirely with the matters that pertained to his work. At Christmastime in 1953, when I sent him a book by a philosophy professor who is forgotten today and who special-ized in Kant, Heidegger responded by saying that I was a master at track-ing down rare and suitable books. That book touched Heidegger's own work. "The very first sentence of the introduction impressed me: 'Think-ing is the element in which a human being flourishes best.' This sentence is not meant as a clarification, as is said and shown by what follows." The work of thinking guaranteed Heidegger his flourishing.

But what has all this got to do with Messkirch, Heidegger's native city, in which the arc of his life begins and to which we now turn? To put it succinctly, Messkirch for Heidegger was synonymous with his work in his last years. Some of the things said and written about his relation with his old home town are accurate; but many of them are regrettably stupid.

To mistake Heidegger's relation to Messkirch for provinciality is possible only from a perspective that is often peculiar to contemporary human beings—a perspective that, I would almost like to say, is reinforced with concrete and limited by that "urban limitation." It seems that the ability to feel the roots of things fails and people everywhere walk on forest paths, *Holzwege*,[15] that do *not* lead to the sources. Where mere intellectuality dominates the field, "homeland" (*Heimat*) is ultimately understood either as a set of syllables or as the sentimentality of a revived folklore.

What Heidegger understood by "homeland" and experienced as such up to his old age had nothing to do with sentimentality. He held memories from Messkirch, as even the most indifferent inhabitants of a big city hold memories of their place of origin. These memories certainly allowed him to see this old, small, provincial town differently than a stranger would—this town with its four-towered castle that belonged to Count von Zimmern and its St. Martin's Church towering high above the jumble of streets. But Messkirch was not the place in the inner Heuberg where he might have pathetically or sentimentally withdrawn—a place that, when seen from the outside, could be called, in part with admiration and in part with light sarcasm, the birthplace of such varied masters as Conradin Kreuzer, Johannes Baptist Seele, Conrad Gröber, and himself— "Messkirch's Corner of Genius." Basically, it was being at home in the native language and being sheltered among its people that gave him the feeling of belonging and from which he had his start. Heidegger lived his early youth in Messkirch. He went to Konstanz in 1903, since his talent was recognized and he was motivated to become a priest; and in 1906 he went from Konstanz to Freiburg in order to attend the gymnasium. Nevertheless, during vacations and later on, during his academic career, he returned frequently to his home in Messkirch.

This loyalty to the country path is a main feature of Heidegger's life. It was on this country path that he reflected on "some or other of the books of the great thinkers," as these books lay on the bench along the country path. In conversation he never betrayed anything more about this than what that sentence in "Der Feldweg" indicates. To be introduced to the reticence of matters that pertain to homeland does not mean that these matters will be straightforwardly exposed. I remember very well my first visit to Messkirch, when Heidegger walked with me through the streets along the south side of the Hofgarten under the linden trees. Ultimately we came to the "Feldweg," which had not yet been paved. Coming back through the dark courtyards of the castle, we returned to the square in front of the church, with its almost repulsive front and its tower with a Roman dome that can be seen from far away. Before dusk set in, we walked through the church, saw the three kings painted in shining gold by nameless masters, and looked for a certain bench in the choir. The stalls were enveloped in darkness; we finally found the one where the small choirboy had secretly carved his initials in the wood as he was beginning to get bored with too much Latin during ministration. These initials are still there today; and the eternal light still shines on the "MH" with which he wanted to "immortalize" himself and with which in a very different sense he reached out beyond his time.

Another path runs beyond the small river Ablach to St. Mary's, a small church with affected little towers. This brought up the subject of the old Catholic community, which held its religious services there. In the 1970s, after the First Vatican Council, this community grew so rapidly that the main church of St. Martin's belonged to the old Catholics for almost two decades. Was this an indication of religious rebelliousness? Perhaps it indicated the intellectual independence of the people of Messkirch, who did not accept anything without reservation. I would have liked to know more about all of this, but I did not like to ask too many questions at the time Heidegger told me about it. This was because I came from the strictly Protestant—indeed, Calvinistic—North and was rather shy and even clumsy in dealing with my Catholic countrymen. Only later, on a long walk, did Heidegger tell me—hinting, rather than explicitly stating—how it was made immeasurably difficult for him to separate himself from theology, to give up the career of a priest and to embark on his own path. (Much of his sometimes-noticeable disinclination toward the power and the influence of the black-clad clergy becomes more intelligible in this respect.) The fact that he nevertheless did not become a renegade, a careless apostate, but remained in the old church—a church that did not deny him a Christian burial—was perhaps one of this life's mysteries that lay upon its sufferings, sufferings that were never entirely overcome. We spoke only once about it. A Protestant religious service in Bremen's cathedral left him cold. In Ronchamp, however, where we visited the new pilgrimage church by Corbusier, he left us to an "examination" of the architecture, because he wanted to follow the mass that was being said in a novel way by a young priest in front of the pilgrims.

When we spoke about Heidegger's childhood and adolescence, his father and mother came up in conversation. Her picture was on Heidegger's writing desk in Freiburg; her features bore the stamp of a goodness born out of suffering. His "Feldweg" indicates only a little of the world of the three children—he did not speak much about it. The writer Hans Bender once wrote to Heidegger, wanting to know his opinion about earlier teachers as he (Bender) prepared for publication a comparison of today's teaching methods with earlier ones. Heidegger responded that this was not a question that could be easily dealt with, because it required reaching back very far. Discussions about Bender's question seemed to center on the issue of whether earlier teachers were actually "caricatures," as they are still thought to be, or whether they endowed the student with something for life.

In a conversation in Heidegger's study in Freiburg, I said that I could not really imagine that the teacher was the man with the slouch hat and the stick, as he is often portrayed. Heidegger's response was that this, regrettably, had been the case: "When I think back to elementary school, I remember the beatings. The teacher needed only to point with his little finger and the delinquent student was spread out for a beating. Teachers beat and beat—with a cudgel."

When I commented that his small piece of reality from Messkirch reminded me about what Rilke, in his memoirs of his terrible school days, reproached his old teacher Major General Sedlakowitz with, Heidegger said, "Yes indeed, but later, in the gymnasium in Konstanz, things were different. In Konstanz teachers were strict, too; but we could learn from them even if they were often quite strange—like our Greek teacher" (the latter was the clergyman Hahn from Rast, whom I have already mentioned).

We spoke about other disciplines and found that what is nowadays called "art studies" was not taught in the schools at that time. Was there no concern for art? Was art completely ignored? Naturally, I was interested in this question, and we had a short conversation on the role of art in the curriculum of those days. Heidegger said, "What is today called art studies was in those days represented in drawing classes, in which all of us boarding-school children had to participate. This took place in a rather large classroom that was also used for choir exercises. The drawing teacher, a strange fellow, would install himself on the rostrum. Actually, he did not care about anything. He faced his own drawing paper and would draw to provide an example. He would be occupied only with his own art throughout the class session. From time to time a student would walk over to him on the rostrum and show him a more or less completed opus, receive a 'Good! Good!' and return to his seat. Until the appearance of another student . . ."

"And what about you?" I asked.

"I would sit as close to the edge of the rostrum as possible, right under the teacher's nose, so close that he actually could not see me when he occasionally surveyed his herd of art-loving and devoted students. In my 'blind spot' I could spread the paper in front of me like a protective shield. I would then get a dismantled ship with lots of sails and rigging as my model to draw from. When my ship was standing nicely in front of me, I could read behind it without being disturbed."

"And what did you read in those days?" I asked inquisitively.

"Adalbert Stifter!" said Heidegger, and reached out to the bookshelf near his writing desk. "You see this old volume? On its front page is written 'Christmas 1905.' For Christmas I had asked for the edition of Stifter's works, and I read it during the drawing classes. Only from time to time I had to present my ship."

"And how did the other students do?"

"I had a friend who was the best in drawing and sat way in the back. Because he drew so well, he was the only one to receive a 'model'—a real skull. But because he drew so nicely and the teacher never looked in his direction, he read Gorky behind the skull. Naturally, this was quite dangerous. Just think of the year—1906! But because I wanted to take part in it, we did the reading together outside of the drawing class, in order not to be discovered. We used to go to the Konstanz harbor and climb into one of the small brake rooms that old boxcars had. There we would read, without showing any interest in the ships that lay in the quay. If only our teachers had known that their pupils were reading Maxim Gorky!"

Messkirch! I still possess a small photo that Heidegger sent me at Christmas in 1952: "The photo shows a place northwest of the castle where I used to hang around a lot as a boy." Was this the improvised soccer field of the Messkirch youth, where little Martin used to play left wing? Even later, he never denied this role of his in sports, although it was generally known that he was a good skier and swimmer. I was thus somewhat surprised when one day, in the early sixties, he asked me whether anyone where I lived in Freiburg had a television set and, if so, whether he could be accepted as a member of the audience to watch a big cup game. No less surprised, my landlord accepted him gladly. When Heidegger arrived on the appointed afternoon, he freely and easily joined the small family circle, which was versed in soccer. When I offered him a cup of tea, he looked at me slyly, smiled, and said, "Okay, Petzet, now go upstairs to your apartment and work—you know nothing about soccer!" With that, he turned to watch the game between Barcelona and Brussels.

Later I heard that at one point he was "playing along" with the teams with his left foot so vigorously that the rest of his tea spilled on his knee. Similar occasions brought him more often to Schwarzwaldstrasse.[16]

Years after Heidegger's death, another incident shed some light for me (as one who knew nothing about soccer) on the extent to which this former left wing of the Messkirch team was still interested in the old sport. The manager of the theater in Freiburg, Hans-Reinhard Müller, told me that one day he had introduced himself to Heidegger on the train from Karlsruhe to Freiburg as Heidegger was returning from a meeting of the Heidelberg Academy of Sciences. Hoping to have an interesting conversation about literature and the stage, Müller tried to draw Heidegger's attention to his own activities in Freiburg, but failed. (Müller did not know that Heidegger was not interested in theater at all.) Rather, Heidegger inquired whether Müller was occasionally involved with television. He explained his question by saying that as far as television (this questionable modern equipment) was concerned, he was actually interested only in television broadcasts of soccer games, especially cup games. While especially praising the English soccer players, he expressed great admiration for Franz Beckenbauer and enthusiastically described Beckenbauer's style, stressing how much he was fascinated by the player's tactics and way of handling the ball. He then tried to show the astonished Müller the subtleties of such a style of play, saying how he also admired Beckenbauer's skill in evading collisions with his opponents. This finally led Heidegger to speak of the "invincibility" of this "brilliant" soccer player.

This went on all the way to Freiburg, where Müller and Heidegger both got off the train. The man from the theater had never imagined that he would carry on such a conversation with the philosopher—and it was to be his only conversation with him. Prudently, Heidegger never told me anything about this conversation, even when later I had the occasion to mention to him the prolific influence of the manager of the theater in Freiburg and Munich. For in the end I did not understand anything about soccer.

In his last decades, Heidegger's native Messkirch was personified for him entirely in his brother Fritz. As an employee of the Volksbank in Messkirch, Fritz Heidegger would never have assumed the role that in the course of time made him the most well known person in that small town. Famous for giving the jester's speech during the carnival in Messkirch, Fritz enjoyed the indisputable fame of an original wit, about whom many stories still circulate—nothing bad, only cheerful things. He enjoyed the respect—indeed, reverence—of the whole community. While the famous "Professor" was at work in Freiburg or at the hut, Fritz could always be seen in the small town. One could talk to him at any time, as long as one was not afraid of getting hit by one of his cordial diatribes, which struck like lightning and left their victims defenseless. Fritz Heidegger possessed an unusual sagacity, which could produce the impression on strangers that *he* had to be the real author of the works that made his brother famous.

Upon entering the small, wood-planked house on Friedrich-Ebert-Strasse in Messkirch and being led into the room where manuscripts almost reached the ceiling in one corner—manuscripts that, as Kommerell noted on his visit to Todtnauberg, were "all unpublished"—one could perhaps assume that these manuscripts were the intellectual treasures of Heidegger's brother Fritz. But Fritz only protected these manuscripts, prepared handwritten copies of them, and kept them in order. Nevertheless, his participation was important because the brothers used to discuss everything with each other, to weigh critical formulations and test each other's knowledge of the classics in Greek and Latin. We cannot imagine Heidegger's work without the assistance of his brother, who occasionally expressed contrary views but never presumed to take a stance against the philosopher. His whole life long, the latter was grateful to "his only brother" Fritz, who was younger and who survived Heidegger only four years. On 1 July 1980, Fritz was buried, with more than half of Messkirch and numerous friends of Heidegger's from all over Germany and even from France attending. This gave the impression that the funeral procession of the philosopher on 28 May 1976 was being reenacted.

Heidegger knew very well that his brother did not have it easy. A small speech impediment handicapped Fritz very much. It was not always without envy that he retreated from speaking when he, too, would have liked to say something. When we would get together with Fritz Heidegger and drink wine—which he liked to do—the longer we were together, the more his speaking and his behavior displayed a deep-seated sadness and pensiveness. His humor, which lacked neither anger nor sadness, had something Shakespearian about it. I had to consider it an honor when, after we got to know each other better, he gave me the tender nickname of "Petzetle." His fantastic coinages of words were and still are in circulation. I would like to mention here one of his unforgettable formulations. It dramatically expresses the hidden genius of this man as well as his inviolable commitment to the world of ideas of his brother Martin. The only time he visited Bühlerhöhe—to him basically an entirely alien world—in order to meet the famous Professor Stroomann and also to hear one of his brother's talks, Fritz was thoroughly cross-examined by a group of curious ladies. They hoped to be able to learn more about the famous but inaccessible philosopher through him. In those days Mao's China was considered a winning card in educated circles. Thus while tea was being served one lady asked Fritz Heidegger what he thought of Mao. She rapidly received the answer, "Mao Tse? That is the *Ge-stell* of Lao-tzu." [17] The ladies were left stunned.

His brother in Messkirch not only guaranteed Heidegger peace and quiet for work, not only kept their native home for him all his life, but also provided him with a third thing—a love that could give rise to the productivity of the philosopher's work in this home. Each depended much on the other and took a deep interest in the other's destiny. Seldom have I seen such an intimate and unsentimental relationship between brothers. Theirs was a brotherhood in the genuine sense.

In the last three decades of his life, Martin Heidegger spent at least two long periods in Messkirch each year—in early spring and in fall, when the days in the hut at Todtnauberg came to an end with the beginning of the colder season. But his intensive work was by no means limited to these periods. Heidegger often took unfinished work with him on his trips. Before we both traveled to Bremen for one of the lectures in the Club of Bremen, he wrote to me (on 4 March 1954), "The work on the manuscripts on Greek philosophy deprives me of a great deal of time. Therefore, I'll have to take some work with me on the train trip, in order to be mostly done with it *before* Bremen." Almost every letter of Heidegger's from the hut or from Messkirch contained similar remarks—about how he was mired in the time-consuming details of his work, how his stay would be profitable for his work, and how pressing work occupied his time. In one of his most beautiful letters from Messkirch he wrote, "We work the entire day. I cannot afford a day of rest, especially as the texts, which resonate surprisingly in one another, press toward new experiences. All around the Feldweg the grain harvest is going on, and the smell of the grain is almost intoxicating. But the walks are at the moment short ones." Harvest—both here in Feldweg and there in Hölderlin.

However, there was another side to those productive days and weeks—it was called renunciation. This word appears frequently in Heidegger's letters. "My work progresses such that I have decided to renounce the trip to Munich. All the hustle at the end interrupts the continuity of work" (13 October 1963). Another time it is pressing work that again forces him to refuse proposals that he would have gladly accepted.

Invitations to Bühlerhöhe also had to be rejected. Once he quotes himself: "Renunciation does not deprive, it gives."

Throughout the years, Messkirch again and again provided the thinker with energy—a thinker whose inexhaustibility in work is comparable only to that of Picasso in our century. No one should underestimate the part that Heidegger's native soil played in his creativity. No one would reproach Chagall for his love of Vitebsk, from where his art received so much power. No one would degrade Theodor Storm to the level of a "country writer" because of his bonds to Husum. Stifter's work did not grow out of the big city of Vienna, but out of Mühlviertel and Waldviertel. And what about Hölderlin's "homecoming?" Like that mythical figure Antaeus, who would lose his power if he did not touch the earth, Heidegger always needed to feel his native soil. What he created was not thought out in the sterile honeycomb of a high rise. Once he wrote to me, "Everyone belongs to his own native soil."

A word by Hebel that Heidegger liked to quote is appropriate here. With that word I would like to conclude my observations on Messkirch—that city of homeliness, industriousness, and brotherliness: "Whether we readily admit it or not, we are plants that must grow from their roots out of the earth, in order to blossom in the ether and bear fruit."

Isolation and Solitude

Writing about Heraclitus, Nietzsche said, "Walking down the road in solitude belongs to the essence of being a philosopher. The walls surrounding his self-sufficiency must be made of diamond if they are not to be broken and destroyed. For everything works against him. His journey to immortality confronts more obstacles and is more difficult than anyone else's. And yet no one but the philosopher can believe with certainty that this journey brings him to his goal, because he does not know at all where he stands other than finding himself on the outstretched wings of all times. . . . He has the truth. No matter what direction the wheel of time takes, it cannot evade the truth. It is important that we know that such human beings once existed."

To whom would these words apply more appropriately than to Heidegger? From the beginning, his path was the path of one isolated. He did not try to take root in an intellectual community. There were the years of difficult struggle to leave theology—a struggle that he had to go through alone against all inner and outer obstacles. Then, after years of

intense philosophical work, *Being and Time* appeared—a book that all
at once made its author famous and put him at the center of every philosophical discussion. Students poured in from all over the world, their
numbers growing every year; the philosopher constituted the center of a
spiritual breakthrough that extended to various disciplines, from theology to the natural sciences, and whose impacts reached across Europe
and overseas. Yet despite all this, Martin Heidegger—the source of this
whole upheaval—remained as lonely as he had ever been.

In retrospect, it looks almost like a hint that, after announcing his
great lecture course for the winter semester of 1929–30 in Freiburg under
the title "World, Finitude, Individuation," he revised this title and replaced "Individuation" with "Solitude." [18] When we read the published
text of this lecture course, we see clearly to what extent this lecture addresses Heidegger's own solitude. The course of his life as an academician—which he traversed among approval and skepticism, frightened reserve and passionate admiration—was surrounded by an aura of seeming
inaccessibility. Some of the students may have initially feared a bit the
small, dark man who spoke from the rostrum, as if something almost
threatening occasionally emanated from him. For was it not so that—
rarely, yet strikingly—something prophetic would come forth in his philosophical assertions? After fifty years, his words still sound as if they had
been uttered yesterday, in the midst of the comfort and the self-satisfied
ease of a world that through its activities is bent upon deceiving itself
about what is essential and what matters. In my old and well-thumbed
lecture notebook stands the suggestion that to take up life explicitly has
nothing to do with some kind of "ideal," but only with affirming Dasein,[19] the burden itself. This suggestion does not mean one should turn
away from reality or from what occurs in each moment: "One cannot get
close to what is essential by making friends with what is inessential."
When the essential pressure is lacking, then it must be awakened; "and if
this makes the good fellow dizzy—that is good, too." And then the following, which almost made the auditorium freeze: "We must call upon
those who can instill terror (*Schreck*) in us. The world war has essentially
passed us by without leaving a trace."

The admonitions contained in these words died out without being
heard. A few years later the man who had spoken them took the center of
public attention for a short while, as if he had betrayed himself. As Jean
Beaufret states in his letter on the occasion of Heidegger's eightieth birthday, Heidegger's distancing himself from German national socialism as
early as 1934—by a kind of "active repentance"—retained for him his

official position as a professor, but condemned him to ten years of silence in publishing. This is certainly correct, and testifies to Heidegger's continuing isolation. During this period he could exercise his influence only in the lecture hall; any extension of this influence beyond the auditorium was virtually precluded. The philosopher was increasingly forced into an unwanted exile, even though beyond German borders—both in the Rome lecture of 1936 (which made public for the first time his concern with Hölderlin) and in the Descartes celebration in France in 1937—he was still at the center of attention. More and more Heidegger became invisible to the public eye, and his "isolation" increased. He characterized his situation at that time quite clearly when later he wrote that after April 1934 he lived "outside the university," inasmuch as he did not concern himself with the "affairs," "but tried to do to the best of my abilities only what was most necessary for my teaching duties. In the following years, however, even teaching increasingly became a monologue of essential thinking. This monologue perhaps succeeded in affecting and awakening some people. But it did not mold itself into the evolving structure of a definite comportment out of which something original could emerge. . . . I was now the target of a suspicion that deteriorated into vilification" (*T&G*, pp. 38–39).

After the end of the war, the ostracism of Heidegger became even worse. There were a few courageous voices, but the worst kinds of slander, ill will, and misunderstanding saw to it that Heidegger's isolation was nearly complete. This isolation went on until it broke down and turned into its opposite, as I have already described in detail. Despite overfilled lecture halls, occasional activity in seminars, numerous lecture trips (which made Benn shake his head), and frequent visits by friends and students, one could not fail to see that the existence of the philosopher had unexpectedly entered, for a long time, a new and colder zone of life. I must explicitly mention that the growing intensity of these experiences had nothing to do with sentimental feelings. What happened here could only be suspected from a certain resignation that resonated in some of the philosopher's later statements. He perceived himself quite clearly in his altered situation, so different from what it had been at first: as one who had been driven out of the university and now "as a solitary individual" was basically "a comic figure" in the world. Heidegger's bitter statement that "at any time" he could again "stop" [teaching] shows the full extent of his inner and outer renunciation.

For Heidegger had left the German university behind long before this. His efforts at rehabilitation, at *restitutio ad integrum,* merely

masked a historical process—namely, that in this case—not rare in the
history of philosophy—a great individual abandoned the usual circumstances in order to mature fully in a living space in which only a few can
follow him and in which he suffers isolation. Nietzsche is an example that
comes to mind. If journalism had not deprived us of any feeling for greatness, the comparison of the peasant from Messkirch with the pastor's son
from Röcken would have made clear to us how similar the decisive
phases of their lives were. And this comparison holds also with respect to
the university. For both were initially shining stars in the university; then
they became opposed to it, and in the end the academic institution could
retain neither one. To survive such an experience, to leave the reliable
support of an official position as a professor of philosophy and to enter
the unprotected and mistrusted realm of "sheer" thinking—and to remain, despite blows and doubts, a human being, not frozen in the iciness
of such an existence—is perhaps the most difficult thing to do. Heidegger
passed this test.

The outward course of Heidegger's life in his last decades, the increased concentration on an unending work, led to the presence of an
appropriate rigor and discipline in all aspects of his daily life. Music
proved to be helpful. Rumor sometimes had it that he was actually no
longer working, but was devoting himself in his isolation entirely to the
enjoyment of his great collection of records. What a misunderstanding!
To listen to a record of a concert, to a symphony of Brahms, especially to
the chamber music of Mozart—these were consolations for a thinker
who in his intellectual struggles would often reach his own limits—
which, as he once said, he would not recognize. He never looked for an
easy way out, but for a soothing dialogue with one of thinking's "neighboring breeds" (Hölderlin). In Heidegger's otherwise-unchanged study,
the visitor would at times notice small and visible aids, like gifts from
friends—for instance, a leaf of Braque's *Lettera amorosa*. And in the
midst of densely written pages of work, the aging philosopher worked
inexhaustibly to continue the path that ran through the immense mountain of thinking of his old age.

Kommerell once showed Heidegger in a characteristic posture when
he described how, on a perfect Sunday, in the austere solitude of Todtnauberg's heights, Heidegger sat at a small table in front of the little hut
early in the morning and wrote. Heidegger, who never considered himself
important but only a traveler to whom the task of thinking is assigned
(we do not come to thoughts, they come to us), appears in Kommerell's
account like one of those sages painted on one of the Chinese folding

screens in the Museum of Ethnology in Bremen, which had inspired Heidegger's great admiration. Each of the sages is sitting in front of his hut, meditating and writing, while a cup—filled by a serving spirit with a refreshing draft from the river that flows by—is passed on to them. Occasionally they engage in discussion, but the river brings them something from the great mystery, without interruption or omission.

"And did he find out anything?" This question, which the customs collector puts to the young companion of Lao-tzu and which Brecht reports in his poem on the origin of the *Tao Te Ching*, will indeed be the question asked by those who would like to receive ready-made answers about the mystery—because they consider the path of questioning too difficult or because they deem themselves to be above the trouble of questioning. However, even when the more than eighty volumes of Heidegger's lifework are published, they cannot be anything but an invitation to new questioning: "For questioning is the piety of thinking."

Once, in Bremen, when we were all together in the evening, the conversation turned to the effects of thinking, its power and powerlessness. Heidegger told us, "Yes, thoughts can change the world. If Leibniz had thought differently, then the world would look different today."

Heidegger loved that poem by Bertolt Brecht. Did he recognize himself in the poem? It was solitude that in the end molded the countenance of the old man. Considering everything ever said about Heidegger, perhaps the lines that a Japanese poet wrote on the occasion of Heidegger's death capture the truth best:

In the depth of the night
The bright moon shines
Alone.

9
Farewell

Between Seventy and Eighty

Soon after his first trip to Greece, Heidegger was stricken for months by a serious illness, which caused a great deal of concern. However, supported by devoted care, his healthy constitution finally allowed him to regain his powers entirely. From that point on, nevertheless, he had to avoid a few things and give up some of the things he much liked. For a long time it seemed as if he were impervious to old age. Only after his eightieth birthday, when I visited him in his newly built residence for his old age in the garden of the house in Zähringen, did I have to admit that Heidegger was getting old. When he himself came to open the door, I noticed how small, thin, and almost fragile he had become and how strongly the big eyes shone through the wrinkles of his face. Not to find him in the familiar environment was at first a shock, although I could easily see that in this well-designed environment two older people would live more comfortably and have better access to everything than in the big house. But when I discovered some of the familiar things—those tutelary spirits, so to speak—I could sense that this was to be only a temporary place of dwelling. For Heidegger was about to set out on the great journey. I could not free myself of these thoughts, which sneaked up on me each time I was there—even with the beautiful view from Heidegger's bed toward the blooming garden and beyond this toward the old house. The attentive eye could also detect Heidegger's changed handwriting; it seemed slightly stiff and no longer as agile as before. It seemed to want to get hold of something that was about to slip away.

Heidegger's seventieth birthday was a great celebration for his family and friends. I have already talked about the gift with which the Bremenians surprised him on that occasion. We came upon the idea partly because the general view on Heidegger's relation to Goethe was not clear. This opinion was strengthened by Frau Heidegger's possessing a loan slip from the university library that showed Heidegger had borrowed several volumes of Goethe. This loan slip confirmed that he did not even own Goethe's works, an essential object utilized in middle-class education.

The back-and-forth exchanges in which all those invited cheerfully engaged while reciting verses of Goethe on the evening before the actual
celebration in the Jägerhäusle, when the exquisite volumes were handed
to Heidegger, culminated in the poet's words: "Years of life are like sibyl-
line books: the fewer they become, the more valuable they are."

Heidegger truly took advantage of this decade and a half of his life,
and not just to read Goethe—from whose work he extracted some provocative words in order to give the lie to the opinion that he was not
interested in the poet. These were also the years in which the plan and the
foundation for the complete edition of Heidegger's own colossal work
were laid. He worked without interruption while calmly looking back at
the past and being concerned with the future.

Heidegger celebrated his seventy-fifth birthday with a larger group of
people than in Freiburg—in the castle of Hagenwil in St. Gallen, which
he had come to like after attending meetings and discussions there. As his
eightieth birthday approached, preparations began on all sides. His
friends from Bremen wanted to honor him again in a special way; we
printed twenty-five copies of a small volume in which Vogeler's initials
and ornamentation accompanied a short thank-you note.

Two pictures adorned this small volume: a reproduction of Vogeler's
Lerche (Lark), which shows a young man who follows the call of the bird
into the dawn of the world; and the old Orpheus in the evening shadows,
who sets his lyre aside—a painting by Hans Leu from the museum in
Basel. The first copy, which was Heidegger's, contained an original copy
of the etching by Vogeler. When the recipient of this gift discovered on
the last page of the volume the nineteenth sonnet from the first part[1] of
the *Sonnets to Orpheus*, the old gentleman said with some emotion that
just that morning he had thought about this poem of Rilke's:

. . . und was im Tod uns entfernt,
ist nicht entschleiert.
Einzig das Lied über'm Land
heiligt und feiert.

(. . . and what withdraws from us in death
is not unveiled.
Only song through the land
hallows and praises.)[2]

The evening of Heidegger's eighty-fifth birthday was serious and
cheerful at the same time. A small mission from Bremen again brought

their best wishes. To our surprise, Heidegger got up and gave a brief but moving speech, which began with the words "Silence is the gratitude of old age." Then he read to us the letter of a Russian philosopher from Leningrad that he had received that morning. "From the land of the coldest abysses," she admitted a strong and serious adherence to Heidegger—from a place where "many carry a great resolve in their souls" and try, despite all kinds of obstacles, to listen to him. The letter concluded by honoring and commemorating Heidegger; it was one of the last great joys for the thinker. It was difficult to bid farewell to him.

This became even more difficult for me when, in the winter of 1975, I called on Heidegger in the Fillibachstrasse. In order not to tire him, this was to be a short visit. But he kept me longer, much longer than the allocated time. As always, I had to tell him a great many things. He inquired with interest about people, things, experiences, and work. His mind was as far-ranging and clear as ever. When evening was about to fall, I decided to leave. Frau Heidegger had already left the room. One more time I turned around at the door. The old man returned my gaze and raised his hand, and I heard him say quietly, "Well, Petzet, now it is getting close to the end." His eyes greeted me for the last time, and I knew then that I would never see him again.

The Deaths of Kästner and Burckhardt

In the spring of 1974 there were two deaths, each of which affected the nearly eighty-five-year-old Heidegger in a different way.

On 3 February, shortly before his seventieth birthday, Erhart Kästner died in Staufen, thereby heeding in a strange way the admonition with which his last book, *Der Aufstand der Dinge*, begins: "Do not become too old, my child." In him the philosopher lost a trusted human being who for many years had resolutely stood by his side through much aggravation and opposition and whom he knew to understand him. For a long time he had feared this loss. How much their close relationship was rooted in a deep agreement is confirmed by two poems that Heidegger sent his younger friend shortly before the latter's death.

In retrospect, the beginning of one of the poems sounds like a presentiment of Heidegger's own approaching end. His days were numbered.

Wo aber sind wir,
wenn wir uns mühen,

Rilkes Zuruf zu vollziehen:
"Sei allem Abschied voran . . ."?
Wohnend im Tod?

(But where are we
when we try
to reenact Rilke's call:
"Keep ahead of all parting . . ."?
Are we dwelling in death?)

That at the end Heidegger surmounted the pain of this loss, too, through "releasement into the mystery" is shown by those two lines that he wrote in December 1975, "In Memory of Erhart Kästner":

Sind, die das Geläut der Stille hören,
Anvertraut der Ankunft einer fernen Huld?

(Those who hear the ringing of stillness—
Are they committed to the arrival of a distant benevolence?)

A few weeks after Erhart Kästner's death, the news came from Basel that Carl Jacob Burckhardt had died. Since as a historian I considered Burckhardt a model and since as a Hanseatic Republican I felt close to him as a *Reichsstädter* from Basel, I was more affected by his death than Heidegger was. Despite his high regard for Burckhardt, Heidegger had little in the way of a personal relationship with him, although a dialogue in the hut had brought them closer. It was different with me. For Burckhardt was the nephew of a good friend of my mother's in Basel; we corresponded with each other, and I was pleased with a cordial dedication in his *Danziger Mission*. And on the occasion of a meeting at which Burckhardt received the Art Prize of Basel, he invited me to La Bâtie, his old-age residence.

All of this may explain why, affected as I was by the unexpected news of Burckhardt's death, I wrote to Heidegger and enclosed a few texts by and about Burckhardt, thinking that Heidegger would read them with interest. Newspapers in those days were filled with laudatory remarks about Burckhardt as a statesman and diplomat as well as about his work as a historiographer. On 12 March, Heidegger responded in such a matter-of-fact tone that it at first scared me. Thanking me for what I had sent him, he added a few words that called for reflection: "Incidentally, one must not exaggerate the glorification of the 'European.' What did he really set in motion intellectually? And what will last? I find that today's journalism has lost all criteria, assuming that it ever had them. *De mortuis nil nisi bene.*"³

On the following day I received another letter. In the meantime, apparently, this topic had assumed a larger and more defined outline for Heidegger. He enclosed his contribution to a Burckhardt festschrift "to be read on a quiet evening," asking that I return the text to him. He added, "The power of the root-unfolding of technology, the destruction of language, and the disintegration of Europe define the destiny (*Geschick*)⁴ to which we are exposed and which calls for a corresponding reflection." A long postscript followed on the back of the letter: "The old Köbi,⁵ who had a more powerful and more rooted nature, writes on 16 March 1883 to his friend Max Alioth, the architect from Basel: 'As I become older, I am increasingly one-sided in certain convictions. For example, I am convinced that the day of decline begins with democracy in Greece. The great force that was accumulated continued to exist for a few more decades, long enough to create the illusion that this force was the work of democracy. *Thereafter, things began to fall apart;* only art survived the terrible later development of Greek life. And in the shadow of a disregard for the artists, it stayed alive.' " Following the quotation from Burckhardt, Heidegger added, "Our Europe is disintegrating under the influence of a democracy that comes from below against the many above."

In his later years, Heidegger's thinking revolved almost exclusively around the power of technology and the destruction of language; a third theme was always contained in these: the disintegration of Europe. But he hardly ever expressed himself about it as clearly as he did in the letter I just quoted. There he used the ideas of the old Burckhardt about the disintegration of Greece in order to indicate what in his opinion is the cause of the decline of Europe. He is not alone in holding "democracy from below against the many people above" responsible for this decline. This view of democracy grasps not only at the frequently renewed and always destroyed dream of a world democracy, but also equally at the instability and powerlessness of those "above." Such issues, however, pertain as little to the field of sociology as language does to linguistics, or technology to the contraptions of the technicians. But what happened to the historiographer who is inclined to the kind of reflection that has been necessary for a long time already? Could Carl Jacob Burckhardt, the descendent and grandson, be such a person in this transformed time?

At that time it seemed to me that an injustice had been done to the man whom I admired so much, and I used the opportunity to discuss the matter with Heidegger when I brought back the manuscript of his contribution to the festschrift a few days later. It was only then that I realized what Heidegger was aiming at. I had to agree with him regarding the tactless "glorification" on the part of the press, especially when I considered that even without such glorification Burckhardt still had enough merits. These showed the deceased to be the last important historian of the old school, who demonstrated his abilities in the realm of action—and not only behind the writing desk. But when I came back to Burckhardt's historiography, it again became clear to me how serious Heidegger was about "history"—which happens always—and about "Geschichte," [6] which occurs rarely. With Carl Jacob Burckhardt, the essential character and mold of another great man from Basel was once again expressed. In retrospect, the descendent embodied the old Erasmian element. But for Martin Heidegger, traditional European historiography stood over against the thinking of what is to arrive, which nevertheless is rooted in what is the oldest of the old.

A little later, a third letter of Heidegger's made the concluding remark of our discussion: "Carl Jacob Burckhardt sees the devastation. But he does not reflect on its origin. However, this was not his concern. More on this in our next discussion!"

The Final Path

Early in the morning on Ascension Day, 1976, I received the news in Bremen that Martin Heidegger had died on the previous day. My first thought was to travel right away to Messkirch in order to pay him my last respects. When I considered things more clearly, however, I realized that the earliest I could arrive there would be a time when the funeral would presumably be over. For it was clear that everything was being done in order to avoid any sensation and to keep the inquisitive public away, so that nothing would deprive this death of its dignity.

And that is how it happened.

I remained in my old native city and remembered the teacher and friend to whom I first became close in my parents' house in Bremen. While the bells rang and announced the holiday, I thought through the long chain of years in which I had received from him so many things that determined my life. On the same day I wrote an obituary, in which I recalled Heidegger's special relation to Bremen and its people. This obituary appeared on the day of the funeral in *Bremer Nachrichten*.

When I returned to Freiburg, I was told that his had been a gentle death, without any struggle. Heidegger died in his sleep in the early morning, whispering the word "Thanks." Did he not say once that thinking and thanking are the same? We read in one of Heidegger's poems for Erhart Kästner:

Stiftender als Dichten,
Gründender auch als Denken
bleibt der Dank.

(More founding than poetizing,
More grounding than thinking
remains thanking.)

My old friend Ingeborg Böttger reported to me later how she managed to attend the burial, being the only one to represent our small circle. She had heard the news of Heidegger's death in Hagnau am Bodensee and immediately telephoned the mayor of Messkirch, to get the time of the funeral service. Thus she was able to travel by car to Messkirch and join the community of mourners—the announcement of the funeral had already been spread everywhere by word of mouth. The letter from this physician, who together with me participated in Heidegger's lecture course in Freiburg in 1929, bespeaks the whole emotional character of that day:

"For me, the most moving event was the burial. Amid the blooming chestnut trees round the chapel flowed the visitors from Messkirch, the group of professors, poets, and friends, among them the old Ernst Jünger. I no longer recall whether there was a men's and boy's choir with a band. There was the ceremony in the chapel. I could not go inside, beside the silent relatives, and stayed at the door of the chapel looking at the coffin. I had the feeling that I should take off my shoes. Then the funeral procession, the coffin carried by the city councillors. With its old-fashioned form and flat vaulting, the coffin reminded me of Les Aliscampes. Wildflowers were thrown over the coffin. I threw a panicle of garden sage (appropriate for a physician) together with an iris from the enchanted garden on the Bodensee that had belonged to my deceased friend Bissier."

The small windwheel from the spring near the hut was placed inside the coffin, and a few branches from around the hut covered it. Hölderlin's poem, read by the younger son, was the last thing before the earth covered the mortal:

Denn manches mag ein Weiser oder der
Treuanblickenden Freunde einer erhellen, wenn aber
ein Gott erscheint, auf Himmel und Erd und Meer
Kömmt allerneuende Klarheit.

(For a wise one may know much
Or elucidate for loyal friends looking on.
But when a god appears, in heaven, earth, and sea,
A brand-new clarity comes.)

A Legacy

Among the many letters and pieces of writing by Heidegger that I possess, spanning almost five decades, there is one letter that has a special character. On the occasion of the publication of a long letter of Heidegger's in the volume of Kommerell's letters, I expressed to Heidegger my reservation about this letter—whether it might be misunderstood and eventually do damage to him. Heidegger's response to me, dated 16 April 1963, is closely related to the letter from Kommerell to Heidegger, dated 29 July 1942 (which is published in his volume of letters) and to Heidegger's response to him on 4 August 1942. Heidegger's answer to me is a continuation and completion of the dialogue that he had started with Kommerell. Written twenty years after the initial occasion, this letter joins retrospectively what belongs to the past with what belongs to the future. In this way it becomes, when read properly, a look at Heidegger's entire striving in life. With a quotation from "The Death of Empedocles," this letter sums up Heidegger's life. The letter reads as follows:

Dear Herr Petzet,
    Thank you very much for your long letter, for the copy of Hofmannsthal's letter, and for returning Gide's text. When I gave Frau Kommerell her husband's letters to copy, I considered everything that you are rightly concerned about. That what is hostile and misrepresentative comes forth everywhere, that people simply do not understand and are not willing to question further, is something that has become so clear to me over the decades that I let all of this rest. This not-willing is a destiny, too. Kommerell may see my efforts decisively differently from others and may understand them not as just philological interpretation, but as fateful dialogues; nonetheless, when it comes to the matter of thinking, he is held captive by the usual lack of understanding.

He takes *Being and Time* as an existential anthropology and believes that my thinking, by encountering Hölderlin, has become metaphysical. On the contrary, what has been at issue, beginning with *Being and Time*, is the question of being in the sense of an overcoming of metaphysics. It is not a question of getting to the same level as Hölderlin, but of preparing in thinking that temporal-spatial framework into which the poet speaks. Despite the significance of his letter, Kommerell fails to see the actual relations. . . . He fails to enter the dimension within which my thinking had been moving since five years prior to the lecture—and within which it still moves. He cannot recognize the 'premises.' Throughout the intervening years, it has become increasingly clear to me that it is impossible for me to make myself understood within the realm of representation that is peculiar to today's opinion. The attempt at such an understanding is already an indication that I misunderstand my own path of thinking. That is how things stand; they are at the mercy of time's god.

As unique as the dominion of *Ge-stell*[7] is and will continue to be in the history of humankind, just as unusual in this epoch and incomparable to earlier possibilities is the determination of thinking. It is, however, always wholesome to meditate on this anew. In this perspective, releasement (*Gelassenheit*) proves to be the way in which one must correspond to the destiny of the world (*Weltgeschick*).[8] Releasement becomes the jointure in which dwelling occurs.

It is part of the strange and inexplicable nature of today's world that with the instrument of an aircraft we procure the precondition for returning to the place of Aeschylus, Pindar, Empedocles, and Plato. This, too, is either granted to us or refused. With two lines of verse, Hölderlin traversed this region:

> Gross ist seine Gottheit
> Und der Geopferte gross

> (Great is his Godhead
> And great too is the one sacrificed)

> ("The Death of Empedocles," first version)
> With cordial greetings,
> Yours,
> Martin Heidegger

Acknowledgments

I cordially thank all those who have contributed to this book's coming into existence. Foremost among them I would like to remember Jean Beaufret, Heidegger's friend, who was willing to write a foreword to this volume but who died, much too early. Death took the pen from his hand. I am grateful to Dr. Hermann Heidegger (Attental), Professor Martin Nagel (Ludwigsburg), Retired Senator Ludwig Helmken (Bremen), Dr. Joachim W. Storck (Marbach), Retired Ambassador Dr. Alberto Wagner de Reyna (Lima, Paris), and Dr. Ingeborg Böttger (Göttingen), as well as Siegfried Schühle, the late mayor of Messkirch. I received encouragement and support from many people residing in various places. From Freiburg, Mrs. Birgitta Elze, Professor Friedrich-Wilhelm von Herrmann, Dr. Ingeborg Krummer-Schroth, Dr. Hildy Berwarth, and Professor Anton Vögtle; from Messkirch, Thomas Schreijäck and Rolando Gehling; from Staufen im Breisgau, Mrs. Anita Kästner; from Gernsbach, Mrs. Hella Sieber-Rilke; from Bonn, Professor Beda Allemann; from Tübingen, Professor Ernst Zinn; from Switzerland, Ernst and Hildy Beyeler (Basel), Professor Heinrich Ott (Basel), and Franz Larese (St. Gallen); from France, François Fédier, François Vezin, Dominique Le Buhan, and Eryck de Rubercy (all in Paris); and from Milan, Walter Strobel. I thank all these people here. For reading the galley proofs, I thank Waltraut Dreier (Freiburg) and Peter Längle (Rast). The photographers deserve credit for enriching the book with pictures: W. Lechner and Franz King (Messkirch), Willy Pragher (Freiburg), Felicitas Timpe (Munich), and Dr. Peter Ziegler (Hanover). I also thank the Erker Gallery in St. Gallen for the permission obtained from Professor Bernhard Heiliger (Berlin) to reproduce his lithograph of Heidegger on the cover of the book.

A book cannot be written mechanically; it needs a suitable atmosphere. I am grateful to Robert and Erna Stadler for the atmosphere in Rast, which was conducive to the native surroundings of Heidegger's life. I am also grateful to Mrs. Elfride Heidegger for the initial encouragement for writing this book, for the generous permission to quote from her husband's letters, and also for the patience with which she attended the slow growth of the work. Finally, I must not forget to thank Arnold Stadler (Freiburg), my friend from Messkirch to whom the book is dedicated. His critical understanding, his patient assistance, and his cheerful encouragement helped this book very much.

H. W. P.
Rast, near Messkirch
Whitsunday, 1983

Notes

Introduction

1. Martin Heidegger, "The Basic Question of Being as Such," *Heidegger Studies* 2 (1986): 5.

2. For a brief discussion of the active character of thinking, see Parvis Emad, "The Echo of Being in *Beiträge zur Philosophie—Der Anklang:* Directives for Its Interpretation," *Heidegger Studies* 7 (1991): 15–35.

3. See Kenneth Maly, "Imaging Hinting Showing: Placing the Work of Art," in *Kunst und Technik: Gedächtnisschrift zum 100. Geburtstag von Martin Heidegger,* ed. Walter Biemel and Friedrich-Wilhelm von Herrmann (Frankfurt am Main: Vittorio Klostermann, 1989), 189–203. See also Kenneth Maly's remarks on translation that appear at the beginning of Hanspeter Padrutt, "Heidegger and Ecology," in *Heidegger and the Earth: Essays in Environmental Philosophy,* ed. Ladelle McWhorter (Kirksville: Thomas Jefferson University Press, 1992), 12.

4. For more on this issue, see Parvis Emad, "Thinking More Deeply into the Question of Translation: Essential Translation and the Unfolding of Language," in *Commemoration: Reading Heidegger,* ed. John Sallis (Bloomington: Indiana University Press, 1992), 317–34. I thank Mitra Clara Emad for suggesting that "root unfolding" be written as one word ("root-unfolding"). It is interesting to note that translating *Wesen* into French as *essence* has become highly questionable. Gérard Guest renders *Wesen* as "l'aître" in his "L'aîtrée de l'être," *Cahiers philosophiques* 41 (1989): 25–44.

5. Martin Heidegger, *Die Selbstbehauptung der deutschen Universität; Das Rektorat 1933–34, Tatsachen und Gedanken* (Frankfurt am Main: Vittorio Klostermann, 1983), 10 (hereafter RR). This work was translated by Karsten Harries as "The Self-assertion of the German University," *Review of Metaphysics* 38 (March 1985): 467–507 (hereafter ET). In what follows I shall alter this translation whenever necessary.

6. RR, 11 (ET, 471).

7. Ibid., 12–13 (ET, 473).

8. Ibid., 13 (ET, 473).

9. Ibid. (ET, 474).

10. Ibid., 17 (ET, 478).

11. Ibid. (ET, 478).

12. Ibid. (ET, 478).

13. Ibid., 18 (ET, 479).

14. Ibid., 13 (ET, 474).

15. Cf. ibid., 31 (ET, 491).

16. Ibid., 25 (ET, 485).

17. Cf. ibid., 28 (ET, 488).

18. Regarding the significant distinction between *volklich* and *völkisch*, see François Fédier, *Heidegger: Anatomie d'un scandale* (Paris: Éditions Robert Laffont, 1988), 192ff.

19. See Martin Heidegger, *Hölderlins Hymnen "Germanien" und "Der Rhein"*, vol. 39 of the *Gesamtausgabe* (Frankfurt am Main: Vittorio Klostermann, 1980), 292f (hereafter referred to as *GA* 39). See also Hartmut Tietjen, "Die Denunziation eines Denkens: Zur Victor Farías: *Heidegger et le nazisme*," *Duiste Kroniek* 38 (1988): 40–56, esp. 43.

20. RR, 27 (ET, 487).

21. Ibid., 5 (ET, 468).

22. *GA* 39:27.

23. Alfred Rosenberg, *Gestaltung der Idee: Blut und Ehre*, 2. Band, Reden und Aufsätze von 1933–1935 (Munich: F. Eher Nachf., 1936), 33, 37.

24. RR, 30 (ET, 490).

25. Cf. Ibid., 25, 26, 33 (ET, 486, 493).

26. See Heidegger's letter to his brother, Fritz Heidegger, dated 4 May 1933, quoted in Hartmut Tietjen, "Martin Heideggers Auseinandersetzung mit der nationalsozialistischen Hochschulpolitik und Wissenschaftsidee (1933–1938)," in *Wege und Irrwege des neueren Umganges mit Heideggers Werk*, ed. Istvan M. Fehér (Berlin: Duncker und Humblot, 1991), 109–28. Because of the *Aufnahmesperrung* (deadline for joining the Nazi party), Heidegger's entry was backdated to 30 April 1933.

27. Cf. RR, 21 (ET, 481).

28. Heidegger in his letter to his brother, Fritz (see n. 26 above).

29. See note 26 above.

30. Cf. RR, 33 (ET, 493).

31. Ibid.

32. Cf. Silvio Vietta, *Heideggers Kritik am Nationalsozialismus und der Technik* (Tübingen: Max Niemeyer, 1989), 46–47.

33. RR, 26 (ET, 486).

34. *Martin Heidegger–Elisabeth Blochmann Briefwechsel, 1918–1969*, ed. Joachim Storck (Marbach, 1989), 69.

35. Quoted by Tietjen in "Denunziation" and in "Martin Heideggers Auseinandersetzung."

36. Martin Heidegger, "Die Bedrohung der Wissenschaft—Arbeitskreis von Dozenten der naturwissenschaftlichen und medizinischen Fakultät" (November 1937), in *Zur philosophischen Aktualität Heideggers*, ed. D. Papenfuss and O. Pöggeler (Frankfurt am Main: Vittorio Klostermann, 1991), 1:23–24.

37. Ibid., 24–25.

38. These accounts are mentioned by Hartmut Tietjen in "Verstrickung und Widerstand: Martin Heideggers konspiratives Handlungskonzept unter dem Nationalsozialismus," lecture presented to the Martin Heidegger-Gesellschaft, Messkirch, 25 September 1988.

39. *Martin Heidegger–Karl Jaspers Briefwechsel, 1920–1963*, ed. Walter Biemel and Hans Saner (Frankfurt am Main: Vittorio Klostermann / Piper, 1990), 201.

40. Martin Heidegger, "Erinnerung an Hans Jantzen; Wort der Freunde zum Freund in die Abgeschiedenheit," in *Erinnerung an Hans Jantzen* (Freiburg: Universitätsbuchhandlung Eberhart Albert, 1967), 19–22.

On the Way with Martin Heidegger

1. The proper names in these two sentences refer to various places and buildings between which *der Feldweg* (the country path) runs.

2. Martin Heidegger, *Aus der Erfahrung des Denkens* (Pfullingen: Neske, 1965), 5; English translation in *Poetry, Language, Thought*, trans. Albert Hofstadter (New York: Harper and Row, 1971), 3.

Chapter One

1. *Existence* in Heidegger's philosophy indicates the specific relations of human beings to the world, to being (*Sein*), and to themselves. It has nothing to do with existentialism.

2. This question is not Heidegger's, but Schelling's and Leibniz's.

3. This course, which Heidegger gave in the winter semester of 1929–30, has been published as *Die Grundbegriffe der Metaphysik: Welt—Endlichkeit—Einsamkeit* (Fundamental Concepts of Metaphysics: World, Finitude, Solitude), vol. 29–30 of the complete edition (*Gesamtausgabe*) of Heidegger's works.

4. A transcript of this debate is included in vol. 3 of the complete edition of Heidegger's works.

5. A place in Switzerland where Nietzsche often stayed.

6. The term *Jugendstil* relates to art nouveau, the ornamental style of art that flourished between 1890 and 1910 in Europe. In Germany this style was named Jugendstil after the periodical *Jugend*, started in 1896.

7. Goldene Wolke, according to the author, was a social-cultural gathering of young Bremenians. It lasted only about a decade.

8. A high school in the German educational system.

9. The title of the English translation is "On the Essence of Truth," published in *Basic Writings*, ed. D. F. Krell (New York: Harper & Row, 1976).

Chapter Two

1. *Aber* (meaning "but" or "however") is here used to express disapproval and skepticism. The phrase "Aber—Herr Heidegger!" has no direct equivalent in English.

2. Literally meaning "being here/being there," *Dasein* in Heidegger indicates the most proper unfolding of human beings. *Dasein,* then, is the word for human existence *in its ownmost and most proper way of being.*

3. The title of the rectoral address was *Die Selbstbehauptung der deutschen Universität. Selbstbehauptung* (self-assertion) was maliciously turned into *Selbstenthauptung* (self-decapitation).

4. This correspondence has recently been published. See *Martin Heidegger–Karl Jaspers Briefwechsel, 1920–1963,* ed. Walter Biemel and Hans Saner (Frankfurt am Main: Vittorio Klostermann/Piper, 1990).

5. This text appeared in English as *Man in the Modern Age,* trans. Eden and Cedar Paul (New York: Doubleday, 1951).

6. *Völkisch* means "pertaining to the people (*Volk*)," but the word was abused and misused by the Nazis.

7. The central newspaper of the Nationalsozialistische Deutsche Arbeiter Partei (Nazi party).

8. Most likely the author is referring to Elisabeth Blochmann, whose correspondence with Heidegger was published in 1989. See *Martin Heidegger–Elisabeth Blochmann Briefwechsel, 1918–1969*, ed. J. W. Storck (Marbach: On the point mentioned by the author, see p. 76ff.

9. A "call" (*Berufung*) was an invitation to a university professor to accept a chair in another university.

10. A suburb of Freiburg where Heidegger lived.

11. The author is referring to 20 July 1944, the day of the last attempt on Hitler's life by Col. Graf von Stauffenberg, a leading member of the German resistance movement. See Alan Bullock, *Hitler: A Study in Tyranny* (New York: Harper and Row, 1964), 738–40.

12. Heidegger's address in Freiburg.

13. A dissertation (in addition to the Ph.D.) required in German universities for attaining the rank of full professor.

14. The complete edition of Heidegger's works begun in 1975.

15. *Abkömmlich* also means "one who deviates."

16. The Nazi equivalent to the National Guard or People's Militia.

Chapter Three

1. A return to wholeness.

2. The distinction between *Historie* and *Geschichte* cannot be readily conveyed in English. Heidegger's distinction goes back to his fundamental ontology, according to which *Geschichte*, unlike *Historie* (history), stems from the *Geschichtlichkeit* of Dasein. On this point see *Being and Time*, sec. 72ff.

3. *Ge-stell* has been variously translated into English as "enframing," "framework," "im-position," etc. Essentially, it designates the sum total of posing-positing-establishing of the calculative thinking of "technics." In *Ge-stell* "things" are preestablished (posited in advance), without letting them appear or unfold in all their disclosing possibilities.

4. According to the author, this is a yearly gathering in Bremen of sea captains who belong to the Haus Seefahrt. These gatherings have been held since the seventeenth century.

5. *Ausgabe letzter Hand* involves a special style of editing someone's works; individual editors are used rather than members of an editorial committee. This style of editing renders a published text that represents the final version available or known—rather than several "readings of a critical edition." In Heidegger's case the decision to publish an *Ausgabe letzter Hand* stems from his giving precedence to *thinking* over mere scholarship.

6. For the distinction between *Geschichte* and *Historie* (history), see note 2 above. The terms "from where" (*Woher*) and "in the direction of" (*Wozu*) refer to past and future understood in terms of *Geschichte*, not in terms of *Historie*.

7. M. Heidegger, *Basic Writings*, ed. D. F. Krell (New York: Harper and Row, 1977), p. 242. Translation slightly altered.

Chapter Four

1. For the remainder of this section, Petzet's style is somewhat elliptical, as befits casual, diarylike notes. We have tried to remain as faithful to his style as possible.

2. Privy councillor, a title of academicians in the old German university system.

3. Orff's main work is a trilogy of stage work called *Trionfi* (Triumphs) in which he employs all three theater arts (drama, ballet, and opera) and celebrates earthly pleasures.

4. A work composed in 1951 that depicts a rustic wedding.

5. A bookstore in Freiburg.

6. The author means the First World War, since that war was close to the time when Heidegger wrote his treatise for his *Habilitation*.

7. See note 13, chapter 2.

8. The term is often rendered in English as "event of appropriation"; it indicates the belonging together of being *(Sein)* and the human root-unfolding that Heidegger calls Dasein.

9. The reference is to Hebel's work.

10. *Sage*—"saying" or "utterance," a "saying that shows"—is a central notion in Heidegger's views on language.

11. "Journey to Canossa." This expression indicates unwilling submission; it has its origin in medieval times, in Henry IV's submission to the pope in the castle at Canossa.

Chapter Five

1. In English in the original.

2. In English in the original.

3. The author mentions only the subtitle of Kästner's work. The full title is *Offener Brief an die Königin von Griechenland: Beschreibungen, Bewunderungen.*

4. The quotation is from Erhart Kästner's *Die Lerchenschule: Aufzeichnungen von der Insel Delos*, 1964.

5. Scholars of Germanic literature.

6. The city in Austria where Ludwig von Ficker lived.

7. The actual title of this speech, whose text is given in Heidegger's *Holzwege*, is "Wozu Dichter?" (What Are Poets For?).

8. "Schluh" was part of the artists' village Worpswede.

9. A place in Switzerland where Rilke lived for a while.

10. From the opening lines of the Fifth Duino Elegy.

11. See note 4, chapter 3.

12. President of the Federal Republic of Germany.

13. Andrei Voznesensky, *Selected Poems*, trans. Herbert Marshall (New York: Hill and Wang, 1966), 29–30.

14. Ibid., 7.

15. Ibid., 20.

16. In English in the original.

17. According to the author (responding to the translators' query), this means something like "There are still other things that come into play."

18. Heidegger is referring to a kind of language appropriate to his hut in Todt-nauberg.

19. The reference is to Fritz Heidegger, Heidegger's only brother.

Chapter Six

1. The German *Wissenschaften* has always included both the "natural sci-ences" (*Naturwissenschaften*) and the "human sciences" (*Geisteswissenschaf-ten*). In English, *science* has for a long time been a more limited designation, referring primarily to natural or physical science.

2. A collection of essays Heidegger published in 1950. The first essay in the book is translated as "The Origin of the Work of Art."

3. *Das Stunden-Buch*, the three parts of which Rilke wrote in 1899, 1901, and 1903.

4. This is a key notion in Heidegger's work. It refers to the way in which truth or being unfolds, in the various epochs. It might be translated as "the way of being that gets handed over," "the handing over itself," "the way of being's un-folding," or, finally, "the handing over of unfolding itself."

5. The word *Dichter* (poet) generally designates all whose vocation it is to be artistically creative. It does not mean only "poet" in the narrow sense.

6. Heidegger discusses the will to power as the "most extreme" phase of the history of being in his Nietzsche lectures of 1936–42.

7. The original title is "Heidegger et la pensée du déclin."

8. The author alludes to what comes "after" metaphysics, the latter term understood not as a discipline in philosophy but as the way of thinking that has shaped Western civilization.

9. The expression Heidegger used, *das Rattenfängerische*, refers to the Pied Piper of Hamelin and has no equivalent in English.

10. The term *Kehre* (turning) in Heidegger implies a turning to being.

11. In section 6 of *Being and Time*, his first major work, Heidegger addresses the issue of the "destruction of the history of ontology" and distinguishes *His-torie* from *Geschichte*. While *Historie* refers to the discipline of historiography, the term *Geschichte* indicates a sending (*schicken*) that is an ongoing work, a process of unfolding; it cannot be studied historiographically or understood in terms of *Historie*, i.e., history.

12. The author has in mind the close connection in antiquity between mask and the concept of person.

13. The German term used is *Erdgeboren*, or *terrigenus* which means "earth-born," "born of the earth."

14. Heuberg is a location in Freiburg.

15. In English in the original.

Chapter Seven

1. The account was, however, published in 1989 by Vittorio Klostermann under the title *Aufenthalte*.

2. This quotation varies slightly from Heidegger's rendition of this statement by Parmenides.

3. C. P. Cavafy, *Collected Poems,* trans. Edmund Kelly and Phillip Sherrard (London: Hogarth, 1957), 29.

4. The author slightly misquotes this title. It actually reads "Aus einem Gespräch von der Sprache" (A Dialogue from Language).

5. This is the title of a short autobiographical essay by Heidegger, referring to *Feld* (field) and *Weg* (path) of thought, as well as to a particular path in a field near his birthplace of Messkirch, which he used to walk in his early years.

6. In English in the original.

7. In English in the original.

8. The phrase "science and industrialization as well" is in English in the original.

9. In English in the original.

10. The entire parenthetical remark is verbatim in English in the original.

11. "Television" is in English in the original.

12. In English in the original.

13. In English in the original.

14. See note 3, chapter 3.

15. Translated by D. C. Lau in *Tao Te Ching* (Penguin Classics, 1968), 108.

Chapter Eight

1. Two restaurants on the Münsterplatz in Freiburg.

2. See note 14, chapter 2.

3. The reference is to "Aus einem Gespräch von der Sprache: Zwischen einem Japaner und Fragenden" (From Language: A Dialogue between a Japanese and an Inquirer), an essay in Heidegger's *Unterwegs zur Sprache.*

4. See note 5, chapter 6.

5. See note 2, chapter 3.

6. The allusion is to the title of and the prefatory note to a work by Heidegger called *Holzwege* (Forest Paths). In German usage, *Holzweg* refers to a path in the woods that suddenly ends or that suddenly comes upon a "jungle"—a kind of chaotic growth. The implication here is that thinking needs to get to this stage, in order to get to the "sources."

7. Heidegger's birthday.

8. In one version of "Todtnauberg," Celan speaks of "eines Denkenden kommendes Wort" (a thinking man's coming word) and in the other of "ungesäumt kommendes Wort" (a word coming without delay).

9. Paul Celan, *Poems,* trans. Michael Hamburger (Manchester: Carcanet New Press, 1980), 241.

10. Translated by Albert Hofstadter as "Thinker as Poet" in *Poetry, Language, Thought* (New York: Harper and Row, 1971), 3–14.

11. *Herrgottswinkel,* the corner in the living room of southern German homes where a cross hangs.

12. According to the author, the expression "Boppeles-Hebel" is not translatable. It does not intend any malice, but only conveys a smile about a pretentious and presumptuous German-middle-class approach to Hebel's poetry.

13. According to the author, *Hebelmähli* means simply *Hebel-Mahl* (a Hebel feast).

14. The reference is to the title of an essay by Heidegger.
15. See note 6 above.
16. The street on which the author lived in Freiburg.
17. Mao Tse and Lao Tse rhyme in German.
18. See note 3, chapter 1.
19. See note 2, chapter 2.

Chapter Nine

1. The original reads "second part," which is erroneous.
2. Rainer Maria Rilke, *Sonnets to Orpheus,* trans. C. F. MacIntyre (University of California Press, 1964), 39.
3. "Nothing about the deceased unless it is good."
4. See note 4, chapter 6.
5. Heidegger is referring here to Jacob Burckhardt, the nineteenth-century historian, not to be confused with Carl Jacob Burckhardt.
6. See note 2, chapter 3.
7. See note 3, chapter 3.
8. Releasement and destiny of the world are crucial notions of Heidegger's later thought. They should not be understood in general terms.

Chronology

Note: Heidegger's works available in translation are cited in English.

1889	Birth of Martin Heidegger (26 September) in Messkirch, the son of sexton Friedrich Heidegger and Johanna Heidegger (born Kempf, in Göggingen near Messkirch)
1903–6	Attended gymnasium in Konstanz
1906–9	Attended gymnasium in Freiburg im Breisgau
1909–11	Studied theology in Freiburg
1911–13	Studied philosophy, humanities, and natural sciences in Freiburg
1913	Received Ph.D. in Freiburg under Schneider
1915	*Habilitation* in Freiburg under Rickert with the treatise *Die Kategorien und Bedeutungslehre des Duns Scotus*
1915–18	Drafted into military service
1917	Married Elfride Petri
1922	Built the hut in Todtnauberg
1923	Held academic position in Marburg (until 1928). Friendship with Rudolf Bultmann and Hannah Arendt
1927	*Being and Time*
1928	Appointed to the University of Freiburg as successor to Edmund Husserl. Lectures in Herder Institute in Riga
1929	Inaugural lecture "What Is Metaphysics?" (24 July). Lectures at Hochschulkursen in Davos (March)
1930	Lecture "On the Essence of Truth" in Bremen (October)
1933	Elected chancellor of the Albert Ludwig University of Freiburg. Gave speech upon assuming the chancellorship (27 May 1933)
1934	Resigned the chancellorship
1935	Lecture "The Origin of the Work of Art" in Freiburg and in Zurich
1936	Lecture "Hölderlin und das Wesen der Dichtung" in Rome
1943	Speech commemorating the one hundredth anniversary of Hölderlin's death in Freiburg (6 June)
1944	Drafted into *Volkssturm*
1946	Banned from teaching by occupation forces (until 1957)

1946   "What Are Poets For?" a lecture (before a limited audience)
        commemorating the twentieth anniversary of Rilke's death
1949   "Einblick in das, was ist," three lectures at the Club of Bremen
        (2–4 December). Repeated in March 1950 at Bühlerhöhe
1950   "The Thing," a lecture before the Bavarian Academy of Fine
        Arts (6 June). "Language," a lecture in Bühlerhöhe in memory
        of Max Kommerell (7 October)
1953   "The Question concerning Technology," a lecture in Munich as
        part of the lecture series "Die Künste im technischen Zeitalter"
        (18 November)
1955   "Gelassenheit," a lecture on the occasion of the Kreutzer cele-
        bration in Messkirch (30 October). Lecture "What Is Philoso-
        phy?" in Cérisy-la-Salle (September). Stayed in Paris. Visited
        Georges Braque in Varengeville
1957   "Identity and Difference," a lecture commemorating the five
        hundredth anniversary of the founding of the Albert Ludwig
        University of Freiburg (27 June). Inaugural speech before the
        Heidelberg Academy of Sciences. "Hölderlins Erde und Him-
        mel," (6 June) a lecture before the Hölderlin Society in Munich
1958   "Hegel und die Griechen," a lecture in Aix-en-Provence (20
        March) and before the Heidelberg Academy of Sciences (26
        July). "Dichten und Denken," a lecture in Vienna's Burg Theater
        on Stefan George's poem "Das Wort" (11 May)
1959   "The Way to Language," a lecture before the Bavarian Academy
        of Fine Arts (January). Named honored citizen of Messkirch on
        his seventieth birthday (27 September)
1960   Seminar sessions in Bremen, "Bild und Wort." Lecture "Sprache
        und Heimat" in Wesselburen (2 July)
1962   Guest of honor at Schaffermahlzeit (Feast of the Captains) in
        Bremen (February). First trip to Greece (April)
1967   Fourth trip to Greece. "Die Herkunft der Kunst und die Bestim-
        mung des Denkens," a lecture before the Academy of Sciences in
        Athens (4 April)
1968   First seminar in Le Thor, Provence
1969   Second seminar in Le Thor. Eightieth birthday
1973   Third Le Thor seminar (in Zähringen)
1974   Eighty-fifth birthday
1976   Heidegger died in Freiburg on 26 May. He was buried in Mess-
        kirch on 28 May.

Biographical Notes

This short biographical index has been compiled to facilitate the reading of Petzet's narrative, which is interspersed with names that may be unfamiliar to the English-speaking reader. The purpose of the index is to assist the reader by relating a name to the person's professional background. The index does not include all the names mentioned in the book, however; considerations of space and time required that we be selective. We did not include the names of authors whose works are available in English and are well known (for example, Hannah Arendt, Ernst Jünger, and Jean-Paul Sartre); and we did not include names of persons whose backgrounds are indicated by the author (for example, Alvar Aalto, architect).

Abraham a Sancta Clara (1644–1709)
    Ecclesiastical name of the Augustinian friar Johann Ulrich Megerle; preacher and writer
Aichinger, Ilse (1921–)
    Writer; reader for Fisher Verlag
Allemann, Beda (1926–)
    Professor of German literature
Altenbourg, Gerhard (1926–)
    Painter; lives in the former German Democratic Republic
Bäumler, Alfred (1887–1968)
    Professor of philosophy; supported national socialism
Beaufret, Jean (1907–1982)
    Professor of philosophy
Bender, Hans (1919–)
    Writer and journalist
Biemel, Walter (1918–)
    Professor of philosophy
Bill, Max (1908–)
    Architect and painter
Bissier, Julius (1893–1965)
    Painter and professor of art
Bollnow, Otto Friedrich (1903–)
    Professor of philosophy
Borchardt, Rudolf (1877–1945)
    Author, translator, scholar, and poet;

known for his translation into German of Dante's *Divine Comedy*
Buchner, Hartmut (1927–)
    Collaborator on the historical-critical edition of Schelling's work
Bultmann, Rudolf (1884–1976)
    Protestant theologian
Burckhardt, Jacob (1818–1897)
    Historian of culture
Carossa, Hans (1878–1956)
    Physician, novelist, and poet
Cavafy, Constantine (1863–1933)
    Greek poet
Celan, Paul (1920–1970)
    Poet, translator, and writer
Chillida, Eduardo (1924–)
    Spanish sculptor
Cohn, Jonas (1869–1947)
    Professor of philosophy
Dessoir, Max (1867–1947)
    Professor of philosophy
Egk, Werner (1901–)
    Director of Berlin Opera from 1950 to 1953; composer and professor of music
Fédier, François (1935–)
    Professor of philosophy
Ficker, Ludwig von (1880–1967)

Editor of *Brenner* and close friend of
the poet Georg Trakl

Fietz, Gerhard (1910–)
Professor of fine arts

Gadamer, Hans-Georg (1900–)
Professor of philosophy

George, Stefan (1868–1933)
Poet

Grass, Günter (1927–)
Novelist

Grimm, Jacob (1785–1863)
Librarian to Jérôme, king of Westphalia; author, in collaboration with
his brother Wilhelm, of famous works
on folklore

Grünewald, Matthias (1460–1528)
Painter; known for the religious motif
in his work

Guardini, Romano (1885–1968)
Professor of philosophy

Gundolf, Friedrich (1880–1931)
Pseudonym of Friedrich Gundelfinger;
a disciple of Stefan George

Guzzoni, Ute (1934–)
Professor of philosophy

Hauptmann, Gerhart (1862–1946)
Playwright and poet; awarded Nobel
Prize in 1912

Heiliger, Bernhard (1915–)
Professor of sculpture

Herrmann, Friedrich-Wilhelm von (1934–)
Professor of philosophy; primary editor
of the complete edition of Heidegger's
work

Huch, Ricarda (1864–1947)
Writer; opposed national socialism

Ionesco, Eugène (1912–)
Romanian-born French playwright

Jacobsen, Jens Peter (1847–1885)
Danish novelist and poet

Jäger, Werner (1888–1961)
Philologist and historian of philosophy

Jantzen, Hans (1881–1967)
Art historian

Kardorff, Ursula von (1911–)
Journalist and writer

Keyserling, Hermann, Count (1880–1946)
Philosopher of history and culture

Kommerell, Max (1902–1944)
Professor of German literature and
member of George-Kreis

Kreuzer, Conradin (1780–1849)
Composer and conductor

Lenau, Nicholas (1802–1850)
Poet and musician

Ludendorff, Erich (1865–1937)
Prussian general; chief of staff for Hin-
denburg

Manessier, Alfred (1911–)
Artist

Mann, Heinrich (1871–1950)
Novelist; brother of Thomas Mann

Marcuse, Herbert (1898–1979)
Professor of philosophy

Meckel, Christoph (1935–)
Surrealist poet

Nishitani, Keiji (1900–)
Professor of philosophy

Picht, Georg (1913–)
Professor of theology

Pindar (518–446 B.C.E.)
Greek lyricist

Podewils, Clemens von, Count (1905–)
General secretary of the Bavarian Academy of Fine Arts

Preetorius, Emil (1883–1973)
Professor of art, stage designer, and illustrator

Ritter, Gerhard (1929–)
Professor of modern history

Schadewaldt, Wolfgang (1900–1974)
Professor of classical philology

Schickele, René (1883–1940)
Novelist, journalist, and poet

Schmitt, Carl (1888–)
Professor of law

Schröder, Rudolf Alexander (1878–1962)
Poet, artist, and interior designer

Schulz, Walter (1912–)
Professor of philosophy

Sellner, Gustav Rudolf (1905–)
Theater director

Shih-yi Hsiao, Paul (1911–)
  Professor in Taipei
Stadler, Ernst (1883–1914)
  Expressionist poet; killed in action near
  Ypres
Stifter, Adalbert (1805–1868)
  Novelist
Storm, Theodor (1817–1888)
  Writer and poet
Szilasi, Wilhelm (1889–1966)
  Professor of philosophy; successor to
  Heidegger's chair
Toller, Ernst (1893–1939)
  Poet, playwright, and pacifist
Trakl, Georg (1887–1914)
  Poet
Tugendhat, Ernst (1930–)
  Professor of philosophy

Ullmann, Regina (1884–1961)
  Poet; a friend of Rilke
Voss, Johann Heinrich (1751–1826)
  Poet and translator
Vössler, Karl (1872–1949)
  Philosopher of language and culture
Weizsäcker, Carl Friedrich von (1912–)
  Physicist and philosopher
Wilamowitz-Möllendorf, Ulrich von
(1848–1931)
  Classical philologist
Wisser, Richard (1927–)
  Professor of philosophy
Zuckmayer, Carl (1896–1977)
  Playwright and novelist

Index

243